'What a privilege to read this immensely inspirational and brave story. Lauren's personality and energy leaps off the page – the mark of a natural and gifted writer.'

David Cohen, campaigns editor and chief feature writer, London Evening Standard

'I laughed, I cried. What a rollercoaster. Lauren weaves her journey into a tapestry of real, raw emotion, humour and courage. Recognising love, cultivating hope and celebrating gratitude are at its core. An inspiring message! Thank you Lauren for so bravely sharing your journey.'

Dr Sumayya Ebrahim, gynaecologist

'Lauren Segal's writing is compelling, fluent and vital. The unexpected triumph of her inspiring book is its ability to portray her battle with cancer as a gift – albeit an unwanted one – rather than a curse.'

Mark Gevisser, author

'I read every word of this memoir and was moved to tears on many occasions. Lauren writes with such an authentic connection to the ebb and flow of her feelings ... often not small waves, but great tsunamis.'

Lucy Draper-Clarke PhD, mindfulness and yoga teacher

'I started this book on Monday night and read until midnight, read the rest until midnight last night and finished it this morning before work. The writing is exceptional. I was hooked from the first page and captivated to the last.'

Jeanette Hyde, human resource manager

'This book is riveting, moving and sometimes surprising. I am in awe of the author's brutal honesty outside the therapy room and how she doesn't dress it up.'

Vicki Broome DSCI, executive life coach and director of the Houghton TM Centre

'I started reading and had to force myself to stop – but only because I needed to fetch my daughter. It's brilliant. Utterly brilliant.'

Kate Shand, author

'I have read this magnificent memoir (twice in fact). This is not just "another" cancer memoir. On a literary level, the author achieves a vibrant homage to the power of literature. So for that alone, the book is worth the read. But its greatest asset is Lauren's remarkable narrative talents: she writes with a scalpel of honesty, her prose is direct and fresh. The tale is engrossing and harrowing and bears an immediacy in the telling that profoundly touched me. What a work! Gorgeous, funny, complex and unsparing. I loved loved loved it.'

Dr Simon Fortin, writer, actor and scholar

'Thanks for sharing this amazing journey. I cried, laughed, self-reflected, and most of all found inspiration to face my own struggles. Without being smaltzy, it felt like a privilege to let us in.'

Zann Hoad, publisher: Sharp Sharp Media

cancer
A love story

LAUREN SEGAL

JAICO PUBLISHING HOUSE

Ahmedabad Bangalore Bhopal Bhubaneswar Chennai
Delhi Hyderabad Kolkata Lucknow Mumbai

Published by Jaico Publishing House
A-2 Jash Chambers, 7-A Sir Phirozshah Mehta Road
Fort, Mumbai - 400 001
jaicopub@jaicobooks.com
www.jaicobooks.com

Published in arrangement with
MF Books
a division of Jacana Media (Pty) Ltd
Originally published by MF Books in 2017
10 Orange Street, Auckland Park
Johannesburg, 2109, South Africa

To be sold only in India, Bangladesh, Bhutan,
Pakistan, Nepal, Sri Lanka and the Maldives.

CANCER: A LOVE STORY
ISBN 978-93-87944-47-3

First Jaico Impression: 2018

Printed by
Thomson Press (India) Limited

'Such is the miracle – a tale about despair
becomes a tale against despair.'

– Eli Wiesel, *Open Heart*

For Jonny, Josh and Katya
– the centres of my universe

Contents

Contents

Author's Note

For the last 30 years, I have written many stories – always other people's stories. This is my profession. I have told these stories first in my capacity as a historian and researcher, then as a filmmaker, and later as a museum curator.

Living as I do in South Africa, my stories have almost always zoomed in on the often traumatic experiences of life under apartheid. These stories have taken me into worlds very far from my own; as far as the oldest prison in Jo'burg where thousands of my fellow countrymen disappeared for weeks on end – their only crime being the colour of their skin and being caught in the wrong place at the wrong time.

In each of these worlds, I am struck by the immense power of storytelling and its potential for healing. I witness the relief etched on people's faces when they feel listened to for the first time.

Now it is my turn to interview myself. The ritual of keeping a daily journal of my cancer journey becomes my lifeline. My life coach encourages me to be disciplined in this practice: 'Writing amplifies the experience.' She is right. My feelings often become apparent through the writing. Much is unanticipated. The words draw the map of my inner world in ways I could not have imagined.

Amidst all the fear and confusion of cancer treatment, making order on a page is the one thing I can control, and the one place where I can find solace. It contains my fears. The words begin to tumble onto the page with feverish intent. Writing becomes my salvation. The upward curves and downward slopes of the characters give shape to my borderless world. They help me to live life in the shadow of death. With them, I carve out a version of my existence. For once, I am telling my own story.

I start to stitch together my journal entries. Whole scenes begin to emerge organically on the page. My vantage point as storyteller is of a terrified person learning to harness her power and inner resources while drawing on the love and resources of those around her to buttress her own.

The pleasures are unforeseen. I am surprised by the fluid nature of the process, and I was amazed at my drive to complete this work. I am also amazed at how liberating it is to tell my own story – free from the constraints of contested histories or clients' needs as is so often my experience. I am the judge of my own memories, the conductor of my emotional cacophony.

Is there place in the world for another cancer narrative, I keep wondering. There are so many. I listen to tens of them when I am filled with the terror and white-hot rage that accompanies cancer. I gain much succour from others' unflinching descriptions of how they confronted this god-awful disease.

Then I think about a kaleidoscope, my favourite childhood toy. I remember marvelling at how the tiny fragments of colour would remain the same at the end of the tube but that, with each turn of the wheel, these same fragments created a wondrous new pattern, beautiful to behold.

I think of cancer stories in much the same way. The components of the story are similar, but each person turns the wheel in a different way and designs an entirely new narrative. This book is the turn of the wheel of my kaleidoscope. It has been unexpected, painful and at times exhilarating to watch the patterns and colours emerge.

My hope is that this story will help people to understand that while there might be universal points in the journey for all cancer patients, the experience of the journey is an utterly private one.

There are experiences that some sail through, while others are felled. There are words that are a salve to some that bring rage to others.

I am all too aware of the privileges that have underpinned my particular journey. I was freed of many of the burdens that so many other cancer patients in South Africa are forced to endure. I am entirely grateful for having my path smoothed in every possible way, and do not underestimate how this has given shape to my tale. I also realise that it is my privilege that has given me the space to write my story.

This book is not just about cancer. It is about how one person decided to tackle an unexpected set of traumas; about seeking alternative healing methods; about the redemptive power of love and community; about discovering courage and different kinds of hope; about soft landings in times of distress; about writing as healing.

If this book helps just one person cross over an invisible line of terror in their lives, it will have served its purpose.

Cancer Lexicon

Breast cancer classification — There are different types of breast cancer depending on the nature of the cells in the tumour and this influences the choice of chemotherapy.

Estrogen receptor-positive (ER-positive) breast cancer — The most common form of breast cancer diagnosed today. These cancer cells have a receptor for the hormone oestrogen which occurs naturally in the body and which stimulates cancer cell growth.

Chemotherapy — The use of chemical substances – which have a toxic effect upon disease-producing micro-organisms – to treat cancer.

Ductal carcinoma *in situ* (DCIS) — This is known as a Stage 0 breast cancer because the tumour is confined to the ducts and has not yet spread to the surrounding breast tissue.

Lobular breast carcinoma — A relatively rare type of breast cancer that accounts for only 15 per cent of all cases. The remaining breast tumours are mostly ductal.

Lumpectomy — A surgical procedure in which a lump is removed from the breast, typically when cancer is present but has not spread, in a way that conserves the breasts.

Malignant melanoma — A cancerous growth that develops from damage to skin cells caused by ultraviolet radiation from sunshine. It's the most dangerous form of skin cancer.

Mastectomy — The surgical removal of all or part of the breast and sometimes associated lymph nodes and muscles for the treatment or prevention of breast cancer.

Skin-sparing mastectomy — The surgeon removes the skin of the nipple and areola, and then removes the breast tissue through the small opening that is created.

Magnetic resonance imaging (MRI) — This machine provides a view of the internal anatomical structure of an organ without cutting it open.

Position emission tomography (PT SCAN) — This machine uses radiation to produce 3-D colour images of the inside of the human body which not only show what an organ looks like but also how well it is working.

Red Devil — The name often used to refer to the chemo drug, Adriamycin, which acquired this label because of its toxic side effects including potential damage to the heart.

Radiation therapy — This treats cancer by using high-energy waves to destroy the cancer cells without damaging too many healthy cells.

Stages of breast cancer — These range from 0 to IV and depend on the combination of tumour size, lymph node status and metastases (secondary malignant growths). Stage I describes a cancer that is less than 2 cm, has not spread to the lymph nodes and there are no metastases. Stage Four describes invasive breast cancer that has spread beyond the breast and nearby lymph nodes to other organs of the body.

Sentinel lymph node — The first lymph node to which cancer cells are most likely to spread from a primary tumour.

PART ONE

Three Diagnoses

Cancer Three
The Car

A Seemingly Ordinary Day

24 JUNE 2014

It starts out as a most ordinary cold winter's day. The Jo'burg sky is a piercing blue. The sun's dull rays are just emerging through the leaves of our large sycamore tree. Dew glistens on the dawn grass. Our warm kitchen is full of the sounds of our morning ritual. The hiss of gas warms the pan for scrambled eggs for my children. Coffee cups, school lunch boxes, computers, unopened post clutter the kitchen counter; the comforting detritus of our lives.

I gulp down my oats and yoghurt, berating myself for not having a Banting breakfast of eggs and avocado instead. Between spoonfulls, I shout into the ether, 'Hurry up! We are going to be late ... *Again*.' My son and I hardly ever arrive at the school gate before the bell. Today is going to be no exception.

Josh saunters into the kitchen without socks or shoes. 'You can't go outside like that. It's freezing.' He begs to differ, as is often the case. Katya appears in the kitchen with her signature thick scarf around her neck. The sun catches the edges of her bountiful curls. I hug her quickly before Jonny and I go our separate ways to drop our children at their respective schools.

The ride to school is harried, and I exhale a deep sigh of relief when Josh bangs the car door closed. The morning ritual is over.

Gym is the next stop. A frenetic spinning class followed by a steaming shower. Then a mad dash for a meeting in Soweto. We are installing a new heritage trail that tells the story of Soweto's first high street. There is no time to stop. No time to breathe.

I arrive on Mooki Street to find my colleague balancing on a ladder leant up against a street pole. The light catches the aluminium surface of the round sign that Tshenolo is struggling to position. 'A bit higher,' I shout to him by way of a greeting, and then give him a thumbs up. As I step off the pavement to get a clearer view, a taxi whizzes past, barely missing me. 'Look where you're going,' I scream at the driver, but he ignores me as he continues to race down Mooki Street. Road rage is a Jo'burger's favourite pastime.

My cellphone rings just after the near taxi debacle. It's Jonny. A red warning light flickers through my mind. He never calls this early in the morning. We had breakfast together less than an hour ago. I don't respond. I stuff the phone into my pocket. I'll call him later. 'My heart is bursting to finally see our history displayed along this street,' Tshenolo says when he is back on firm ground. 'It is a moment that I have always dreamed of.'

My own heart bursts with pride when I think of what our team of artists, historians and community members have created. An open-air museum, a heritage trail. History. Tangible. Accessible. We move to the next street pole directly in line with the entrance to Orlando Stadium.

This sign is my favourite. The photograph is of a group of young Orlando Pirates supporters who are dressed in the soccer team's famed black-and-white regalia. They are hamming it up for the camera. The girl in the front of the photo is in fishnet stockings, a short mini skirt, and an iconic skull-and-cross-bone miner's hat. She stares straight at us.

Jonny's name again flashes on my phone. Again, I choose not to answer it. The honking of the taxis and the bustle of life makes it hard to hear anything.

As I get back into the car, Jonny's name lights up the screen for the third time. Maybe something is wrong. 'Why haven't you answered your phone?' he implores. 'I've been trying you for over two hours.' I am defensive. 'I was in the middle of a street in Soweto. It's a difficult place to talk. Anyway, what's wrong?' My irritable retort feels absurd as I hear Jonny saying, 'La, the biopsy results ... The lump. It's malignant. I am coming home now.'

The furthest thing on my mind has been my biopsy. I have not thought it possible that the lump being investigated on my chest wall is anything but scar tissue, as my radiologist has calmly assured me over the past two years.

There is no good place to hear this news. The first time I was in the bath. The second time, I was in a school hall. This time, I am driving back from a township far from home. I had assigned Jonny the task of phoning the lab for my test results. I am too terrified to do this myself. My husband accepts this role because he is a doctor and a very kind person. He likes to ease the path of difficulties for others, particularly for his wife and children. Not that anyone can actually ease the passage of this news. For me, the recipient, it is the reverse of being born, a flight back up the birth canal into darkness.

The vivid blue of the sky fades as I hurtle along the Golden Highway towards home. The gold mine dumps that tower beside the road shrink and turn grey. The sharp outline of the Johannesburg cityscape with its familiar contours blurs. The trees along Jan Smuts Avenue, once sculptural in their bareness, are now bleak protrusions. All familiar tableaus in the world outside are rendered indecipherable.

Inside the car, the word C-A-N-C-E-R hangs heavy. Dense. Palpable. Malevolent. 'It is not possible,' I mutter to myself over and over. It is just not possible that a survivor of a Stage III melanoma, a dangerous type of skin cancer, a previvor of a ductal carcinoma in situ (DCIS) – a Stage 0 breast tumour, is also now the same person with a malignant lump on her chest wall. Melanoma. Carcinoma. Malignant. Words that feel as invasive, as uncontrollable, as deadly as that which they signify. They suck at the air in my car and leave me searching for breath.

'A third diagnosis of cancer,' I find myself saying aloud. 'And I am not yet fifty.' I clutch the steering wheel too hard and my knuckles turn white. It is fortunate that home is fast approaching. I no longer trust my ability to steer through the traffic. As I fling open the car door in my driveway, my face is instantly stung by a gust of cold air. I desperately want to rewind the day. Be late for school. Take that spinning class all over again.

I am not sure how I reach the couch in our bedroom. Instinctively, I collapse into the round puddle of light that filters through the window onto the dense woven cloth. But there is no comfort to be drawn from this illuminated circle. I am never good at waiting. The minutes that tick by while Jonny makes his way home are unbearable. The room tilts. The cupboards warp. I am untethered. It is just not possible that this is happening to me *again*.

Deep breaths stop my heart beating faster against my chest wall, bringing with them the odour of fear. The fingers of my left hand reach for the lump under my layers of winter apparel. This mass of flesh is hard and cold to the touch as if nothing can bring it warmth. It has been growing and changing steadily over 18 months, causing me to sleep on my left side. I quickly pull down my jersey. A hadeda's shriek from the garden echoes my own internal scream.

At last, I hear the car gate rattle open. Jonny's footsteps on the wooden floor that leads to our bedroom have a particular urgency. Then he is beside me, holding me tight. 'It's an invasive lobular breast carcinoma,' I hear him saying. I don't know what this means yet. The words sound ominous. Unfamiliar.

Each diagnosis has become progressively worse. Each came as a surprise, and with it a wish that the experience would never be repeated. My memory scours back to the first episode of cancer. Like most cancer stories, the point of diagnosis is always the beginning of the narrative. It is the point at which the metamorphosis from person to patient happens.

Cancer One
The Bath

Yeoville

28 NOVEMBER 1989

This story begins in the bath in the small hours of the morning, after one of those late-night parties. I was a 23-year-old student living in an apartment with two friends in the bohemian enclave of Yeoville, Johannesburg. In between the delicatessens and eateries on Rockey Street, then an all-white suburb, bars and clubs for young revellers flourished. Parties went on late into the night, and I seldom attended a university lecture before 10 am. Youthful melodrama and intrigue dominated our lives. So did the struggle against apartheid. This was 1989, and we were living under a State of Emergency. Our campus was a battleground. I was part of an organisation that fought against a cruel and unjust system. I gave only a passing thought to the blood seeping into the water from a mole on my right thigh at 2 am one morning.

Something about the streaks of red steered me to the doctor the next day. I hated doctors, even though I had a penchant for dating them. The GP assured me: 'This is a blood blister. You have nothing to worry about. But I am sending it to the lab just to be sure.' Little did I know then that he was starting a trend in misdiagnosing the signs of a serious disease.

The next day, Jess and I were lying on the chocolate brown

carpet in the entrance hall of my flat. We were part of an intricately entangled group of friends with a thumbnail's width between one person's life and another's. When the phone rang that day, we were dissecting our somewhat reckless behaviour of the night before. The phone was an old-fashioned instrument with an extremely long cord that allowed me to meander around.

I lifted the receiver absentmindedly but adjusted my position as soon as I heard the doctor's voice: 'I am afraid that mole is a malignant melanoma. It is already Stage III. You need to go to the surgeon right away.' And then he added, 'You are very lucky to have caught it.' Luck. Such a small word that was to become such an outsized motif in my life.

Jess saw me stiffen and mouthed to me, 'What's wrong?' I put down the receiver and tried to repeat the doctor's words. Neither of us knew anything about malignant melanomas. Or what 'Stage III' referred to. These were innocent days. Cancer had not yet insinuated itself as a deadly disease in our lives. There was no Google, no Wikipedia, no Yahoo. So instead of trawling the internet as one would today, I ranted to my friend in machine-gun style: 'How dare that doctor tell me this kind of news over the phone? Why didn't he tell me to come there?' I then declared: 'Whatever this melanoma thing is, it is not going to interfere with my summer holiday plans.'

Jess listened sympathetically as she bundled me into her tiny blue, rather fragile VW Beetle. We sputtered our way to the surgeon's office. He was a friend's father, a rather typical South African coincidence. His wife, who doubled as his receptionist, was friendly in the way that people are when they are in possession of bad news. Dr K cut to the chase: 'This is serious ... We need to excise the tumour with a very wide margin of both skin and muscle. It's a fairly large surgical procedure which will create quite a cavity in your leg.'

My body shook as Jess helped me back into her car. But this was not the cataclysmic moment that it was to become later in my life. My own mortality had not yet entered my field of vision. My focus lay elsewhere. Just a few months before, I had met the man I instantly knew I would marry. We were at a party in Mayfair, a so-called Indian suburb which students across the apartheid colour line had recently begun to occupy.

My star-dusted memory of our first encounter was on the dance floor. I was wearing a tulip-shaped short summer dress with a pattern of wild blue roses against a plain black backdrop. My dance moves were energetic and unruly, unconstrained by the thought that love loitered between the beats of the music. Jonny made a beeline for me. His resolute overture both surprised and intimidated me.

The man dressed from head to toe in black was five years my senior. I knew him only as the leader of Habonim, the progressive Jewish youth camp that I had attended in the December holidays from the age of 13. He had a commanding manner and held a God-like status among us youngsters. I can still hear his calm voice announcing the daily news through a megaphone to 1 300 young people gathered on a dusty patch at that three-week seaside camp. He was in charge and completely unattainable. After that, my main memory of Jonny was when he drove my best friend Carol and me to Habonim meetings every Sunday morning. We sat at the back of the car giggling between ourselves rather than talking to the imposing figure behind the wheel.

Jonny had studied abroad after finishing medicine and had just returned to Jo'burg. He came back to specialise in neurology – although he quickly switched out of clinical medicine into a career in public health. If my gran was alive then, she would have called him a real '*ghap*' (pronounced with a long guttural 'g'), a Yiddish word roughly translated as 'an excellent catch'. His educational pedigree would have been enough to earn him this accolade. He was tall, dark and handsome to boot. He had some early flecks of grey hair, which gave him a sense of gravitas rather than age.

I never dreamed of him in romantic terms until the impossible-to-ignore frisson between us on the dance floor. We ended up watching the sunrise from the roof of my apartment building. My physical attraction was soon matched by my attraction to his complex and penetrating mind. The next day, friends arrived at my door. 'We approve,' they said one after the other.

As I got to know Jonny better, I was more convinced that we were a perfect case study of opposites attracting:

1. *He is serious. I am lighthearted.*
2. *He is contained. I am mainly uninhibited.*
3. *He is highly responsible. I am insouciant.*
4. *He owns his power. I tend to diminish mine.*
5. *He is single minded about career. I am single minded about life.*

Like many men at that age, Jonny suffered from commitment issues. My life became consumed by making sure that Jonny knew we were each other's north and south poles. He lived in the house at the end of my block. I used to drive past every morning, surveying the cars parked outside to see if anyone had usurped my place in his bedroom.

This preoccupation with the cars outside Jonny's house remained all through the days of my first cancer diagnosis and even after a vast area of my upper thigh was excised to remove the melanoma. 'Will you be at the hospital when I wake up from my operation?' I asked gingerly of my sometimes boyfriend.

I don't remember his response. He wasn't there. I went to my parents' home to recover. They had been only peripherally involved in my unfolding cancer saga. I still took my laundry home to be washed, but I was determined to claim my emotional independence. I didn't know how vulnerable I was and, even if I did, I would not have shared this with my parents. I forced them to stand by quietly on the periphery.

Now that I have children of my own, I can imagine how awful it must have been for them to wait in the wings in the face of a threat to their daughter's life. My mother recently confessed that they found it extremely difficult to deal with 'my rambunctious behaviour'. Indeed, I was an exuberant, slightly out of control young adult – with cancer. In fairness, it was age appropriate to possess a fervent desire for independence. And my parents were hardly the greatest of communicators, glued as they were to their own silences.

Despite my stridency, I eagerly imbibed my mother's chicken soup and other delicacies that arrived on a tray while I lay recuperating in my childhood bedroom. My bandaged leg was hoisted up on a cushion and I spent hours staring through the large windows that overlooked my mother's verdant, prize-winning garden.

It wasn't the delicious food, however, that brought me solace. It was Jonny's voice on the other end of the phone. Just hearing him ask, 'How are you?', made the sun come out from behind a bank of clouds. How weird it seems now that a truly serious, life-threatening cancer took such a backseat and that my worries zeroed in on my romantic endeavours. The lasting consequences of this episode were threefold:

1. *I have a big dip in my right thigh.*
2. *The sun forever became my enemy.*
3. *Big hats and umbrellas became de rigueur.*

Back in that summer of 1989, there were many things I didn't know:

1. *Cancer was to be part of my life story.*
2. *Mortality was to be my recurring shadow.*
3. *My life force was profoundly important.*
4. *Jonny was to be my saviour.*

The first inkling I had of my luck in surviving that melanoma was when I stood at the death bed of Kevin, a much-adored older first cousin. He had gone to the doctor with a bleeding mole just like mine. The malignancy had spread by the time his mole was excised. As a terminally ill and bed-ridden cancer patient at home in a modified hospital bed with drips attached, he decided to get married to the woman whom he had loved and lived with for the past ten years. The wedding canopy was erected over his deathbed. The scene of him and his wife taking their vows haunts me to this day. Kevin died a few weeks later, just shy of his 40th birthday.

Standing by Kevin's graveside, in and amidst my grieving family, I realised how this could have been my fate. Still, the true impact of my melanoma eluded me.

Cancer Two
The School Hall

The Second Time Around

19 FEBRUARY 2011

Twenty-two years later, I receive my second cancer diagnosis. I have just turned 45. Happily, I am now married to Jonny, the focus of such emotional turmoil during my melanoma episode. Now our cars stand side by side in the driveway of another kind of enclave – this time suburban. We have two beautiful children, Josh and Katya, aged 14 and 10.

As before, I receive the diagnosis on the phone. This time, it's a cellphone. I am in the worst possible setting. I have invited Jann, an old friend who is a well-known writer and film director, to speak to my daughter's Grade 5 class about the memoir she has just written. The irony. Jann's father, a famous anti-apartheid activist, had been assassinated in front of her when she was 10 years old – the same age as the kids she is talking to. As she shows the enthusiastic class her beautiful old diaries that she kept as a child, Jonny's name flashes on my cellphone. I would not have answered if I had thought the news from my breast biopsy results were bad. It seemed impossible to be diagnosed with cancer for a second time at such a young age.

'I can't really speak,' I whisper into the phone. 'I am with Kat's class listening to Jann.' Jonny's response is firm: 'La, listen. The biopsy results show that your lump is malignant. It's a Stage 0 ductal carcinoma *in situ*. Call me as soon as you can.'

Again, I don't have a clue what the diagnosis means. The word, 'malignant' and the urgency in Jonny's voice are enough, however, for me to understand that it is entirely possible to be very unlucky. The unforeseen and unforeseeable are happening – again.

My heart thumps violently, but I have to keep my composure. 'That was amazing,' I tell Jann when she is done. She does not seem to notice the slight tremor in my voice or the fault line that is cracking my brain open bit by bit.

After dropping Jann at home, I grab my cellphone. Jonny answers immediately. 'Jon, what is a Stage 0 ductal carcinoma? What does this mean?' I am sobbing and the words barely squeeze through my windpipe. 'It's a sleeping kind of cancer where the anomalous cells may or may not mutate into invasive cancer cells,' my husband says. 'It's a good diagnosis if you are to have breast cancer, La. We have an appointment to see Dr Carol Benn early tomorrow morning.'

'How come she is working on a Saturday?' I come to discover that this is a really stupid question. Dr Benn is not only the best breast surgeon in the country but has a missionary zeal to ensure that no woman dies of the disease. There are no limits to her working hours.

My body heaves with gigantic sobs. How, in a nanosecond, has my life plunged in this impossible-to-believe direction? After a flood of tears, and Jonny assuring me, 'La, this is genuinely the best kind of breast cancer diagnosis,' I create a scenario for myself that goes like this:

1. *Because the tumour is small and in its early stages, it can be removed in the same way that my malignant melanoma was removed two decades ago.*
2. *I will go into hospital on Monday and be out by Wednesday.*
3. *I will be back at work the following week.*

Undressed Barbie Dolls

20 FEBRUARY 2011

I am shocked when I enter the breast surgeon's rooms early the next morning. Already, over forty women of all ages sit on gently curved chairs that are joined together in a jigsaw pattern. Most have partners or friends with them. Many have surgical drains secreted away in bags around their shoulders, although I don't know what these are yet. Many have bald heads. Some wear scarves. 'There but by the grace of God,' I murmur to Jonny, thinking how I would never cope if I had to have chemo.

I first catch sight of Dr Benn when she breezes into the jam-packed waiting room to call in her next patient. She is nothing like I imagined. She is very striking, tall and blonde, dressed in an Ed Hardy jumper and black jeans. Most importantly, she radiates energy and warmth. More messiah than surgeon. 'The lovely Mrs Sibaya is next,' she shouts as she grabs her file.

When at last she calls us into her office, Dr Benn hugs us both. This simple gesture opens my floodgates. 'Forgive me,' I say. 'I am highly anxious and I cry a lot.' Her response is typical of the woman I come to deeply admire: 'I am the most anxious person on this planet. And tears don't scare me in the slightest.' Through my misty veil, I scan the array of anatomical model breasts, undressed Barbie dolls, abstract images of nude women in paintings and multiple photos of her family in exotic holiday destinations that fill her office. Breast cancer and her life are clearly entwined.

'Tell me about your medical history,' Dr Benn starts off. She raises her eyebrows when I say, 'I had a Stage III melanoma when I was 23,' but goes on to explain the different treatments for ductal carcinomas *in situ*. At some point, Jonny cuts to the chase: 'What would you do if Lauren was your daughter?'

Her response is instantaneous: 'Given her previous history, Lauren is a high-risk patient. Science is slowly uncovering a link between skin and breast cancers ... If Lauren were my daughter, I would advise her to have a double mastectomy.'

I only vaguely hear what comes next: 'A preventative double mastectomy is the gold standard in breast cancer treatment,' she says. 'An average woman's risk of a recurrence is about nine per cent but for Lauren, it is significantly higher. A mastectomy will reduce her lifetime risk to about one per cent.'

Nothing can prepare you for this moment. Not Angelina Jolie's high-profile preventative double mastectomy. Not a memoir, film, television show or podcast. I have read how some women respond with courage and witty repartee when they hear this news. They rush out to buy one of those 'Fuck Cancer' T-shirts. I am not that brave. I can barely speak. I am ignorant of how the surgical procedure works and imagine both my breasts being chopped off. (I later learn that the breast skin, except for the nipple and areola, is actally preserved.)

I manage to choke: 'I thought that mastectomies are to save people from a very serious cancer diagnosis.' Inside I am thinking: 'I love my breasts and don't want to lose them.' It is true. I don't love that much about my body but I have always loved my breasts. They are a good shape and sit well on my chest wall.

Dr Benn's answer makes me slide down deeper in my chair: 'You are not an ordinary patient. Your father and young cousin both died of cancer. Your two paternal aunts have both had melanomas and breast cancer. But this is still a highly personal decision. I recommend that you seek a second opinion.'

Every last fantasy of my cancer being a simple problem that can be fixed like a burst water pipe disappears. A raft of decisions that I had not anticipated just a few minutes ago loom before me.

Katya

20 NOVEMBER 2000

This ever-deepening spiral of medical dread is part of Jonny's and my DNA as a couple. I have a flashback to my daughter's diagnosis over a decade back.

Katya was six months old when we discovered that she had very serious heart defects. We were told that it was a miracle that she was still alive. Time, however, was running out. Her heart would ultimately fail. Our daughter needed urgent surgery to correct the many defects. When the heart surgeon rather bluntly told us, 'Katya has a 30 per cent chance of dying as a result of the lengthy surgery,' Jonny and I entered the hell of recognising our child's mortality. It did not take long for us to decide that Katya could not have her surgery the next day as planned.

We fled the ward with our baby in our arms, just a few hours after checking her in. Many phone calls later, we found a surgeon at the Children's Hospital in Boston who assured us, 'We have done many more complicated operations than this one. Katya's risk of dying from the procedure is around five per cent.' I am eternally grateful that we had a medical insurance that allowed us to secure Katya her treatment overseas for procedures that could not be performed in South Africa.

We flew to Boston a few days later and were met by our friends Paul and Susie who had flown from New York to meet us. They made us laugh at a time when our hearts were in shreds. Handing Katya over to the anaesthetist remains the single hardest act of my life so far. We did not know if we would see our tiny baby alive again. My brother, Mark, came to be with us during the long hours of the operation.

When the surgical assistant came and told us, 'Your daughter is in recovery. All went very well,' the three of us wept. The surgeon had repaired all of the defects, and Katya suffered no complications. Today, the faint scar down her chest and her fierce determination are all that is left of this story. Katya is a gorgeous, smart and powerful young woman, forging her own way in the world.

Those 10 days in the ICU changed us, her parents, forever. They laid a template for dealing with highly traumatic medical emergencies. We learnt to accept the help of others. Paul, Jonny's brother, arrived a few days after the operation to do our washing and shopping followed by Simon, a good friend from New York. I can still taste the buttery scallops that Simon made with so much love. Our friends, Penny and Ilana, who lived in Boston, delivered a daily dose of chicken soup to the ICU.

We came to know our different strengths and weaknesses. Jonny's medical acuity, networks and drive blended well with my emotional strengths. For many, catastrophes tear love asunder. For us, it became part of the glue that binds us. We know the tastes and smells at the top of the precipice; the experience of staring into the abyss; the prodigious joy and exultation on the other side.

Something else stuck with me from that time. Words were then, as they still are, conduits for my healing. The fragmentary emails that I wrote from Boston became the connective tissue with those back home. In the year 2000, Facebook and Twitter were not yet on our radars, nor were blogs or websites to communicate updates to friends and family. In the parents' room at the hospital, I poured my heart into emails. Those that we received energised us in the gruelling days while breastfeeding my daughter in the ICU.

I have kept every email and I still look at them periodically. The one I read most often is the very first that I sent a day after Katya came out of the theatre:

On 23 November 2000, 2:51 AM,
Lauren Segal < lsegal@iafrica.com> wrote:

We are so relieved. It has been an unspeakably long day – easily the longest and hardest day of my whole life but the news is very good thus far. We are going to be spending the next days right beside Katya in ICU. It is very difficult to see my little baby girl hooked up to a ventilator and other machines. The unbelievable thing to know is that Kati is working far less hard to breathe and stay alive than she has been for the last six months of her life. Her heartbeat is now like 'Plett at low tide' as our doctor friend from South Africa told us. Thanks for all the love and support that you have been beaming into our lives. We have cherished every last drop of it.

That is why, when I receive my second diagnosis of cancer, when my world loses its longitude and latitude yet again, I instinctively draw on our Boston experience. I invite my nearest and dearest to become my stars and moon, my external navigational system.

For some, openness of this kind is an acquired taste. For me, the strain of hiding a trauma is more daunting than laying bare the precise delineations of the situation. I needed to be buoyed during my new medical tsunami.

The Cancer Club

15 FEBRUARY 2011

For the second time in our marriage, we are confronting a potentially life-threatening situation. This time I am the patient. This time there are different questions to confront. Will my sleepy pre-malignant cells wake up and become invasive? Might the cancer have spread already? Should I have a preventative double mastectomy which would remove both my breasts to prevent the cancer from recurring?

Or should I have a lumpectomy, a surgical procedure that removes only the malignant lump and preserves my breasts but then requires that I have radiation to kill any stray cancer cells? Radiation has its own potentially severe side effects from the high-enery waves that are beamed into the area of surgery.

In time, there may be answers to my questions. For now, we are playing a dangerous game of Russian roulette. I am weighing choices with no predictable results one against the other. I quickly learn why 'decision fatigue' is a term invented for us cancer patients.

The appointment a few days later with a geneticist is a new low point. This kind young professional blithely takes notes about my family tree that is littered with tales of cancer. In my extended family, cancer appears to have the gravitational pull of a small planet. As she excavates the rubble of my past and charters each death or near death in her neat child-like print, I become increasingly irritable and staccato in my answers. By the time that this 'tree of death' has taken shape on the page, I am mute.

'Have you heard of the BRACA cancer gene?' she asks.

'Yes,' I answer. Twins I know have recently been diagnosed with it.

'For women who have this gene, there is almost a 90 per cent chance that they will develop breast cancer. There is also a direct link to ovarian cancer. This gene is very prevalent among Jews.' How predictable that I fell into a special niche category of possibility, I think. 'Testing positive for this gene would mean a double mastectomy and then having your ovary and uterus removed.'

At this point, my face resembles the woman in Munch's painting, The Scream. This polite geneticist quickly tries to reassure me: 'Many women's lives have been saved in the last five years as a result of testing for the BRACA gene.'

This dramatic medical leap forward is undoubtedly a cause to celebrate. But when it's your insides and entire reproductive system that may have to be vacuumed out, it's hard to see this. I am simply horrified at the thought. Later, I learn that this combination of eviscerating surgeries is known as 'debulking'. An awful word for an awful process.

The radiographer's office is just across the way. Dr P tries to calm me down: 'It's unlikely that you are BRACA positive. Let's wait for the results before we worry.' (She turns out to be correct.) She counsels me: 'I strongly believe you should have a lumpectomy rather than a mastectomy. If you have a mastectomy, what will I tell other patients with a more serious diagnosis than yours?' And then she adds. 'I will personally take responsibility for checking that you are cancer-free.' These moving words come back to haunt me.

I drive home with 'mastectomy, lumpectomy, mastectomy, lumpectomy,' galloping through my brain. Which is it to be?

My quagmire deepens when I meet Sue, an old friend who was diagnosed with breast cancer ten years before. In her studio teeming with paintings which incorporate stitches and bandages, she tells me: 'I immediately elected to have a double mastectomy. I just wanted the cancer out of me so I booked my surgery four days after I was diagnosed.' I was awed by her certainty. She went on to have an extremely unlucky recurrence of the cancer despite this.

I meet another friend with the same diagnosis as mine. I know her more peripherally but this didn't matter in the slightest. Once you enter the cancer club, you are instantly connected to its members. Jenny was far less certain than Sue: 'I didn't know which way to turn after my diagnosis,' she said. 'I interviewed ten different doctors including plastic surgeons, oncologists, radiologists. They were divided down the middle. Five told me to have the double mastectomy and the other five told me this was way too radical an option for a relatively minor cancer. The breast cancer survivors who I spoke to were equally divided. In the end, my high levels of anxiety made the double mastectomy a better route for me.'

Unexpectedly she asks, 'Do you want to see my breasts? I must warn you that I have never had my nipples reconstructed.' I am not prepared for this moment. My heart starts beating as if I have just encountered a lion on foot. She gently lifts her shirt and, I confess, I am shocked. Nipple-less breasts are an anatomical oddity if you have never seen them before. My eyes mist with tears. We hug each other tightly. 'Thank you,' I say. 'I really appreciate your openness and generosity.' Jenny then repeats to me something reassuring that her breast surgeon had said to her: 'Nipple-less breasts look like sleeping kittens.'

As I drive away, the image of Jenny's breasts is a new piece of visual shrapnel that pierces another layer of my innocence. I am not yet prepared for the physical disfigurations that are to come.

Jonny and I search for our own clues to stop the merry-go-round we are on. The stats make a double mastectomy seem like an obvious choice. A mastectomy has a five per cent risk of recurrence of breast cancer, while a lumpectomy has a 27 per cent risk.

But the situation is more complicated than these figures suggest. Long-term studies reveal that there is absolutely no difference in the mortality outcome of those patients who choose a lumpectomy or a mastectomy over a ten-year period. Many doctors in the United States are vehemently opposed to radical preventative surgery to solve my particular diagnosis. Some whom we speak to say, 'A mastectomy should not be offered as an option'. My surgeon and radiologist have opposite beliefs about the right treatment for me.

I turn to writing to make sense of this all. By typing words on the screen, I hope that my confusion will untangle itself. I am feverish. I write at odd times during the day and night. The subject line for an email to a small group of close friends is: 'List of an unruly mind'.

I don't know it then, but this is to be the first of many lists and emails I write in an attempt to work through questions and confusions and to help me select and prioritise my next steps. I come to rely on the way that streamlining my thoughts in an ordered way on a page helps me to organise my sense of inner chaos and create a sense of mastery over life.

On 22 February 2011, 12:49 AM,
Lauren Segal <laurensegal3@gmail.com> wrote:

In the wee hours of the night, I am typing my 'cancer list' to try and capture the events of the last few days. They seem to keep slipping away. They are too large, too overwhelming, too unfathomable, too unfair to keep hold of. I am flummoxed (what a nice-sounding word). So I am sending you these fugitive pieces of anxiety that have emerged over the past 96 hours. Maybe by sending them, and by asking you to hold them, I can adjust a little better and arrive at the last point on the list.

If my list were a poem, I would call it, 'And that's not all'. I would insert this title in between each item on the list. If I sung my list, it may even start to sound humorous:

You are due for your annual mammogram.
You have small calcifications in your right breast.
You need a biopsy.
You are told you have a Stage 0 ductal carcinoma in situ (DCIS).
You are one of every nine women who is diagnosed with DCIS.

You will need a lumpectomy with radiation.
You have to go on a pill that brings on early menopause.

You are a high-risk cancer patient.
You can't have radiation. It will mask recurrence.
You may have other tumours.

You have something on your liver. Something is in your groin.
You need an MRI so we can see if the DCIS has spread.
You need an ultrasound to check.

Your cancer hasn't spread but it is in 3 ducts not 1.

You need to go for genetic testing to see if you have the breast cancer gene.
You will need a hysterectomy if you are BRACA positive.

You can have a lumpectomy without radiation and have MRI's every 3–6 months.
You will always be anxious and wondering if it has come back.
You are the only one who can decide.

You can't have a single mastectomy. It leaves a high-risk of recurrence on the left breast.
You will also look lopsided.
You could have a double mastectomy and get total peace of mind.
You can have reconstruction at the same time as the mastectomy.
You are the only one who can decide.

You will get through the operation just fine.
You will feel very tired for a long time.
You will need another operation to sew on the nipples.

You may have to have a mastectomy and then a reconstruction.
You will have to wait and see what is possible during the op.
You are the only one who can decide.

Your husband will not love you less without your breasts.

Your children won't mind.
You will feel different and life will never be the same.
You will be thankful to be alive.
You are the only one who can decide.
You will be alive.

I end the email:

Jonny and I are entirely hollowed out. It is my greatest wish for this all to be over and for me to go back to my life and for Jonny to be relieved of his best supporting actor role. My kids who know only the faint outlines of this situation are doing really fine for the moment. Thank you for receiving this.

Not-A-To-Do-List

25 FEBRUARY 2011

When I wake up, I continue with my list-making frenzy. My day-time list is messy and confusing. It can't be ticked off as neatly as my usual 'to-do's'. It is a list that should not be written too many times in one's lifetime.

My Fears List

Lumpectomy

The lumpectomy will be more difficult than imagined.
They will have to make a bigger incision to clear the margins.
They will have to take tissue from my back creating another site of trauma.
The cancer is more diffuse.
They will have to close me up and do a mastectomy a few weeks later.
There will be more scars.

I will not be able to tolerate the radiation.
I am scared of being burnt.
I will go into early menopause.
My body will lose all elasticity.
I am only 45. It's too early for this.

I will lose my lightness of being.
My life will become medicalised.
I will need an MRI every six months.
I will lose my peace of mind.
I won't be able to cope if there is a second time around.
The cancer will become more invasive.
I will have to have chemotherapy – I don't want this at all.
They won't detect the cancer the second time around.
I will die.

Mastectomy

I will lose the part of myself that I like the best.
My most intimate part will be sucked away.
I will lose my sexuality.
Katya is an adolescent. How will she be affected by this?

Jonny will stand by me but will he really feel the same?
I will not be the same. Can I really ever be the same?
Jonny will be waiting outside the theatre just like we did with Katya.
He will be carrying too much.

I will be frightened by what I see when I wake up.
I will not have nipples.
I will not be able to look at myself.
I will not be able to love myself or let Jonny love me.

My kids will be scared to look at me.
I will turn away from my life force.

Others will look at me differently.
The operation will go wrong.
All my fears are irrelevant.
I won't be here. I am dying.

The cancer will still come back.
I will have chemotherapy and more operations.
I will have to go through more of this.
I won't be able to find the strength and resilience.
Life will never the same.

Thoughts of a Diminished Self

27 FEBRUARY 2011

After many painful hours of soul-searching, Jonny and I decide that I should have a bilateral mastectomy instead of a lumpectomy. In the end, our decision comes down to four factors:

1. *I have an extreme needle phobia and am constricted by fear of any form of medical intervention.*
2. *I don't want the future rhythms of my life to be dictated by scans and endless medical investigations.*
3. *I don't want hormone therapy. I am not at all ready for menopause.*
4. *Losing my breasts is better than losing my life.*

'I will love you with or without your breasts,' my gorgeous husband assures me.

Amidst the tears, I am distracted by new thoughts. Where will my breasts go, I wonder? My mind drifts to a visit I made to Carol, my oldest friend, after she had her tonsils out. Carol greedily gulped down the ice cream and jelly that I had brought her while my eyes fixated on two strangely shaped mounds of tissue in a bottle of formaldehyde next to her bed. The image of her tonsils has never left me. Should I be asking to keep my nipples in a bottle as a keepsake? Would I ever want them on display? My inner eyes avert at the thought.

A very different set of dilemmas awaits me when I go to see the plastic surgeon the next day. 'What shape and size do you want for your new breasts?' Dr S asks soon after I step into his office.

How naïve of me! I hadn't even considered this question. I am not one of the millions of women who obsess about changing the proportions of their chest. I am a classic 34B and have never entertained fantasies of bigger or smaller, perkier or more rounded.

So the surgeon's question isn't a zone of opportunity as it may be for others. It is only a zone of loss. In subsequent months, I discover a massive research study that shows the ideal proportions for new breast implants are those of the famous Venus De Milo, the beauteous statue by the artist Michelangelo that resides in the Uffizi museum in Florence.

But without this knowledge, I tell the surgeon: 'I want my breasts to be exactly the same as the ones you are taking away.'

He casts his eyes over my chest area and then walks over to a stack of silicone implants lying haphazardly on a side table. As he rummages through them, they absurdly wobble around and remind me of the mounds of luminous red and green jelly served inside orange peels at children's birthday parties. It doesn't take long for Dr S to place two small silicon objects in my hands. 'These are the right size,' he announces.

I have no way to judge. I simply nod and rush out of his office for fresh air.

What to Expect When Expecting a Mastectomy

6 MARCH 2011

I have no idea how to prepare to undergo such radical surgery. All I can see before me is a diminished version of myself. The castrated image of my torso isn't easy to hold. Annette suggests she comes around for some yoga. We roll our mats out on the shady vine-covered patio of my house. A bird sits chirping on the ancient twisted branch that weaves around the column of the *stoep* (verandah). Something about its innocent singing makes me cry convulsively. Annette soothes me by holding a rope across my thighs and raising my body into downward hanging dog. She is literally holding my body afloat. My raging fires subside momentarily.

Carol, Neil, Nicola, Indra and Steve bring lunch. Carrie and Tana arrive with baskets of love. We lounge on the worn brown leather couches on our deck. Much of the conversations pass me by, but I am grateful for the chatter that creates the edges of a bubble that I am floating in. Jonny fields calls from far and wide to wish us strength.

My mother is in the house feeding my children and helping them with their homework. I am so grateful to have her loving presence to take care of my kids, although I am equally glad that my father is not alive. He would not have borne the pain of seeing his daughter in this moment.

I write to my colleagues telling them to expect me back in action after a week. My business partner, Clive, wisely responds to this unwise email that I should perhaps give myself a bit more time.

In the evening, Roz phones: 'Should I come over and take a portrait of you?' I wish I had taken her up her most thoughtful and generous offer. The photograph would have been a better keepsake than nipples in a bottle.

The final bath with my whole anatomy intact induces more tears for both Jonny and me. We stare at my reflection in the bathroom mirror, terrified of the erasures to come. We take a mental snapshot.

The day of my mastectomy dawns. Dr Benn has ensured that I have high doses of anxiety meds at the ready to cope with the extensive procedures that take place before the surgery – all involving long needles into my nearly gone breasts. My needle phobia is on red alert.

Adam, my beloved brother-in-law, flies in from London to be with Jonny. They walk besides the gurney as I am wheeled into the operating theatre. 'Why am I not asleep?' I keep asking with growing desperation. 'I don't want to be awake right now.' Jonny promises, 'You will be asleep soon.' These are the last words I remember through my blinding terror.

My next memory is waking up on a morphine high. Why has no one ever told me the euphoric effects of this drug? Through the gentle mists that envelop me, I see Jonny, Adam and two of my closest friends, Steve and Phil, around my bed. Steve and Phil have come bearing a tray laden with delicious food from my mom. She hates hospitals and is staying at home with my kids instead.

I love my mother's food deliveries in times of trouble and today is no exception. She has selected food for the soul – chicken soup, deseeded grapes, ripe figs, slithers of cheese with a mild tomato relish, small pieces of barbeque chicken. Both my appetite and my *joie de vivre* hours after such major surgery amaze the assembled coterie. Neither they, nor I, realise quite how happy I am just to be alive and to be feeling no pain. My absent breasts are of no immediate concern.

When my loved ones go home, however, the relief and the morphine are not able to conquer my inner fears. That first night in the high-care ward turns into a proverbial nightmare. There are eight women who have just had mastectomies and are awake throughout the night in various states of distress. High as a kite, I am not able to distinguish between my own suffering and that of the others. The women's muffled cries next to me blends with mine. 'Do you think I am going to die?' I murmur to the heroic nurse who tends to us all. She holds my hand for what seems like hours and assures me, 'You will see the morning'.

Friends create a solid ring of love around me for the next days. The morphine pump that dangles over my shoulders and allows me to control my own dose keeps me euphoric. I later learn that Dr Benn is concerned that I am 'hypomanic', a medical term meaning 'a mood characterised by persistent disinhibition and pervasive elevated elation'. She calls in a psychologist to check that my exuberance isn't hiding something more sinister. Doctors clearly underestimate the terror that surgery such as this can induce.

After three days, I arrive home with two drains that protrude from each side of my chest. They are attached to a vacuum pump mechanism which sits in a wooden box that I carry around. The vacuum pump assists with healing by draining fluid from my surgical sites. The tubes, which are attached to my body on the one end and to the pump mechanism on the other, are extremely uncomfortable. Not to mention the nausea I feel as they fill with the debris created by my own body. I cannot bear to look at the bits of flesh and blood that gather nor can I bear the smell and so I place this whole contraption in a large Ed Hardy bag adorned with a colourful skull. Every half hour or so, the whirring sound from the pump is exhaled through the mouth of this multi-coloured effigy.

There is only a single moment of light relief in relation to the drains. Janine arrives for a visit and without realising what the contents of the bag are, she moves it aside with a single swift motion. My body lurches forward. 'That's not a handbag,' Tana, who is often on my bed during these days, cries out in alarm. 'It has Lauren's drains which are attached to her.' Janine and I laugh for months over this incident.

My devoted sister-in-law, Ilana, flies in from Toronto to look after me during that first week back at home. She is the domestic traffic controller, shepherding friends in and out of the house at allotted times. She makes endless cups of tea, and trades in endless conversations. She is the most comforting presence along with many others who buoy me up at this time.

Such is my desire to be well again that I host a work meeting with French clients who are in Jo'burg to put the finishing touches to a museum and guest house we have created in the house that Mahatma Gandhi once stayed in. As a *satyagrahi* (passive resister), Gandhi believed that the physical suffering he endured in prison would make him stronger and more determined in his moral cause.

I wonder if he would have approved of my working on a museum in his honour in my lounge in my bandaged state, hooked up to a box that whirred every few minutes.

When the drains come out after a week, I dance around our bedroom in celebration. I am preoccupied by many other incursions into ordinary life as I once knew it. I still have to sleep bolt upright with pillows all around me as well as under my knees. The two breast implants feel like alien forces have landed in my chest wall. I am preoccupied with the twinges, unexpected pulls and weird pangs of these foreign objects as they are still to knit into the cavity of their new home. Months go by before these feel seamlessly integrated into my anatomy.

I remember the exact day that I experience a sense of my oneness again. I am relieved that I am no longer an occupied territory.

Cancer Lite

Around the same time that my chest region is re-integrated into my body, I discover a new label. Cancer invents new languages and a new word has been formulated to describe the rising number of us women who have chosen radical surgery in order to prevent the reoccurrence of cancer. I am now deemed a 'previvor'.

I have always loved unusual words. When my father was alive, he would send me a new word each day, each email forming a silent connection between us. I record the words that I like in a journal on my bedside table. If they happen to be seven letters, I get a visceral pleasure imagining the high score I may get in my next scrabble game. With other words, I simply love hearing the unfamiliar new sounds roll off my tongue to create an audible splendour – like 'sesquipedalian'. Often I discover a word that captures a feeling so perfectly that I wonder how I could have lived without it.

The word 'previvor' has no appeal. It gains a particular intimacy nonetheless, as it is to be worn by me for the rest of my life.

I find ways to embrace my previvor status and welcome

mortality as my new friend. I tack this quote by a Talmudic sage onto my pin board: 'It is incumbent on you to live as if you were to die the next day.' Next to it, I pin a list of ten injunctions:

1. *Spend as much quality time with your family as possible.*
2. *Go on adventures.*
3. *Climb every mountain.*
4. *Break new ground every day.*
5. *Do something that you never thought you could do.*
6. *Love your life.*
7. *Focus only on what's important.*
8. *Pursue pleasure.*
9. *Eat healthily.*
10. *Resist cake.*

I spend hours scouring the internet to fulfil the first two injunctions as well as to find a place to recuperate. How lucky I am to have this kind of choice. Our family and my mom end up winging our way to Zanzibar, the spice island off the coast of Tanzania. There must be an unconscious impulse that leads me to a place that represents more than just escaping to a paradise. Zanzibar was once a slave colony with a history of profound suffering. The story of the emancipation of the slaves is a fierce emblem of the sweet tastes of freedom that I am experiencing as a previvor. I have won my own battle against the forces of darkness – even if it bears absolutely no resemblance in magnitude to slavery.

Zanzibar is also an exotic place. Each day, we discover the most beautiful sights, sounds, smells and tastes. I am compelled by the way that this island enlivens my body and mind, which have been dulled by weeks of lying on my bed. Each day, the brilliant azure blue ocean swallows me in its gentle swells. I look at my husband, mother and children with a heightened sense of appreciation. The holiday marks the end of me being a patient. Or so I think.

When we return to Jo'burg, I develop an infection in my right breast. I am shattered. It arouses a violent set of raw emotions as I have to endure needle aspirations in my newly reconstructed right breast to remove a pool of fluid. I reach out to my fellow travellers, Carrie and Sue, to keep me sane. The incident is short-lived, and I regain my internal equilibrium.

As part of my rehabilitation, Annette takes me for a session with an extraordinary yoga teacher and friend, Carla. I can't lift my arms higher than my shoulders but the three of us commit to weekly yoga, which we do every Thursday to this day. Carla cajoles my body into calming stretches which I drink in with relish. I begin to unfurl and we all have tears in our eyes when my arms can reach over my head once again.

In these months, I am generally on a natural high. My second cancer leaves me intent on squeezing every last bit of sap out of the bark of life. Despite undergoing a double mastectomy, I feel lucky. This has been 'cancer lite'. No chemo. No radiation. No death sentence.

The trauma does not induce me to ask any penetrating questions about the meaning of life; or the impact of illness on the body and mind; or the nature of the demands the body makes of us. I do not link my suffering and vulnerability to new pathways of pleasure. Besides the ten points on my pin board, I do not ask what it is that I truly want. I do not seek solidarity with other previvors.

I believe that I have dealt with the issue of cancer in my life. I have fought relentlessly and won. I have done my time. 'Cancer Two' is a temporary hiatus and I return to normal life. I am overjoyed.

Cancer Three
The Bedroom

It's Not Scar Tissue

24 JUNE 2014

Given my triumphant ending to 'Cancer Two', it is not hard to imagine how shocked I am driving home from Soweto on that cold blue-skied winter's day. It is unbelievable to me that all my fears from my 'worst fears list' – including that 'the cancer will still come back' – have come true. Despite having chosen the most radical treatment option, my breast cancer has reappeared. My post-mastectomy sense of wellness was a blind folly. Now it seems like my smile was forced, my enthusiasm had a desperate, hard edge.

I sit in my bedroom with my hands firmly wedged between my knees. Tears trickle down my cheeks. Primo Levi's words about the Holocaust swirl through my brain. 'It happened, therefore, it can happen again.' This is an entirely false equivalence but at that moment, it is as if my own internal Holocaust is recurring.

I hear Jonny pulling up at the gate. His car has a particular purr. The gate rattles open. These are usually happy noises signalling Jonny's arrival home from work. Today they spell impending doom.

My husband's footsteps are intimidatingly purposeful on the wooden floor of our passage. He enters the room with that look of dread carved into his face that I have only seen twice before. Once when the doctor told us that our Katya had multiple heart defects, and again when I learnt of my second cancer. This time, it accompanies the diagnosis that the lump in my chest wall – that my radiologist was '100 per cent sure' was scar tissue – is a malignant breast cancer.

I am gutted. Split in half. Shocked and disbelieving. Jonny explains: 'The tumor is too large to remove surgically at this stage. You need hormone therapy to block the production of oestrogen.' I will be thrust into precipitous menopause. This is exactly what I had tried to avoid by choosing the preventative mastectomy.

The world is muffled. 'How do we know that the lab hasn't switched the sample?' I ask feebly. 'I checked that already,' Jonny replies. 'They are your results, La.' Jonny is equally disbelieving.

My husband is not the sort who brings me tea in bed in the morning. He does not arrive home with bunches of flowers. He does not cook. He does not make wildly romantic gestures. He seldom plans surprises. He is over-controlling at airports. He can be very impatient. But he has loved me passionately from the day that we committed to wed. He is loyal. He has given me boundaries and created an unrivalled sense of safety. His calm spirit is a ballast for my frenetic nature. He has loved my scarred body, even more so after my breasts were removed. He is my fulcrum. A fixed point. My rock.

Neither of us could have anticipated under the *chuppah* how often we would have to redeem our pledge, 'through sickness and health'. 'The ghosts of repetition' – a beautiful phrase by the writer W.G. Sebald – have haunted us in our 22 years of married life. In our case, it is the ghosts of a potentially fatal illness that do not leave us alone.

All marriages have their trajectories, different rhythms and patterns that mark their texture. Ours has been a swing between extreme highs and extreme lows. In the outside world, Jonny is a double doctor – a medical doctor with a PhD in economics. In my world, his PhD is in being my husband.

That night, Jonny and I find ourselves back in the car on our way to the breast surgeon. The sense of 'Groundhog Day' is overwhelming. The waiting room is just the same as three years before. Too many people in too small a space. Too many women with their heads in scarves. Too many with drain boxes secreted away in bags.

Jonny and I stare just at each other. 'We have done our time here,' I say. I pick up knitting needles to add rows to a scarf – a common project in doctors' waiting rooms. I am not a knitter. Each row is a desperate attempt to calm my jittery nerves.

Dr Benn pops in and out of one of several consulting rooms. Her kind and hyperactive manner is just the same. Her uniform is still jeans and trainers. She has not lost her extraordinary touch of picking up the next file and adding something nice like, 'Gosh! You have got your colour back!' When it's my turn, she gives me a big hug. 'You look beautiful,' she says.

But when we sit down on her couch, she has no answers. She is as surprised as we are with my biopsy result. 'I thought the lump on your chest wall might be a kind of melanoma. Another breast tumour is a completely unlikely outcome. There is almost no breast tissue in which cancer might occur again ...' She speculates: 'There is a chance that some of the cancer cells could have moved to the chest wall during your first biopsy when we found the DCIS.' This seems unlikely, as does the other option: 'Some cells may have been there before the mastectomy and were simply left behind in the breast tissue that remained post the surgery.'

'What will happen to me this time?' I ask in a small voice. I am waiting for Jonny to ask, 'What would you do now if Lauren were your daughter?'

'We have to wait for an MRI to find out more about the tumour,' Dr Benn says. 'Thank God, I forced you to have the biopsy. At least we have caught it. We should not have waited this long.' There is no blame or self-aggrandisement in this statement. On the contrary. If she had not called me to say, 'I am driving around with your file on the front seat of my car. It's keeping me awake at night. Please go and have that biopsy,' who knows what might have transpired.

I appreciate her forthrightness. I am naturally optimistic. My oldest friend describes me as someone who perpetually turns lemon into lemonade. But the shock of being diagnosed with cancer for the third time before I am fifty has left me reeling. I no longer know how to live by the optimistic watchwords that were my inner mantra for so long. I am stiffening under the attack of a malevolent God in whom I do not believe or find solace. My spirit is disfigured.

I still want to believe though that the MRI will actually tell me that the lab results have got it wrong. That this is all a bad mistake and that life can carry on. But this wish is as naïve as it was after 'Cancer Two'.

Two days later, I am in a yoga class hanging upside down from ropes in the wall when Jonny's name pops up on my phone. This time, I answer the call immediately. His voice is thin: 'The MRI scan shows a 6.5 cm tumour.'

'Are you joking?' I yelp as my voice coasts upwards from the floor. And then again: '6.5 centimetres?'

'La, remember the pathology results. It's lobular and slow growing. It's a good cancer to have. It is hormone sensitive, and HER-receptor negative. These are all good for the prognosis. It means that the tumour will respond to targeted hormone treatment that saves thousands of lives.'

I don't quite understand this yet. It seems like a meagre consolation prize, a somewhat 'optimistic tragedy', the paradoxical description given to Shostakovich's 5th symphony. I hoist myself up on the ropes and turn my body the right way round again. My feet give way slightly as they touch the floor.

I had imagined my tumour to be smaller and more contained. I would have been better off if I had been a pessimist. News of this potent single cell that, even though slow growing, would have been less shocking. Now I have to come to terms with a cancer that has been exquisitely adapted to survival and has managed to produce billions of malignant cells that have taken occupation of my chest wall.

My yoga teacher, Carla, and my yoga partner, Annette, have watched the very visible lump morph over the last two years. It has been red and angry some days. Calm and better behaving on others. Sometimes, I can do some of the postures that involved twisting the right side. Sometimes, I can't.

'How is this possible?' Carla asks. She has regularly inspected my chest wall. She has observed the changes but has never doubted or questioned the diagnosis that this was post-operative scar tissue.

'I am so sorry, my friend,' Annette adds, her eyes overflowing with tears.

I leave the class in a daze although the irony of doing yoga when I receive this news strikes me. Yoga is a practice of listening to one's body, finding the edges, going to a place of safety with awareness and connection. My body appears to have been yelling and performing for two years now without me hearing. Instead, I preferred to listen to the reassuring inflections of the radiologist after each scan: 'This lump is not another tumour. I am prepared to bet my life on it. I will hang up my stethoscope if this is malignant.'

To rewind. For the past 18 months, I *have* been worried about the lump protruding from my body. When I finally went to see the plastic surgeon, he took one look at it and said, 'This is another malignant tumour. It needs to be removed immediately.' Dr Benn was less sure and sent me straight to Dr P for an ultrasound.

Dr P looked hard at the image on the screen. 'This is scar tissue. We can do a biopsy,' she said, 'I don't think it is necessary, however. Rather, come for a scan every few months so we can keep an eye on this.'

I skipped out of her office that day. Of course, I didn't want another biopsy. The first one before my mastectomy had been utterly traumatic. I fainted so many times while they tried to plunge an extraordinarily long needle into my breast that I had to be sedated. Why on earth would I put myself through that trauma voluntarily again? Dr P had given me the confirmation bias I was seeking.

I carried on happily with normal life. I returned for scans on a regular basis – every three months or so. Each time, the radiologist assured her colleagues and me that, 'The hard mass is not malignant.' Each time, I believed her with all my heart. She is a brilliant diagnostician, with a deservedly excellent reputation, and the most caring of human beings. God would undoubtedly declare her among the righteous on earth. Her gentle manner was a balm to me at each and every step of the way during my mastectomy.

But she has made the wrong call. And I have chosen to listen to her. Human fallibility is staring me in the face. Mine as well as the doctor's. I had shut my eyes to the growing and changing lump on my chest wall. I had ignored the pain when I lay on my right side. I simply turned over so as to be able to sleep more comfortably. I had no other signs of illness. Nothing else was amiss. I believed I was really well. Why shouldn't I have? My radiologist, husband and I were all participating in a complex triangulated dance of avoidance. A potential death dance. We did not know that then.

Now, 18 months later, I am alone with this misdiagnosis, this monumental mess, and this potential life sentence. My mind is pulled thin. I circle like a vulture around the question of blame. I wonder if my own fear of the biopsy has actively clouded the radiologist's judgement. Had I persuaded both Jonny and Dr P to ignore the warning signs? I can't rule out my own complicity, but I am not willing to take full responsibility. There was conflicting information at my disposal. I had not computed the risks, not realised that I was playing a game of Russian roulette.

Would a statistician have chosen to have the biopsy instead? What is the probability of getting cancer for a third time, and breast cancer for a second time *after* a complete risk-reducing bilateral mastectomy? The medical odds are extremely low. The surgery has been shown to reduce the risk of breast cancer by at least 95 per cent.

Anyone in my position would surely have come to the same conclusion – that this was not another malignant tumour and that its behaviour could be monitored by scans. Surely others too would have ignored the clamorous signals of my tumour?

I later learn of the 'Bayes' Rules'. This governs how subjective probabilities are updated as new information becomes available. Once I learn that it is entirely possible for one person to have recurrent malignant tumours, and that there are other people who have suffered my fate, I begin to see how I could have so radically misjudged my situation and how Jonny and I could have colluded in believing the radiologist's assurances.

At that moment, however, I do not want to become ensnared in this controversy and I simply tell myself, 'There is no space here for would have/should have/could have'. There are bigger issues to confront. I say this again and again over the next weeks as the implications of my avoidant behaviour become starker. In hindsight, I am relieved that I did not play a blame game. I did not give in to my vicious superego that was waiting in the wings to transform 'It was done to me' to 'I did it to myself'.

To Tell or Not to Tell

26 JUNE 2014

That night, Jonny and I are due to board a plane to Israel with my family for my nephew Benji's Bar Mitzvah in Jerusalem. What do Jonny and I do with the news that I have cancer again, for the third time? Out of the 30 trillion cells in my body, one irregular mutant cell has triumphed. My world has turned on its head.

In *Cancer Ward*, the Russian writer, Aleksandr Solzhenitsyn, writes how being diagnosed with cancer is like entering a borderless 'medical gulag', a state more invasive and paralysing than that which he had left behind. Jonny and I are in the heart of this medical gulag, utterly outcast and desolate. But we decide that we can't drop this bombshell in the midst of a major family celebration, an event planned for years. Family has gathered from every corner of the globe. I can't imagine walking into the hotel and telling my brother, 'We are so glad to be here. And by the way, I have cancer again but please let that not spoil the moment.'

I am also not ready to become *that* person, the one with cancer in the room, the one that people look at with such tenderness. The one who people lower their voices around and speak in dulcet tones of love and concern. I want to try out just being me for a few more days before my whole world changes. Just recently both my children reflected on this decision: 'Thank goodness you didn't tell us,' they say. 'We wouldn't have coped.'

And so Jonny and I stand in the airport queue with my mom and kids who are blissfully unaware of our tempest brewing. We have donned firm carapaces to ensure that no untoward signs escape. The mundane and frustrating rhythms of an airport check-in happen amidst the chaos of the *El Al* counter. Passports in and out. Boarding passes issued. Security checkpoint reached.

'What was your Bar Mitzvah portion (the reading a Bar Mitzvah boy is assigned from the Torah)?' an officer asks my unsuspecting son. Presumably, he is checking that Josh is really Jewish. It is one of the few times I have seen my son at a loss for words. He stumbles, but then manages to access the name of his reading that he did four years previously. Jonny and I are genuine in our laughter.

Next are the endless queues at passport control. This humdrum officious tedium rolls on while my head screams that I am carrying a lethal disease. I wonder if the metal detector will pick this up and if the siren will scream, 'Cancer! Cancer! Cancer!'

Is it a pure coincidence that Jonny almost chokes to death on a piece of biltong while we wait to board the plane? I think not. The incident is shocking. Josh and I are casually strolling out of a shop when we see Jonny in front of us turning deep red and struggling to breathe. He barely manages to gasp, 'Get water. Hurry!'

Josh and I both freeze in fright. Thank goodness Jonny has the wherewithal to rush up to a complete stranger and grab his bottle of water which Jonny glugs down in a second. Thank goodness the piece of biltong goes down and the colour returns to Jonny's face.

We are all in shock, not least the poor man who has had his water snatched from him. 'Thank you for saving my husband's life,' I say and offer to replace his bottle of water. 'Really don't worry,' he tells me and I know that he means it. It is not often that one is unknowingly presented with an opportunity to save a life.

Of course I assign a symbolic meaning to the incident. In our 24 years together, nothing like this had ever happened. Jonny is usually the one doing the Heimlich manoeuvre, including to his own mother who once almost choked on a piece of meat during a family celebration. Now it is he who is choking on a diagnosis that is impossible to swallow. Our children chuckle about the episode: 'Did you see the man's face when Dad took the bottle?' Josh asks. Katya adds: 'Dad has saved so many people from choking that it is now his turn to be saved!' Too true.

I catch Jonny's eye. We both know that we can't quite escape the medical gulag we have been assigned to. Nonetheless, we carry on with our pretense. We remain silent while our insides are in tatters.

As we step out of the taxi into the blinding heat of the Israeli summer, small beads of sweat gather below my hairline. Will I be able to maintain our vow of silence, I wonder? When the cousins rush into each other's arms and Mark and Ilana welcome us with delight, I know that we have no choice. The secret must stay in its vault. I plaster on a beaming smile and I exclaim, 'It's amazing to be here!'

This cheery disposition is what I cling to over the following days as a large pack of us tour this beautiful but haunted patch of land where peace is so evasive. The sun illuminates the white stone walls of the ancient city and imbues their physical weight with a sense of holiness. The spiritual landscape is a balm, and I marvel at the Jerusalem that is claimed by so many.

Meals are a raucous affair with over 30 of us gathered to celebrate over an array of dishes of hummus, tahini, falafel, pickled cucumber and other delicacies. Although we do not share the religious way of life that governs most of this large extended family, the bonds that transcend time and space are very moving. I love the way my own family is absorbed into this circle of love. Our differences evaporate.

In my state of vulnerability, it is the unspoken gestures and emotions that strike me most: the adoration between grandparents and their grandchildren; the ease with which one of the cousins who had leukemia when he was seven years old conducts himself; the joy expressed by a child born with serious developmental abnormalities and how her cousins protect her.

We commune late into the night. We laugh and chat. My pleasure is genuine. My husband copes less well. The space around him is heavy. He is tense, distracted, often talking on his cell. He is organising second opinions and a genetic test of my tumour. This requires that a tissue sample of my tumour be couriered to the United States. Up to now, I have not been aware that my medical aid facilitates this at all. Jonny is trying to convince the laboratory to conduct the test in less than usual time so that my treatment is not delayed.

I am struck by the luck and un-luck of this situation. Jonny's medical training and his position in the healthcare industry ensure that I will get the finest medical care in the world. Yet despite all the access, neither he nor I is able to orchestrate a better diagnosis. Despite our enormous privilege, we are powerless.

In our stolen moments together, we are assailed by paroxysms of fear for our future. We interact with the tenderness that comes with confronting a dreaded disease. We are not able to assume that a good outcome will simply come our way, although we are both geared up to make it happen.

The sun is unrelenting on the morning of the Bar Mitzvah. The temperature soars past 40 degrees. As we wend our way over the path that takes us to a small ancient synagogue in the heart of the city, our makeup melts and our high heels crunch on the ancient stone path. It is an utter relief to enter the cool white interior of the synagogue. From the moment that I am in this holy place, I am captivated by a woman's plaintive voice of prayer while her body moves back and forth, her hands open in supplication before her. I long for this connection to religion. It would provide such comfort at this moment.

The same wish repeats itself the next day at the Western Wall, the holiest of holy space for so many. Even though I inwardly rail against being on the other side of a divide where we women are forced to stand, watching my male family in their black-and-white prayers shawls moves me. The sound of the Hebraic *davening*, a primitive chant in a bid to connect humans with the divine, echoes in the vast space around us. My nephew sings his way into adulthood surrounded by the most important men in his life.

The religious fervour stirs me and I write a note asking God: 'Please look after my family and me.' I press the folded piece of paper into one of the cracks in the Wall that is crammed full of notes written by so many different hands seeking the comfort and assurance of a greater being.

Not Quite the Land of Milk and Honey

28 JUNE 2014

Jonny decides to fly home early with Josh, who has to return to school to write exams. 'Why are you leaving?' my brother asks. Jonny wishes he could answer truthfully but instead he says, 'Sorry, Mark. There is a crisis at work. I have to be back.'

I miss my husband's presence by my side, but I go on to explore the vibrant and sassy beach city of Tel Aviv with my mother, daughter and niece. When I am alone in my hotel room, there is mental fraying. I feel split off and angry. Over lunch, I shout at my mother for no reason whatsoever. She accepts my behaviour with equanimity. For many years now, my mother has been at the end of my sharp tongue. I can't seem to grow out of my adolescent habit of snapping at her over the smallest thing. This is our infantile bond, a bond that I suspect is part of many a mother–daughter relationship.

My mother and I are different in so many ways. My exuberance is in stark contrast to her deep restraint. She shares little of her feelings. I wear mine on my sleeve. She is well coiffed at all times of the day and night, elegant and edgy for a woman of her age. I am shabby chic, 'a hippy in Gucci' as one friend once described me. I love my career. My mother loves her bridge, although she has recently discovered her considerable power in her role as President of the Union of Jewish Women. We do, however, share important passions – raising children, cooking, decorating our homes, tending our gardens and shopping.

The shopping gene is something that my daughter and niece have both inherited and we especially adore shopping with my mother. It is an art form that she has perfected, and she is very generous too in spoiling us. So while in Tel Aviv, I depend on retail therapy to get me through. My fellow shoppers are delighted by my energetic inclination to trawl through the shops. My daughter is treated to an unusual number of pairs of shoes. She looks at me oddly but cannot realise the true weight of these purchases and the forces that are spurring me on to get a black belt in shopping.

While I am manic by day, I cry and fulminate by night. I am so afraid of my unreliable body. These chameleonic shifts, the highs and the lows, are to become a pattern of the next months.

Susie is in constant touch with me by phone. Jonny and I had shared my news with her before we left. As a trained psychoanalyst, she is gifted in her insights and wisdom and is often the emotional gateway for both of us. She coaches me through my bubbling rage and madness. She helps me to bridge the two realities I am trying so hard to yoke together in a land so far from home.

'Your anger towards your mother is so understandable. You are besieged. You are reverting to a child-like state and you lash out against the one to whom you are closest. It is important at this time to be kind to yourself.'

The only other person I share my story with while in Israel is

Jonny's sister, Mandy, who lives in the north of Israel. She is a loving and sensitive human being. We meet in Tel Aviv at the museum of Yitzhak Rabin. I tell her my news over mint tea before we visit the exhibition about Israel's greatest leader whose assassination changed the entire geopolitics of the region.

I have not meant to tell her. But when she mentions that I am looking good, tears well up in my eyes. Such is the problem with an invisible disease. On the outside, I look entirely normal. There are no signs of my rapidly dividing cancer cells multiplying all too quickly. I make a crude attempt at a preamble before I let out my secret. In a faint echo of the story we are about to encounter in the museum, I explain that my own family's geopolitics is also about to be rearranged.

The shock on her face is unbearable. I wish I had never uttered a word. The stuttering exchange is a foretaste of what is to come with others in the weeks that follow. 'You are amazing to have carried this diagnosis secretly. How have you managed?' she wants to know. I tell her I have no option.

Our departure from Israel is calamitous. The dishevelled bureaucrat behind the screen tells me: 'Sorry. Your tickets are not showing in the system.' I start to screech: 'Then something is wrong with your system.' My daughter turns bright red. 'This is embarrassing. Calm down,' she mutters under her breathe. I am now more enraged. I want to scream out, 'I have a potentially fatal disease. I am going home to learn my fate. Please show me some consideration.' Instead, I get Jonny on the phone. 'If this man doesn't find our seats, I will implode.'

Jonny's attempts to calm me down from a million miles away and fails. My shouting takes on a life of its own. It bubbles over from the weight of my situation. Jonny gets it. Just as I am about to decompose entirely, the computer seems to register what is at stake. Everything in the system suddenly aligns. Our tickets click out from a slot in the desk. Katya and I scuttle off. 'Why are you behaving so badly?' my daughter asks. How do I answer with any kind of integrity? I try to apologise. Katya wants none of it. I suggest we go to duty free.

If Not Me, Then Whom?

1 JULY 2014

Something about flying through the clouds at high speed makes me dwell on the possibility of dying. I become fixated on the mundane rituals of our lives and who will fulfill my role: Who will make my children's elaborate daily lunch boxes for school? Who will invent creative ways to celebrate their birthdays? Who will scour cookbooks for healthy recipes to cook each night? Who will fantasise about the next destination for the family holiday? Who will keep the stationery drawer full and the gift cupboard stocked? Who will trawl the shops with Katya for her dance dress? Who will take Josh to university next year? Who will read my children's essays and remind them to use full stops? Who will make sure that Jonny doesn't work too hard?

In fear of Katya getting wind of my volatile emotions yet again, I make my way to the tiny cubicle at the back of the plane. Sitting scrunched on the toilet seat with my legs against my heaving chest, my mind skips from these daily concerns to the special occasions that may take place without me. Letters start to write themselves; letters for Josh and Katya on the day of their graduations; letters expressing my happiness for them on their wedding days; letters to be opened on the day of the birth of their first children. Would an untethered maternal voice be a comfort or a dagger in the hearts of my children? What is the proper role of a dead mother on these occasions?

The last time I found myself in a toilet cubicle like this was after being told that my father had an inoperable Stage IV brain tumour. 'Your husband has between three and six months to live,' the neurologist said to my mother before he proceeded to answer a call on his cellphone. I took refuge in the toilet outside his consulting rooms and my uncontrollable sobs were so loud that a nurse in the next-door cubicle asked if I needed help. 'Thanks. It's okay,' I stuttered. What I really should have said was, 'Do you have pills to mend a broken heart?' I was 41 years old and was not ready to lose my father.

My son is 17 and writing his final high school exams in three weeks' time. My daughter is just 13 and in her first year in high school. Both are at such vulnerable points in their lives. How can I tell my kids that their mother has cancer *again*?

The pilot's voice over the loudspeaker interrupts my thoughts. 'Please fasten your seatbelts. We are expecting some turbulence.' I don't care; turbulence is where I fly these days, I say to myself. While I make my way back to my seat, I think how pilots are trained to handle all kinds of emergency situations. Parents need better schooling in disaster management. We need to learn how to create soft landings for our children in times of distress and how to sew internal parachutes into the fibre and sinews of their beings.

The rest of the trip is uneventful but my arrival home is not. As I pull into the driveway and Katya runs into the house, my floodgates open. I answer a call from a beloved friend who knows of my predicament. When Janine hears my shaky voice, she insists that I meet her at our local coffee shop. I haven't slept or showered but I follow her instruction. Her son was diagnosed with a brain aneurism when he was just 11. He is my son's best friend. I walked the miles with her when he was having his operation. He is a healthy and beautiful young adult today.

Now the baton has passed from her family to mine, and it is Janine's turn to provide solace. She tries to hold my heaving shoulders as big tears plop into my hot oats, left untouched. Susie rushes into the coffee shop between her sessions. Because she has been speaking to me throughout my time away, she knows the extent of my distress. Her face bears the look of concern that comes only in times of great suffering.

'What am I going to tell my kids?' I wail. 'How can I reassure them that all will be all right when my whole world is crashing down around me?'

'How did you tell them last time?' Janine asks.

I think back to the busy restaurant in Rosebank. I remember the conversation vividly. Jonny did the talking just after we ordered breakfast. He was unusually hesitant. 'We have some bad/good news,' he began. 'Your mom has cancer and needs to have an operation.' He paused to take both their hands. 'But if you are going to have cancer, this the best kind you could have. The cells are still asleep. They are not the bad kind of cells that have spread.' I took over at this point. 'I am lucky to have caught it so early. I am going to be just fine … I promise it is not like Normie's cancer (my father) where there was nothing to be done.'

Josh, who was 14 at the time, started to ask a lot of questions. We answered them as honestly as we could. It did not seem necessary to lie – a ductal carcinoma *in situ* is genuinely a good kind of cancer.

'At 10, Katya was too young to absorb the import of our utterances,' I tell Janine and Susie. 'Her memory of that time seems to be the abundance of flowers that filled our house and friends bringing special tea and cake and making a fuss of me. It will be so different for her now.'

I walk back home to shower and unpack. The rest of the day is consumed by thoughts of how best to shield my children from the new foreign words that will soon invade their innocent world. There is no way to stop our next exodus from the promised land.

A New Kind of Cancer

3 JULY 2014

After dinner, we ask our kids to come into our bedroom. It is by far the favourite room in our house. It is large and inviting with doors onto an indigenous garden on one side, and a courtyard on the other. During the day, red-breasted robins perch on the aloe trees and become the onlookers to our lives.

Many nights have passed with the four of us lying together on our king-sized bed piled high with soft downy cushions that receive our imprints. Old steel pressed ceilings form an intricate canopy over our conversations and dreams. Friends are also drawn here, where an evening often ends with us clustering on our bed.

Tonight, our children sense that something is wrong. Unspoken signs litter the space. Although I take my usual position on the bed, my face is not my own. There is a pile of tissues on the bedside table. Instead of lying next to me, Jonny sits stiffly on the pink striped chair in front of our fireplace. Neither of my children can anticipate what they are about to hear. We can still barely comprehend it. 'Mom has a new cancer. A tumour has grown in the small bit of breast tissue that remained after her mastectomy,' Jonny starts.

Katya's face crumples. She rushes over and hugs me tightly. I beckon for Josh too. I squeeze both their hands too hard. I wish for an equivalent of white noise to cancel the pain. 'This is very unlucky and very unusual. But like before, Mum has the best possible prognosis. The tumour is very slow growing and has not spread ... She is going to be just fine.'

These words are thinner than the first time. It is a small white lie to say that the tumour hasn't spread. That confirmation still awaits us. For now, it is a hope we share.

As with my first diagnosis, it is Josh's brain that switches on first, even though I know that his heart is racing. He needs answers. He now has a fairly advanced knowledge of the anatomy of the body through his study of Grade 12 biology. Jonny responds diligently to each question while my mind is screeching, 'Why do my children have to go through this again? Surely they have been tested enough?' The 'ODTAA Syndrome' – the 'one damned thing after another syndrome' described by the doctor and writer, Atul Gawande, in his book *Being Mortal* is a good description of my family when it comes to medical traumas.

I don't want cancer to be my children's constant chaperone, but I am not given this choice. The news of my illness cannot be rescinded. It has already contaminated our domestic space. It has liquefied the walls of our home, and our job as parents is to try to stem the flow of the tsunami as best we can. I already long for the solidity that minutes before characterised our dwelling.

I cling to the fact that we have resilient children. They have been forged in a strong family unit with a beloved granny close at hand and another beloved set of grandparents at the other end of a phone. I know that our brothers and sisters will erect a solid fortress around us as they did before. I know that a community of godparents and friends will fortify this structure with sandbags and other braces to guard against the floods to come. Together, we will support my children as they are fast-tracked into a premature confrontation with mortality.

After Josh and Kats escape back to their rooms, Jonny and I fold into each other like flimsy tissue paper. The worst is over but there is still so much to come. We have to inform our family and the rest of our friends.

My mother is still with my brother's family on their post-Bar Mitzvah adventure in Israel. I know that I can't speak the words, 'I have cancer again' so Jonny is burdened with this unenviable task. He calls my brother. I imagine the words, 'Lauren has another malignant tumour', making their way slowly through the airwaves then speeding up as they traverse the telecommunications cables under the oceans that separate us. I imagine them swirling around inchoately before they are neatly reconfigured and reach the restaurant by a shimmering blue lake in the north of Israel where my family is sitting with the moon spreading light rays across the pool of water.

I can't bear to picture what happens next. The scene goes blank. This is surely a mother's worst nightmare. My hope is that my brother, and the other close family surrounding her at this moment, will buffer the harsh tidings.

I don't know what transpires that night. I learn that in the days after that my mother, my brother, my sister-in-law and her extended family say prayers for me during their visits to ancient synagogues and gravesites of their relatives who are buried in this holy land.

This touches me – one does not have to be religious to appreciate the prayers of others. My mother is in my heart even if she is not an active player in the drama that unfolds over the next days.

The only call I attempt is to my brother-in-law Adam in London and I fail dismally. My tongue is not yet habituated to forming the necessary sounds that will communicate my fate. All that comes out are uncontrollable sobs. Jonny takes the receiver away from me and I hear him say, '... another tumour'. He hands back the phone and now Adam is sobbing too. Jonny's parents and his two other siblings are equally devastated.

I tell my closest friends the news by email. As I start to fill in the addresses in the space bar, I find myself adding more and more names. Every person who is in our lives needs to know what is happening to our family and they need to hear it from me. We will need all the fortifications that we can get over the next months, including our colleagues and our children's friends. The drill is familiar by now and I know that by sharing this kind of information with others our burden will ultimately be diminished.

But the letters are still arduous to type. It is hard to find the right tone, the delicate balance between communicating the severity of my situation and my determination to stay afloat. It is hard not to be overwhelmed by history colliding. The subject line is a particular challenge. I settle on, 'Bad news' which seems like an adequate warning for the contents of the mail. I hesitate for a long time before finally pushing 'send'.

On 3 July 2014, 10:24 PM,
Lauren Segal <laurensegal3@gmail.com> wrote:

This is a hard email to write and I wish I were closer by and talking to each of you in person. I discovered last week that I have another primary site of breast cancer. It is off the breast actually in an area I have been scanning for the last two years. We thought that the hard lump that I have been feeling there was scar tissue caused by the infection that I had after the mastectomy. The radiologist assured us on every occasion of the scan that there was absolutely no chance that this was a malignant tumour. She was wrong.

Luckily my breast surgeon had a bad feeling and kept calling me. Eventually, two weeks ago Dr Benn forced me to do a biopsy, which revealed a 6.5 cm malignant tumour. Luckily, it has not spread. This time, I need hormone treatment to shrink the tumour, an op to remove it and then radiation. Not sure about chemo as yet. Not fun.

We chose not to tell anyone so as not to spoil the Bar Mitzvah week for my family in Israel. Kats and I arrived home this morning and Jonny and I just told our children.

We are all in deep shock. The kids are trying to absorb what this all means. It is too soon to know how they have reacted. I am disbelieving that I have to do this all over AGAIN.

Jonny is a champion as always. A rock in my life. But he is taking strain. I feel for him that he has to deal with yet more of this stuff. Luckily, we are a strong unit and together, like the last time, we will find the positives of this journey. Believe it or not, there are some positives to having to (keep) facing one's mortality. I might have to be reminded of this going forward.

I am flooded with relief at the moment that the email is sent. This disease is no longer mine alone. Despite the late hour, my computer starts to ping almost immediately. Gusts of love rain down. Our fragile dwelling is bolstered. The shock and disbelief I receive is tempered by an insistence that I am particularly well equipped to deal with this situation:

Oh my darling friend I am in such a state of shock. But since you are absolutely the epitome of everything that is full of life, courage and hope and joy, I know if anyone can cope with this dreadful illness, it is you. Michi

Words fail us. We are gutted that you have to find the strength to tackle this cancer all over again. But you will. Your bravery is deep inside you from the last time. And we will be right behind you, Jonny and Josh and Katya every step of the way. Pam and David

Jonny's inbox starts to fill up too.

> *I am all too aware that the shock and burden of Lauren's news must weigh very heavily on you, and my heart goes out to you both at having to face this yet again. Hilary*

The phone also starts to ring despite the late hour. My dearest friend Phil calls from Cape Town. We usually speak for hours. Tonight, our conversation is much shorter and comprises only tears. Jess calls from London. She was with me when the doctor phoned about my melanoma in my flat in Yeoville all those years ago. I hear the intense worry that underlies her attempts at assurance.

Jonny and I go to bed, bodies leaden with exhaustion but also wrapped in an extraordinary blanket of love. The scaffolding that we so longed for is now being erected. We can confront the gruelling days that await us in the full knowledge that our family and community are holding the ground firm. This provides us with a tiny tincture of courage.

The next day, the walls around our house evaporate. The doorbell buzzes repeatedly as friends drop in to give me a hug. They come bearing flowers and tea and cake but mostly they carry with them friendship and concern.

It is very important to me that my children bear witness to the generosity of our community. The acts of kindness that shower down on us are a testimony to the redemptive power of love. More emails pour in and love continues to radiate off the screen. I am so struck by the repetition of the words describing me as brave and strong and courageous.

Inside, I do not feel brave or strong or courageous at all. On the contrary. I am not being propelled forward by bravery. The simple fact is that I have no choice. There is no freedom involved in walking this well-trodden cancer pathway. No one is saying to me, 'I can reverse the diagnosis. I can make this all go away'.

Atul Gawande describes two kinds of courage in aging and sickness. The first is the courage to confront the reality of mortality when there are so many reasons to shrink from it. The second is to act on this reality even when a wise course forward is so frequently unclear.

He relates how Socrates and two Athenian generals discuss the question, 'What is courage?' They engage in a long and complex conversation about courage being the 'endurance of the soul', and about the differences between 'foolish' and 'wise' endurance. Their exchange helps me come to my own conclusion. I think that courage is pursuing life to its fullest even in the knowledge that my time may be limited.

This is more challenging than I imagine. Without a sense of what lies ahead, I feel stumped, devoid of courage and not ready to confront my mortality. Nor do I feel I have the strength to pursue my life's course in the face of this large obstacle that has been thrown my way. I am at a crossroads and I'm struggling to harness my 'glass-half-full courageous self'.

PART TWO

From Person to Patient

I Am No Longer I

4 JULY 2014

It is all downhill from after sharing my news. Besides the emotional upheaval, my body is now flung onto a medical rollercoaster with no safety belt. This is my moment of sharp transition from person to patient. 'Your life is the ship others steer,' says the author, Rebecca Solnit, after she was diagnosed with breast cancer. In her book *The Faraway Nearby*, she goes on to beautifully capture the voyage that all of us in this position are destined to travel toward or away from our mortality.

'You must be patient, must become a patient, must take up residence in waiting rooms, must learn to wait for experts and results, must grow accustomed to being laid out upon tables and invaded, described in unfamiliar language and treated with methods that may seem like illness is injury, though they are intended to cure.'

Just as Solnit describes, I take up residence in waiting rooms which invariably try to create a false cheer. My cracked and fragile vessel has to be scanned to assess if the tumour has spread. I undergo the procedures that I so desperately wanted to avoid when I elected to have a double mastectomy. As I am pricked and prodded and pushed and pulled, the irony of this still makes me wince.

I am no longer I. What I took for granted just a few weeks ago is no longer. My 'Goldilocks life' that was neither too hot nor too cold, neither too soft nor too hard, neither too good nor too bad, is permanently altered.

꩜

The nadir of my voyage away from all that is known is the PET CT scan. It takes months before I can write down what happens during this 'position emission tomography' process.

The day starts off innocently enough. 'What a beautiful cloudless sky,' I say to Jonny as we drive to the hospital. But the image of this rich inky blue expanse soon disappears as I enter the hospital. I am grouchy from an enforced 24-hour fast and my mood is not helped by the taciturn nurse whose bosom is squashed into her too tight uniform.

'Your husband cannot stay with you,' she tells me as she ushers us into a small darkened space with a faint odour of disinfectant. 'Why not?' I shoot back in horror. I am relying on Jonny's presence to get me through this ordeal. 'The radiotracer we inject you with over the course of the hour makes you radioactive,' she replies.

I have no idea what a radiotracer is or what it means to become radioactive. My only association is with the song by Imagine Dragons called 'Radioactive' with its seemingly appropriate line about the apocalypse. My own apocalypse starts with Jonny squeezing my hand tightly before making his enforced departure.

The next thing I feel is the nurse inserting the drip into my arm without a single word of comfort. 'Don't talk or move,' she says. 'If you need the toilet, it's over there.' I am horrified to see another person hooked up in a chair just outside where she points to. This is one of the best private hospitals in the city. Is it possible that a patient's dignity and comfort is so overlooked?

I try my best to get through the next 60 minutes while my inner voice is screeching, 'Unfair, unfair, unfair.' (I am later to stop using this word but for now it seems appropriate.) There are no physical clues to becoming radioactive although my arm gradually gets heavier at the point where the drip is running into me. When the hour is up the same lacking-in-empathy nurse leads me into a large room. An equally surly technician enters and pins me down to a cold slab by pulling a series of straps across my torso, my waist and my thighs. They are too tight but I have given up protesting.

'Do not move an inch,' is all that I am told. Again, no reassurances, no words of comfort. As she goes into her booth, it strikes me that I have no way of calling them if I need something. There is little wonder that the original meaning of the word 'patient' in Latin is 'one who is suffering'.

The scanner starts to whirr up and down the length of my body. I am overcome with claustrophobia. My panic levels rise. My throat constricts and my breathing quickens. To calm myself down, I think of what Katya had to endure as a baby. I often use her experience as an anchor for myself in situations of stress. Her tenacity gives me courage. It helps me to surrender to a medical process.

After 40 of the longest minutes I can remember, the whirring stops. I am unstrapped as unceremoniously as when I was tied down. My legs judder as I stand up and walk back to where this day started. I am so relieved to see Jonny. He is holding me tightly against him when a technician comes in and announces, 'You need an ultrasound of your liver.' I search Jonny's eyes. What is the import of this statement? Is it an ominous indicator of spread? My husband's lips are white. He clearly cannot offer me any assurances. This isn't happening. This can't be happening.

This is happening.

'Let me go into the scan room alone,' I say to Jonny. I want to protect him from more bad news. But when the radiographer descends into silence and his mien becomes grave, I wish Jonny had been with me. I know the signs. Reticence spells trouble. All that the doctor says is, 'Have you ever had an ultrasound of your liver before?' I can't remember. What is he seeing in the fuzzy white lines on the screen that are so hard for me to decipher?

Afterwards, the doctor refuses to answer Jonny's questions or to give us the encouragement that we are looking for. In his uninflected voice he tells us, 'There is a shadow on Lauren's liver.' He pauses but does not meet our eyes: 'I will send the report to the oncologist later today.'

Jonny and I don't need the report to tell us what we know – that the shadow means that the tumour has spread. This is my death sentence. I have read Steve Jobs' biography. His pancreatic cancer killed him once it had spread to his liver and other parts of his body. There is no hope of a cure for these kinds of malignant metastases.

Flashes of my life masquerade before me. In that moment, I long for the simple and predictable life cycle of all animal species. They are born, grow up and die in marked out periods of time: a few weeks for insects, longer for cold-blooded reptiles; shorter for the more frantic warm-blooded birds; over two centuries for sea urchins. Humans go through the same stages of life in the same order but the variation in our life span is far greater. Wealth. Nutrition. Disease. Too much uncertainty to pin down a timeframe. Is death my biological destiny?

We walk up to the hospital café and each step is like treading up a sand dune with the ground slipping away beneath our feet. The tea and food we order remains untouched despite the fact that I have not eaten since the night before. We are too overwhelmed by the sudden proximity of my mortality.

The silence between us is filled with the unsayable. Time becomes thick. The bustle in the hospital lobby is slowed down to a dull thud. Jonny makes repeated calls to our various doctors to see if they can talk to the radiologist and get the results sooner. It is unjust to be made to wait to hear that you are going to die. As the minutes tick by, our hearts and minds become unmoored. We simply cling to each other. At some point, Jonny phones Susie so that there is someone else who knows what we are enduring. 'Come over,' she says. 'It's not good for you to be there alone.' We leave our table, forgetting to pay for the meal. I am not sure how we get to the car.

Jonny's cell rings as we pull up to our friend's house. It is Dr G, the oncologist. She must have the results. I cover my ears. When Jonny gives me a thumb's up and a wild smile crosses his face, I cry out in relief. 'It turns out that the shadow on your liver is a benign mass known as a hepatic haemangioma,' Jonny beams. The 6.5 cm tumour that has grown steadily for two years has miraculously remained localised.

Susie comes out of her house to see the tears of relief streaming down our faces. We sit with her, debriefing. We can't go home quite yet. Our bodies are too heavy from being in the vicinity of death. We need to remain cocooned. We need to talk about our lucky escape. In our tin capsule, Susie gives us the language to describe what has happened to us: 'The trauma is massive. In a few hours, you experienced what human beings fear most – the loss of life and the loss of love. You feared your children could lose their mother, and Jonny his wife. It is important to allow this trauma to have its place so that you can regain a sense of hope.'

Some months later, I read about different kinds of hope: sadistic hope (You are going to be fine, everything is okay); manic hope (You feel a great sense of triumph but it is not a true recovery); and mature hope (You've been through hell, a lot has changed but there is still a lot to hope for.) After my last diagnosis, I fell prey to a manic hope. My quest for the next months will be to discover mature hope.

Right now, however, my capacity for any kind of hope is severely impaired. I am relieved that there are no metastases but my circumstances are graver than I imagine. Any sense of optimism is truly bleached out of me.

I am not ready to exit the current story of my life and step into a new one – particularly one where the middle and ending are so uncertain. I don't want the starring role in this particular movie script. Way out on the edge of my comfort zone, I continue to spiral downwards.

My cancer induces self-contempt. I am consumed by ugly thoughts and internal lacerations. 'I am a cancer factory,' I tell myself and become transfixed by self-pity. How is this possibly happening to me *again*? What evil have I done to deserve this? Like Icarus, have I flown too close to the sun? Is my illness a sign of my bankrupt spirituality?

Alone, I alternate between convulsive crying and unfathomable rage. Cancer is a disease that is as elusive as it is emphatic. I am wrestling with the unknown, the unknowable. It is made of silence and yet induces a roar of inner noise. Voices crowd my head. How many more sunrises and sunsets will I see? I feel closer to my own mortality than ever before.

The torments of damnation in Hieronymous Bosch's triptych, 'The Garden of Earthly Delights', a painting that mesmerised me on first sight, dance before me. My inner roads are populated with Bosch's fleeing figures, cities on fire, torture chambers, infernal taverns, and mutated animals feeding on humans. The painter's dense scene of hell portrays what my words cannot.

My diagnosis forces me to cross an entirely imaginary boundary between what Susan Sontag designates as 'the kingdom of the well' and 'the kingdom of the sick'. When entering this kingdom of the sick, there are no prescribed recipes for how to cope. There is no cancer 'toolbox'. There is complete discontinuity between my yesterday, today and tomorrow. My worst nightmares have come true. I am on the edge. How do I re-find my inner compass?

Cancer Warriors

As I begin to read about others who have trodden my path, I am alarmed at how much of cancer speak is peppered with references to us patients as 'warriors' and 'heroes', 'soldiers' and 'combatants'. These labels appear to be strictly reserved for those of us with the 'big C'. I have never heard talk of a patient 'going into battle' when diagnosed with an angina, TB or polio. Among the endless descriptions of cancer patients, our malignant cells are deemed our 'enemy' and we are urged to 'win the battle' against them. Obituary after obituary euphemistically declare the famous and not so famous people who have died from the disease as having 'lost the fight'. A cartoon next to the basin in the washrooms at the chemo centre shows a woman dressed in gladiator gear with the caption, 'Cancer – you have messed with the wrong woman'.

I am fascinated by this bellicose portrayal and am thankful to come across Siddhartha Mukherjee's 'biography' of cancer, *The Emperor of all Maladies*. This provides the best explanation of why the disease is 'languaged' in this way. Mukherjee describes how early fundraisers created this combative language in order to shift cancer from a disease that existed in the shadows to one that occupied a central place in the world of public health. The new marketing device – 'the war against cancer' – initiated by President Nixon in 1971, succeeded in drawing the public into the crusade for public action and funding to find a cure.

It is equally fascinating to learn that real wars were entangled with the prolonged and intense fight to discover a cure for cancer, and this also explains the linguistic framing. I had no idea how difficult the problem of cancer treatment really is. Unlike other diseases that come from outside of the body, cancer grows from the inside. A cell that has functioned normally for many years wakes up and becomes a cell of excess, dividing in an unregulated and unfathomable way. Generations of doctors have puzzled over how to find a drug that can destroy specific cancer cells while sparing normal tissue. A selective poison of this kind proves highly elusive.

I read about the growing arsenal of possible treatments that created glimmers of hope. For over a century, however, the efforts to perfect chemotherapy seemed *ad hoc* and chaotic. Many leading scientists who developed breakthroughs in treatment regimes became outcasts because they were seen as imposing solutions that were medically cruel and untenable.

It was the German's use of the monstrous mustard gas – a toxic mist that caused hundreds of thousands of soldiers to die writhing in the trenches during the last years of WW1 – that took the story forward. Examinations of the survivors revealed that the gas targeted the bone marrow and wiped out only certain populations of cells. This fact was forgotten in the amnesia of war. It was not until the use of mustard gas during WW2 that doctors were again alerted to the gas's unique properties. An experiment was carried out with a patient with lymphoma and indeed the cancer cells were wiped out. It was a Dr Faber who dreamed up the notion of chemotherapy – a chemical that could cure cancer outright, 'cancer's penicillin'.

This startling narrative leaves me marvelling at how it took a team of scientists three years to perfect the manufacture of an atomic bomb that killed hundreds of thousands of people, while it took scientists over a century to discover a form of chemotherapy that would work imperfectly on both solid and liquid (blood) forms of cancers. It is also now more obvious why the association between war and cancer is so prevalent and why this warring terminology is used to describe this particularly strange condition that involves our bodies' own cells going rogue.

The story of chemotherapy makes me realise how lucky I am to be living today rather than in the last century. But this knowledge speaks to my head and not my heart. When one is confronted with a serious diagnosis, the same age-old terrors apply despite advances in science.

I fall back on the well-trodden path of the warring metaphor, and I set out to devise a 'battle strategy'. What I really have to contend with is the idea that my battlefield is my own body. My foe is not in lines of trenches on the other side of a field. It is in close vicinity. Some cells have lost the checks and balances that control and limit cell division in normal cells. Stripped of my armour, I need to find new defences as well as safeguards. Just like parliament is supposed to protect our country from an overbearing president, I need to devise rules for my intrusive disease.

There are as many battle plans as there are cancer patients. Some patients go into instant retreat. They hand the reins to their doctors. My father was like this. After he heard that he had a fatal Stage IV brain tumour, he accepted that he was going to die and let the doctors dictate. He never asked about the nature of the disease growing in his head, and he wasn't interested in alternative treatments. He simply never went into battle at all.

Other cancer warriors go into knowledge overdrive. They scour the Internet to learn everything there is to know about their condition. They become their own doctors and use their new knowledge to discuss treatment protocols with their oncologists. This is their way of taking charge of their bodies. My friend, Caroline, wrote to me about her own approach: 'To me, knowledge is power, and I wanted to feel in charge of my treatment, and to make my own choices. In order to do so, I had to be able to have informed conversations with my doctors, understand what was going on, and challenge their position when necessary ... So David and I did a lot of studying.'

Other patients try to bargain with the disease. When Oliver Sacks was diagnosed with an ocular melanoma in his mid-70s, he made this agreement with his malignant cells: 'Take the eye if you must but leave the rest of me alone.'

I thought I had done my bargaining the last two times. I have already given up my breasts. Clearly, that was not enough.

My battle plan is bifurcated. Jonny takes care of the medical front. Over the years he has been the Commander-in-Chief of countless war rooms that have been set up in the face of a medical crisis. He diagnoses; advises on treatment plans; phones his network of specialists; follows up with the results; assists with health insurance problems. Recently, while away together, Jonny answered a call from my oldest friend close to midnight. He did not sleep until he could ascertain that she was suffering from severe viral meningitis. Jonny says he would never have been a good doctor had he remained in clinical practice. When I watch him in action, I disagree. He has an excellent bedside manner. Now it is for his wife that he creates a war room.

Jonny sets off with his ferocious intensity to uncover the latest treatment protocols for my specific cancer. He works with my team of doctors in Johannesburg to arrange consultations with the breast cancer specialists at the Massachusetts General Hospital in Boston and at the Cleveland Clinic.

This involves sending emails to doctors across the globe. Every one of them who hears of my medical history is perplexed. It is very rare for one person to have been diagnosed with three primary cancers before the age of 50, and the occurrence of a new lobular cancer, with a different cell type from my initial DCIS after a total mastectomy, is very puzzling. A world-leading oncologist who runs a large clinic in Los Angeles writes to Jonny of the 'oddity' of my situation. She could not have described it better.

Jonny reports back to me how the current, standard treatment of all cancers – a one-size-fit-all approach – is fast disappearing. The rapidly shifting cancer battlefront offers exciting possibilities. Indeed, whole new frontiers of medicine are opening up and new achievements being recorded continuously. My husband identifies a laboratory in San Diego that has developed a detailed genomic screening test for breast cancer, and he arranges for the tissue sample to be dispatched.

I am lucky and entirely grateful to have him do so. It is a great privilege to be able to access this cutting-edge medical frontier through the daily work that Jonny does. Nevertheless, the intricacies of my diagnosis and the exact nature of the treatment plans are not my current preoccupation. At this moment, these are not the weapons that I need to protect myself. I am satisfied with the knowledge that the cancer has not spread beyond the primary site of my rather large tumour.

Even if Jonny had not pursued this medical path with such rigour, I don't think I would have delved into knowing the intricacies of my disease. I am a big-picture person, preferring the broad outlines to the granular details. It is enough for me to know that my body has produced a single cancer cell that has reproduced itself in a limitless fashion and found ways to outwit the inhibiting forces that stop the disease. My right chest wall has been colonised. Every medical website that I engage with is an assault on my senses.

My energies go elsewhere. I am in search of a different kind of artillery. I start reading every book I can lay my hands on about the psychology and healing practices surrounding illness in general, and cancer in particular. I want to understand what is happening to me outside of a purely western scientific medical paradigm.

The questions I ponder are focused on the psychology of my body. Wittgenstein's words, 'What you say, you say in a body', take hold of my imagination. If nothing is outside of the physical realm of my body, what is the cause of the corporeal civil war that has been unleashed inside of me – not once, but three times? I ask myself:

1. *What is my body telling me?*
2. *What meaning does this diagnosis have for my life?*
3. *What answers are buried in the irregular cells that are so restless and agitated, so fierce and adamant?*
4. *Why did this illness choose me?*
5. *Did I choose this illness?*
6. *Am I ever going to win internal cooperation?*
7. *How can I use my illness to help me grow?*

I am flummoxed by these questions and have no ready answers. I remain convinced that these are the right questions to be asking and that the rejoinders are lurking somewhere in the crevices of my body and mind. My job is to find them. These conundrums need to be solved if I am to live. I have a new quest.

I read and re-read the lists that appear in different books that try to define the 'C (cancer) Personality'. These lists suggest that there are common threads detectable across all cancer patients:

1. *Always putting others first*
2. *Low self-esteem*
3. *Bottling up emotions*
4. *Living in fear*
5. *Harbouring resentment*

This list does not speak to me. In fact, if any one of my family or friends were to read it, I doubt that they would assign any of these characteristics to me.

Red Hair and a Temperament to Match

I set myself the task of making a list to describe myself – or rather the self that I am before 'Cancer Three'. The journey I am to go on changes this list considerably but it starts off as follows:

I have red hair and a temperament to match.
I have a limitless capacity to cry in circumstances both happy and sad.
My family is at the heart of my world.

I am happiest when my house is full of children.
My feet are firmly planted on the ground.
I am ebullient and an optimist by nature.
I am tenacious.

I will always choose a route to my destination with the least number of traffic lights.
I have never worked in an office. I don't do bosses.
In fact, I don't do rules.
Or tax returns or car insurance.
I HATE being told what to do. (Tell me to go right and I'll go left.)
If I smell order and routine, I run a mile.

I can efficiently multi-task.
I often think I can be in two places at once.
I struggle to say 'no', preferring to keep my options open.
I love to travel and discover new worlds.
I have an appetite for aliveness.
I am tuned into the world around me.
I am an inveterate networker.

I look like I am a person where the world flows my way.
I struggle with anxiety and vulnerability in others.

I like challenges.

I love tomatoes and hate raw onions.
I have never tasted coffee.
Cake is my greatest delight.

I believe in retail therapy.
I have a shoe fetish.

My favourite place in the world is our house in the Magaliesberg.
My worst place is any beach at noon.
I am not a morning person.

I don't plan ahead.
I don't mind being teased.
I prefer process to outcome.
I am an opener and not a closer.
I don't like murk and shadows.

I hang upside down every day (in my yoga ropes).
I find a reason to throw a party as often as possible.
I prefer walking up a mountain to down one.

I prefer a sprint to a marathon.

As I start to absorb a range of stories about illness and healing, I am prompted to add other qualities to this list:

I have a propensity to be irritable.
I get flustered and bothered when things don't go right.
I have an easy way with anger.
I can easily overcome being angry.
I am not afraid to ask for help.

I read Louise Hay, herself a cancer survivor. She went on to became a metaphysical lecturer who teaches people to use their powers for personal growth and self-healing in times of illness. She asks her cancer patients to tell her what has prompted their illness. Her core belief is that we are completely responsible for every experience in our life.

At the back of her book, a chart correlates diseases and their probable causes. Hay instructs us to look up the mental cause of our illness. 'See if this could be true for you,' she says. 'If not, sit quietly and ask yourself: "What could be the thoughts in me that created this?"'

I run my hand down the list to the word 'breasts' located between brains and breathe. It reads: 'Breast problems are a refusal to nourish the self. They are about putting everyone else first. Over-mothering. Overprotection. Overbearing.' Cancer is the very next item on the list. For Hay, this disease is about, 'Deep hurt. Longstanding resentment. Deep secret or grief eating away at the self. Carrying hatreds.' She tells us cancer patients to embrace alternative statements which focus us on filling our world with joy, love and approval.

In my previous life, I might have rolled my eyes at Louise Hay. I probably would have rejected the idea that my disease is linked to certain personality traits. But in my new state of helplessness, I am open to all possibilities for self-empowerment and taking back any vestiges of control. Inside the vacuum of my soul, her list gets me thinking:

1. *Do I harbour deep hurt and resentment?*
2. *Do I refuse to nourish myself?*
3. *Could it be that our souls choose our parents with those faults and weaknesses that we need to learn to overcome?*
4. *Could my disease be linked to my hot temper and rebellious nature?*
5. *Could it be that my hunger for new experiences and my restlessness can explain my tumultuous constitution?*

Perhaps Hay did not mean me to take her so literally, but I am on a mission to find the right questions and any possible answers. A welter of memories of my early self bubble up from the shadows of my despair. It proves helpful to look backwards when looking forwards is so difficult. There is comfort to be had in trying to decipher the clues that may have landed me in this particular life circumstance.

The Sweet Cupboard

JO'BURG, CIRCA 1970

On the surface, I grew up in the happiest of households. We lived in the leafy suburbs of Johannesburg in the height of apartheid. I was 10 years old at the time when army tanks rumbled down Corlett Drive, the main street near our home during the 1976 Soweto Uprising. Few of us white children had a sense of what lay just beyond the white picket fences of our happy and innocent childhoods.

My mother, who in a later era might have been the CEO of a large corporation, poured her vast organisational capacity into the domestic realm. Her garden won first prize in the annual garden show. The smell of jasmine infused the pathway to our front door. The numerous collections of musical instruments, antique scientific implements, old Afrikaner farm utensils and much else besides, were all perfectly arranged in harmonious patterns on the wall. She dressed impeccably and her large wardrobe of fashionable attire could easily have been converted into a small retail outlet.

Clothes and food were part of our connective tissue, and both were played out on a grand scale. While most other little girls I knew were taken shopping at Woolworths, my mother took me to a children's boutique called 'Freckles'. How I wished that I could have been the eponymous little girl on the shop's sign above the door. My freckles were perfect and my smile cheekier, I remember thinking.

The shop was a fairyland. My mother would perch on a round

ottoman in the centre of the shop and I would sashay in and out of the change room in one outfit after another. My mother's ample sartorial wisdom allowed her to pronounce: 'That really suits you!' She always encouraged me to be bold and different. In those moments, I felt very special and adored. The feelings were amplified when I would walk out with several more packets than necessary.

Her generosity in the clothes realm was matched by a gastronomical abundance. Both signified her special brand of maternal care. My school lunchbox was the envy of the class. It was jam-packed with different sized containers of chicken wings, carefully cut sandwiches, fruit kebabs, assorted nuts and a range of treats. The golden honeycomb bar was my favourite, followed closely by slices of rich chocolate chiffon cake with thick chocolate icing made by my great aunt. I would often share these delights with the teacher, which helped to maintain my status as 'teacher's pet'.

Meals at home were an equally elaborate affair – breakfast, lunch and supper. We all ate our eggs with carefully poached kippers, a colourful sugar-drenched fruit salad and steaming hot tea from a tray with an embroidered tray cloth in bed in our own rooms. In the evening, my mother rang a bell just before 7 pm. The family would sit down to savour her constantly changing menu of culinary delights.

The *piece de la resistance* of our home was the sweet cupboard. This is where all meals ended. The three-shelf wonder was built into the wall of the living room. It outdid Willy Wonka's factory of delights. Every possible variety of sweets and chocolates spilled out of boxes onto the shelves. My friends loved being at my house for this cupboard alone – especially because we had free reign.

It strikes me now that this enormously generous bounty, and the lack of restrictions pertaining to it, may have reflected a darker pattern of life in my household. The absence of limits with sweets was mirrored by my parent's inability to assert boundaries in other realms too. This may explain why, from my earliest memories, I cannot tolerate the word, 'No' being said to me, either internally or externally. All roads appeared to be open. It also explains why my friend assigned me the Rolling Stones song, 'You Can't Always Get

What You Want,' when we sat around choosing the soundtrack of our lives.

Mick Jagger crooning that you can't always get what you want makes me reflect that I might have taken a bigger slice of pie than was my right. My brother, just 18 months my senior, found this justifiably difficult. I won the verbal fights. He won the physical ones. The violence of our confrontations and our jealousies prevented me from taking responsibility for my rivalrous little-girl self. Only now do I realise how lonely it was to assert my 'rightness'.

My mother, who did the bulk of the child rearing as was the norm of this era, was often at a complete loss as to how to contain the passions of two strong children. She was, after all, very young when she had us. She married at 19, and had her children at 21 and 23. I remember her chasing my brother and me round the garden one day with my father's leather belt. 'Try and catch us if you can,' my brother and I taunted. Of course she never hit us. Ever. But to this day, I struggle with consequence.

My father arrived home at 7 pm at night. I always felt like his little girl, the cute little redheaded daughter, and the one who could do no wrong. My father was my saviour. I would tattle-tale 'Mark hit me today.' My father safeguarded his cute daughter who looked like she was the one getting a raw deal. But his generosity and conviviality were matched with an explosive temper. I stepped out of the way of his rage. I watched from the sidelines with a sense of triumph that this anger was not aimed in my direction.

I, however, inherited my father's fiery traits. My own tantrums were volcanic. The eruptions would endure for hours. My parents looked on helplessly, as if I were a strange specimen. They failed hopelessly to douse the flames of my inner fury, or to contain me.

I did not understand any of these dynamics at the time, or the damage they would carve out in my future life. Instead, I revelled in my father's attention and was deeply drawn to his unbounded enthusiasm. My favourite activity with him was to blaze down the highways of Jo'burg perched on the back of his motorbike. It was exotic and unique to have a father who dressed in leathers and loved speed.

Motorcycle riding was just one of the many of my father's varied passions. I was taken along on archeological digs, photographic courses and clay-pigeon-shooting expeditions. I was often the only child amidst a group of adults pursuing their hobbies. My red hair constantly attracted attention, and I loved being photographed endlessly in the park with my beloved Maltese poodle, Gambit, when my father's obsession with photography was at its peak. My precociousness grew.

Well into our adulthoods, my brother and I carry the scars of a relationship that was never guided out of the stormy seas of early sibling rivalry. My mother and father were silent about emotional troubles. I don't blame them. They were of a generation that seemed to have skipped those classes that taught the emotional consonants and vowels that could have helped them build bridges between their children. Their parents also did not help them to articulate their emotions.

My mother and father had also married very young, and lived in a world well before therapy was the norm. Their parents were indirectly and directly survivors of the WW2 and the Holocaust. They had no emotional road maps of their own. They did not know how to deal with damaged parents who had buried their traumas in the easy rhythms of suburban life in South Africa.

Our family's habit of bypassing troublesome emotions meant that I grew up thinking that happiness was the main goal in life. The illusion of perfect happiness deftly carved the unspoken assumption of my being. My world was that of the *Sound of Music* before the Nazis made their arrival. The hills were always alive. They had to be. In the outside world, my smile and merry disposition were an important antidote to the stormy volatility that sometimes tore through our home.

When distress of any kind reared its head, I was told that I had no reason to dwell in sadness. To succumb to unhappiness was tantamount to moral failure. And so the silences became entangled in my body, and the demons that are an inevitable part of growing up, got buried deep inside my psyche.

These unmetabolised feelings have provided me with a treasure trove of discovery, as I get older. They are especially important to me now. As I delve into my family past, my list of 'Who I am' starts to grow:

1. *I was much loved as a child.*
2. *I was showered with attention.*
3. *I grew up in seeming abundance.*
4. *I was spoilt with possessions.*
5. *My happiness was a gift and a burden.*
6. *I was often not contained.*
7. *I often felt out of control.*
8. *I treasured my father's affections.*
9. *I grew up with secrets and riddles that haunted me.*

Is it too far-fetched to discern parallels between this list of qualities and my cancer? For a start, cancer is a disease of excess with cancer cells endlessly replicating themselves. Unlike TB, which for centuries has conjured up images of 'fading away', being hollowed out, and leading to what Byron called a 'beautiful death', cancer has always been cast as a disease that leads to an 'ugly death'. Cancer is also a secretive disease. Its subterranean forces play themselves out far from the human eye in much the same way that my dark feelings throughout my life have been pushed underground. They are split off and out of sight.

I long to enter into a conversation with my undesirable killer cells. I want to ask them:

1. *Is my body 'in excess' an expression of the excesses that I became accustomed to as a child?*
2. *Is it an expression of the rage that still inhabits my body?*

3. *Is my body challenging an inner world that has no ways of signalling 'enough'?*
4. *Does cancer's secretive and silent nature relate to the dark crypts of my childhood?*
5. *Is the vessel that I inhabit so secretive in nature because the secret part of me had triumphed?*
6. *Did my parent's insistent striving for our happiness mean that my brother and I did not learn to bear suffering?*
7. *Would I be less felled now if suffering was bred into the sinews of my being?*

There are no ready answers available. The only thing I am now certain of is that real strength and robustness are not born amidst the Disneyland smiles of my childhood. For the first time, I deeply understand how the ordeal of being human must also focus on the dark and dank backroom that controls the rides. I would not have wanted to be raised under the German philosopher Arthur Schopenhauer's severely melancholic view that children are condemned 'not to death but to life' but I do wish I had been given a small peak behind the curtain of darkness and encouraged to understand that a greater elasticity of emotions is the real state of the world, and that pain is unavoidable.

These childhood meanderings intrigue me. They throw up shards of truth but they do not provide an automatic well of clarity. They seem to be too narrow a lens to decipher the civil war that is again raging in my body. Besides, I have Louise Hay's wise warning ringing in my head that we must take responsibility and not blame others for the events in our life. Resentment, she believes, is part of the reason why we get cancer.

I understand that my challenge is to own my disease *without* blaming my parents. I must not succumb to the sweet and intense relief to be derived from the three simple words, 'It's your fault'; words that are much like diving into a swimming pool on a boiling hot summer's day. Blame is the easy reflex that I must overcome. The rest is rather confusing and requires a lot of work.

My psychological musings are rudely interrupted by my first

appointment with the oncologist. It is time to decide on the treatment strategy. I genuinely think that I am going to see Dr G to devise a hormone therapy plan. It's amazing to see in retrospect the extent to which I am hiding away the realities of my situation – even from myself.

Not for Me

7 JULY 2014

My body goes rigid as Jonny and I enter Dr G's oncology rooms and I catch sight of the chemo treatment room through a large pane of glass. Until this moment, my image of this setting is entirely drawn from Hollywood movies. Everything I see conforms to the celluloid tropes of the black lazy boy chairs, the rows of intravenous stands, the nurses in their starched uniforms, the lethargic-looking bald-headed patients. What does not conform, however, is the thought of me in one of those chairs.

I grip Jonny's hand, 'Please assure me that I will not need chemo.' I am genuinely hopeful that because my tumour has not spread and is hormone receptive, I can be treated in other ways. Jonny squeezes my hand tightly but no words emerge from his mouth. Months later, he tells me that this was a unique moment in our relationship, one in which he could not speak that which he knew. He knew from the beginning that I would need chemo but he elected to spare me that reality for a while. I never hold it against him. At least he does not lie.

An unthinkably long hour passes before we are called in to see this oncologist who is nothing like I imagine. She is small and petite, full of the ravishing beauty of a woman of Mediterranean origins. Her thick dark hair hangs loosely, and is well coiffed. Her nails are manicured. Her manner is soft and inviting. She seems young and fresh, unburdened by the weight of her job.

After a brief exchange of pleasantries and without warning, she begins to talk about chemotherapy and the options for different regimes. She resorts to medical jargon and speaks with a scalpel-sharp precision: 'You will need four rounds of AC – the standard therapy combination for invasive breast cancer – followed by 12 rounds of Taxol to shrink the tumour before surgery and target any circulating cancer cells.' A brief pause. 'There are some alternatives, but this is the standard therapy for your type of breast cancer. We could contemplate Gemcitabine and Carboplatin, but this is unlikely given the nature of your malignancy.'

These unpronounceable names mean nothing to me. They tumble out of her mouth in an avalanche of sounds that shoot past my ears and ricochet off the walls. Dr G begins to morph into an ogre as she moves seamlessly from explaining these drugs to the most effective ways to prevent nausea, potential side effects of the drugs, hair loss, the best wig shop. A long dark crack appears on her desk.

I rehearse several questions, but they are trapped inside my mouth. I know she is trying to be kind, but I hate her in that moment. Her words are too simple and skate over their import. What does chemo mean for my life, for my prognosis, for my family? Is she worried? What lies behind the statistics that she rattles off in machine-gun style?

The idea of *me* sitting in the chemo treatment room just beyond her door is also too horrifying to contemplate. I am wholly unprepared. In a feeble voice, I manage to ask, 'Are you talking about me having the "Red Devil" treatment?'

I am familiar with that colloquial slang for the drug she calls AC (Adriamycin, Cyclophosphamide). I know several people, including a close friend, who have had this treatment. I am to learn that it gets its name from the florid red colour of the chemotherapy agent in the infusion bag, but the real meaning of its name is in its awful side-effects, which include possible heart damage. Somehow, it is this particular drug that represents the very worst possible outcome for me.

Dr G nods her reply at which point my heart begins to hammer uncontrollably against my ribcage. 'Is there an alternative?' I stammer. She shakes her head and says a phrase I am to hear often: 'Chemotherapy works according to the tried and tested protocols.

This is the best standard treatment for now ... there are not enough trials on patients with lobular breast cancer to understand the impact of different forms of chemo. All of the current evidence is based on treatment of all invasive breast cancers, both ductal and lobular, with no ability to differentiate between them.'

As the room spins around, I hear her voice floating towards me: 'I would like you to start the treatment tomorrow.' The twinkles from the glitter on the endless thank you cards that adorn her desk transform into glaring lights. I am the spider crack spreading across an icy lake.

Thankfully, I have the wherewithal to say, 'I am sorry Dr G I am simply not ready.' Jonny adds, 'I think we should wait for the genetic test results from the tumour sample that I have sent to the US laboratory. The results might offer us a more definite sense of what drugs the tumour is most responsive to.' Dr G reluctantly agrees, even though she tells us, 'I don't think the result will be that influential in deciding on the treatment. In the meantime, Lauren needs to be put into instant menopause. Given that her tumour is ER-positive, oestrogen is dangerous for her as the hormone stimulates the cancer cells to grow.'

In retrospect, I am truly thankful that my oncologist, whom I come to like and admire, is open to us waiting for the test results. I imagine that many of the other oncologists, whom I later see strutting around the treatment room with their outsize stature, would have insisted that I report for duty the next day.

In that moment, though, I have no such gratitude towards the doctor sitting in front of me. Rather, I feel like I am drowning and someone has brought me up for air in the nick of time. Jonny helps me off the chair.

One of the darkest hours sets in during the journey home. My anger is so vast it fills up the entire car and seeps out of the windows into the cold night air. I am mute – other than to say as we approach home, 'Please drive round the block. I don't want to go inside. I can't tell my mother and children that I need to have chemo in this frame of mind.'

'Are you ready now?' Jonny asks after circling the block several times. 'No.' I say. I don't know how many more times we drive around our suburb before I am forced out from beneath a continent of darkness into my reality. Jonny tries to reassure me: 'We will tell your mom and the kids a version of your news.'

My family is gathered around the supper table. I give no sign of my inner state of laceration. Instead, I plaster my face with a rigid smile and a mask of self-possession. 'I am waiting to hear about the genetic testing and then we will be able to decide on the best option for treatment,' I say, in response to their anxious looks.

After dinner, my kids escape behind closed doors and I retreat to the winged-back chair in my bedroom. I am reeling, bouncing between mute anger and despair. 'How the fuck is it possible that I have been dealt this card? Why am I being tested in this way?' I ask myself. The rage mounts, along with mental disintegration. I don't want to talk to Jonny or anyone else. I cannot resort to the well-worn verbal façade 'that everything will be okay'. I am utterly alone and even my husband can offer no consolation. I am facing an 'unGoogleable' problem.

In this state, a new me is being born, full of internal defects. In a diamond, the cracks and imperfections are white, but mine ooze a dark black. The longer I sit there, the more the light leaks out of my body and the darker the defects become. From within this black hole, I hear repeated pings on my phone noting a string of text messages asking about the outcome of my visit to the oncologist. I cannot possibly answer in this state of mind. Instead, I write an email to a small group of close friends:

On 7 July 2014, 10:55 PM,
Lauren Segal <laurensegal3@gmail.com> wrote:

My worst nightmare came true. I have to have chemo. I am in another kind of state of shock. I do not feel like talking or saying much. I am too overwhelmed. I know your thoughts are with me.

Although everyone will know soon enough, I do not want to talk about this to other people yet. Please don't say anything.

Somehow, this feels harder than my diagnosis. I have told my mother and kids that I am still considering options until I have digested this and can face it bravely without the fears that are right now so strong inside.

While my fingers hit the keyboard with sullen rage, Jonny is writing emails of his own. He wants advice from a range of cancer specialists around the world on the most appropriate drug regime. I realised later how lucky I was that Jonny was in a position to fire off emails of this sort: 'Given that my wife's tumour has been so indolent and slow growing with such a slow Ki (rate of multiplication of the tumour cells) is there a difference in the shrinkage effect of AC versus Taxol? What is your sense of these options?'

1. *Four cycles of AC (the Red Devil) followed by 12 weekly cycles of Taxol.*
2. *Starting with the Taxol and then the AC thereafter.*
3. *Just Taxol x 18 weeks and no AC.*

Jonny ends his emails: 'I personally feel that Lauren should have the treatment most likely to assure a complete cure here, and do not want her to avoid anything just to avoid side effects, but equally we should avoid using chemo that is of little efficacy.'

Jonny shows me one immediate response which states, 'There is no need for haste'. I cling to this. It is essential that I have the space to learn to breathe again.

The Day After

8 July 2014

For the first few seconds as I open my eyes the next morning, I do not remember my fate. Slowly, fragments of the discussion the night before start to filter back into consciousness. Yet again, the world as I know it spins from my grasp. I still cannot absorb or transmit light. In this darkness, I find myself stranded on an ice floe of my own making. My disorientating paradox is that chemo is my route to health and yet I feel nothing but complete and utter dread of it. Jonny calls me and tries to tug me back in with love, but I am too far from solid ground and struggle to respond to him. We end the conversation. I am unmoored. Cancer does that. It untethers you and leaves you floating in a place far away.

While my internal monologue continues unabated, Walter the central character in the hit TV series *Breaking Bad* comes to mind. I replay the scenes of how, after his diagnosis of lung cancer, this rather insipid teacher frenetically tries to find a way to pay for his expensive chemo treatment. His solution is to use his chemistry skills to cook Crystal Meth. The travails that follow form the basis of hours of sometimes darkly hilarious and poignant television. How lucky I am to not be in Walter's position. How lucky I am to have medical insurance that will pay for my treatment. How lucky I am to have Jonny sending all these emails. Perhaps that's part of my problem - all this excessive 'luck'. I desperately wish for some kind of incentive of my own. Instead, my tongue is literally stuck to my palate and my feet are cemented to the ground. Where will my call to action come from?

If I had been asked to write my 'Who Am I' list at this moment it would be full of black energy:

1. *I am extremely angry.*
2. *I am desperately sad.*
3. *I am overwhelmed by anxiety.*
4. *My heart is full of unremitting fear.*
5. *I still don't want to know an oncologist.*

From the growing library of cancer literature that I am reading, I understand that my enfeeblement is not helpful in the slightest. Every self-help book about illness stresses the importance of a positive attitude. But all I can see is a monstrous image of my invader that alternates between taking the form of a gigantic Tyrannosaurus Rex baring its ragged teeth and a terrifying dragon breathing out long bursts of fire into my beleaguered body. My adamant intruder is perpetually in motion, churning inside me without respect for any borders or boundaries. Its unstoppable malevolent force produces a cancer fatalism – a sense that there is absolutely nothing I can do.

Zorba the Greek described the human condition, especially the moment when one is subjected to difficult things that we have not signed up for, as 'the full catastrophe of life'. It is years before I can put a name to my state of mental agony – it is called trauma and it arose in me from the severe rupture of hope.

I marvel at how we are living in the midst of a big data revolution that is transforming the way we live, think and work. We are able to measure just about anything these days with monitoring devices – the number of steps that we take in a day; our heart rate at any given moment; how many grams of carbohydrates in each type of food; how many calories we imbibe; when we are in the right 'heart zone' to achieve the best workout; what part of our cortex responds to being in love; how many steps people take in winter compared to summer; how much more we walk if we have friends beside us.

Amidst all of these advances, there is still no accepted scale to measure fear. I know of no scientific words to describe the size or shape of it. I have not, to date, found a way to communicate the terror I am experiencing. I can't tell others that I possess 'a hundred metres of fear' or '60 kilograms of panic'. It doesn't work to say, 'I have taken 100 steps of fear today'. There is no guarantee that comparing what I feel to the immense flukes of a whale will describe how tightly fear grips me.

My inner thoughts turn to metaphor. My fear is an onion. As one layer is peeled away, another emerges. Some layers are easy to deal with. Funnily enough, I dispense with my terror of dying, so pervasive at the time of the PET scan. That fear does not take hold of my mind any longer. I also dispense with my anger around entering the world of cancer again. I do not focus on the fact that I am being thrust into instant menopause. I have stopped asking

'Why?' I am buckled up and ready for the ride. But a whole new list of fears around more immediate physical challenges related to the chemo starts to take shape:

1. *I will get fat and bloated from the steroids.*
2. *I will look disgusting without my hair.*
3. *My nails will turn black and fall off.*
4. *My hands will bloat from the intravenous drips.*
5. *My veins will collapse.*
6. *I will no longer be able to exercise my body or my mind.*
7. *I will get sick because of my compromised immunity.*
8. *I will end up in hospital.*
9. *I will not be able to be a mother.*
10. *I will not be able to be a wife.*
11. *I will be a shrivelled shadow of my former self.*

It is clarifying to itemise these 'outer layer' fears. Once on paper, they lose some of their magnetic charge. The list, however, reminds me that my real challenge lies elsewhere. In the heart of my onion is my deep and enduring fear of needles. Like a hungry vulture, my needle phobia circles around my body and dominates my mind. It is so prominent at this moment that dread parades in front of me if I so much as imagine a needle piercing my skin. My left arm goes numb instantly. The conduction of senses to my mind is slowed. How on earth am I going to deal with having multiple injections and a drip every single week for the next six months?

My phobia is as old as I can remember. There have been times when Jonny has had to force me onto the bed to have an injection. I have experienced a range of involuntary physical reactions from tachycardia to sweating hands to a severe vasovagal reaction (a steep rise and then drop in blood pressure) and sometimes even fainting. One or other of these gets reenacted every time I see a syringe. As a result, I have spent my life avoiding medical procedures involving needles where possible.

Years later, I realise that I am struggling not only with these fears at this moment but also with profound grief. Grief at the life I am about to lose. Grief at the uncertainty of whether I will live or die. I can't access this grief. Grief is a difficult emotion that requires strength of character. Anger and fear are far easier to access. They do not require turning inwards. And so I use anger and fear to paper over the long dark void that is opening inside me. They are a valuable means of self-defence.

Buddhist healers preach that one has to let in the things that one most fears in order to heal. I listen intently to Pema Chödrön's lecture *When Pain is the Doorway.* Instead of following any of this Buddhist teacher's wisdom, I am dancing with my devils and letting them dictate the rhythms of my response.

Shame at my primitive behaviour helps propel me forward. I try to imagine the terror Jonny must be feeling, and the impact of my silence. This is his pain too. My petulant refusal to engage in the face of his immense care is reprehensible. Yet again, I turn to the one thing that helps me correct my despair – writing. Words on the screen refract and transform my black beams into faint colours of a rainbow.

On 8 Jul 2014, 7:37 AM,
Lauren Segal <laurensegal3@gmail.com> wrote:

Darling Jon

Deep apologies for my silence. In Dr G's office last night, I crossed over an invisible line of terror. I have entered a realm that has left me without words.

In the prison of my fear, I don't know how to act on this new road that we are travelling. I am not used to a sense of defeat. It doesn't sit easily. Dr G's words felt too matter of fact, too routine for my whirling mind. Wigs, bandanas, scarves, blood tests, low white blood cells, etc. all came too quickly for me. I walked out feeling that suddenly everything had irrevocably changed even though the drive home and the motions of life are just the same. It is very disconcerting.

Just now, I was reading this line in the book by Kafka 'that the healthy flee from the ill but the ill also flee from the healthy'. Right now, I am in full flight even though in my rational mind, I know that chemo is not an illness and is ultimately a journey to health. I am so angry to be here. I am full of rage at Dr P for letting us down. I am full of shame at my own inadequacies in relation to having the biopsy. I am full of sadness for what I am putting you all through.

I trust that from everything I have been hearing about myself refracted through the eyes of others, and what I know of myself deep down, that I will find the strength again to deal with this. Of course I will – for you and Josh and Kats.

Just right now, I might need to dwell a little longer in this place of uncertainty and fear. Please be a bit patient. When I am in your arms, I feel very safe. I promise not to let you down as a wife or mother.

Months later, I read a brilliant description by the journalist Jenny Diski that confirms that bad behaviour is a common response at this point of diagnosis: 'Sullen rudeness is a possible option handed to us cancerees. It institutes a period of bad behaviour as one's own private glumly gleeful saturnalia, world turned upside down, lord of misrule regulated havoc, for a short period before the great slog of getting on with it began ...' Jonny doesn't need any of this kind of reminding. He is his usual considerate self:

Hi my love
I can't pretend to know or understand the road you are travelling on right now – I do know that on some level it is a road you have to travel alone and that it must feel very lonely. But you also know, deep deep down, that I and the kids and so many others love you so very much, and we will be by your side all the way.

You are fully entitled to whatever reactions you need to have, including silence and have no need to apologise to me or to anyone else. But as you know, I personally find your silence very hard to deal with. But that's my problem, not yours. I love you.

This email makes me determined to unlock my melancholia. I am aching to be consoled. The question of 'How?' remains. What will help me build bridges to the other side of my panic? Which angles and ratios will allow me to draw in and reflect the maximum amount of light? Why are we all so masterful at composing 'manuals for living with defeat', a brilliant phrase by the late singer Leonard Cohen, rather than manuals of hope? I think about ancient cultures that have songs and dances to illuminate their universe in times of need. I think of the 'mother goddesses' in Asian culture who provide a constant support to those on earth. Why have we no altars in our home to pay homage to our protectors each day?

Those of us who are not religious are bereft of these rituals. Conventional psychotherapy does not feel appropriate right now. Its modality is too focused on the mind rather than the body. Caroline, who has just been through chemo herself, recommends that I make contact with her life coach who has survived Stage IV pancreatic cancer, the prognosis of which is far more serious than my own. I am open to any and all interventions at this point. I email her immediately, and arrange a free online meet-and-greet session. I reach out to the first of many healers.

Stop Kvetching

Marissa's voice is strange when she answers the Skype call. Her American accent bothers me. I am encouraged, however, by her responses to my litany of woes. After listening to my medical history, she asks me, 'What relationship do you want to have with these circumstances? Do you want to step into a place of low energy and take the line that this shouldn't be happening to you?' She answers her own question; 'You don't want that. You want to be able to use your mind as a valuable resource. You might not choose this illness but it is full of unlimited possibilities. The greatest opportunity to grow and live in an authentic place is through the challenges that life presents you.'

She goes on to speak about the value of 'disconnects' as points of insight, of the power of our mind as an anchor, of chemo as a gift from the universe, of my body being 99% healthy, of all fear being on the edge of something new. She finishes off the conversation by saying, 'You will not just survive. You will thrive.'

This is the perspective I need so desperately right now. I commit myself to ten sessions, immensely grateful that I have the resources to do so. Marissa gives me an exercise: 'Write down your dreams and a vision for your life. This will become an anchor in the journey that lies ahead.'

A deep sigh escapes me as I put down the receiver. Although Marissa lives thousands of miles away, she feels very close to me right now. Seeing chemo as 'a gift from the universe' is definitely stretching things, but I appreciate her spirited encouragement to get me out of my intense state of resignation.

I set about the exercise of 'How I see myself now, in a decade, and in 30 years' time' as a way of breaking my psychological gridlock. At some point, I might have dismissed this exercise as really corny. Right now, I see the point of illustrating my future on paper:

Journal Entry
My Vision

I see myself as strong, well and healed. I love the scars on my body as they tell of my story of survival.

I see myself with my husband and children in our home in the Magaliesberg, sitting in front of the fire, playing 30 Seconds and laughing madly.

I see myself snuggling in bed with Jonny, watching one of our endless television series, talking, being held.

I feel myself reaching out for Jonny's hand every morning, the first thing I do every day before I open my eyes. His hands make me feel so safe.

I see myself climbing the long, sandy road up the Magaliesberg mountain all the way to the top where a wondrous world is revealed.

I have completed part of the ancient pilgrimage route in Spain, where so many have sought absolution before me.

I see myself cooking a meal with Josh and Kats in the warm open-plan kitchen at the farm – the happiest room in my world. We take chances to be chef and sous chef.

I see myself in Cape Town, with Jonny, Josh and Kats watching the boats bobbing in the harbour, one of the most enchanting sights in the world.

I see myself wandering the small streets of Kalk Bay, exploring the treasures and eccentricities of this small seaside town where we holiday.

I see myself climbing the mountains of Kalk Bay, reaching heights that make me feel as if I am bird, soaring in the sky. I revel in being so high above the world.

I see myself in a dance class, feeling the pulsating music and the aliveness of my body responding to it. I am so free.

I see myself being kind to my mother who is becoming frailer. I am learning to forgive her for her inadequacies. Instead, I treasure the emotional gifts she gave me as a child.

I see myself with Josh just before he sets off for his matric dance. I am marvelling at what a good-looking and funky young person he has grown up to be.

I see a photo of Josh, Jonny, Kats and myself, a family woven together in multiple ways.

I see myself shopping with Kats for her gradutation dress, revelling in her beauty inside and out.

I see myself at both of my children's weddings. Josh is ultra slick in a beautiful Italian suit with a tie and an attitude to match. Bride Katya is a fairy with her long tussles of wild curly hair carefully reigned in for the occasion but not quite tamed, revealing the strong and beautiful child that she is.

I see myself holding my grandchildren just after they are born. I can feel the newness of their breath. I am in awe at how the generations renew themselves. I feel the fresh possibilities of life.

A Path Forward

This wish list becomes an indispensable tool in the days ahead. I start to call people who have recently been through chemo. I listen intently. I tear through cancer memoirs that plunge me into gloom but also inspire me.

In David Rieff's book, I learn that his mother, Susan Sontag, was diagnosed with cancer three times. I am strangely comforted that someone else, especially someone of Sontag's stature, has suffered my fate. Her three diagnoses allow me to feel like less of a failure. David's descriptions of his mother's refusal to accept that the cancer would beat her gives me courage. So does his descriptions of Sontag's insistence on her own exceptionalism – she got through both advanced breast and uterine cancer that had metastasised. She eventually died from leukemia at 73.

It is Sontag's extreme behaviour that fascinates me most. Each time that she was diagnosed, she negotiated with her doctors for the most radical interventions possible. How did this woman summon the strength to urge her doctors to prescribe the harshest chemotherapy regime that brought her close to the brink of death each time?

Something else amazes me when I learn that Sontag died in 2004. This was the same year that I had the honour of showing her around the heritage site of Constitution Hill. I was intimate with the site's history and its transformation into the home of the Constitutional Court, and often guided visitors around this true exemplar of our young democracy. I was unusually nervous to lead the tour with Susan Sontag and her hosts, the Nobel Prize-winning author, Nadine Gordimer, and Pippa Stein. Sontag had a formidable presence, as did Gordimer. I worked out that Sontag must have been diagnosed soon after that visit and died just a few months later. Pippa died five years later from a recurrent breast cancer. Had each of us known of our fates on that day, the conversation might have veered away from the transformation of our country to something far more personal.

From my intelligence-gathering exercise, I discern two kinds of responses to chemotherapy. Some people say to the doctor, 'bring it on, the more radical the better'. Others are terrified like myself. In general, most accept their predicament. I am incredulous at the equanimity of the people I speak to, their upbeat courage and their cavalier attitudes towards treatment. How is it possible, I keep asking myself, that their voices are so strong and vibrant when they speak to me about their chemo, that they are so utterly matter-of-fact about hair loss, wigs, severe nausea and vomiting? My own voice tends to trail off, in much the same way as women might have done when speaking of sex in the Victorian era.

People I don't know call me to offer advice: 'I spent hours in a wig salon frequented by religious Jewish women,' a lovely sounding friend of a friend tells me. 'I was fascinated by the streams of women having their *sheitils* (the wigs worn by observant Jewish women to hide their real hair) washed.' She goes on to instruct me: 'It is vital to look and feel good when going for treatment. Dress up and put on the best makeup that you can.' Her tone hushes slightly when she describes the towelling turbans she buys for the nights so her husband does not see her balding head.

Jonny's colleague, Penny, who is starting her second round of chemo in her short life, delivers me the book, *The Fault in My Stars,* a beautiful love story about two teenagers in the terminal stages of the disease. Despite their predicament, they share romance and laughter in their tragic and circumscribed worlds. They understand pain and suffering, but also rejoice in joy and tenderness. I devour the book.

These real and fictional stories begin to lure me out of my truculent terror. They force me to rethink the 'Who Am I?' list:

1. *I am open to listening.*
2. *I am willing to learn.*
3. *I am hungry for help.*
4. *I want to take charge.*

These new additions to my list enable me to tell my kids about my needing chemo. For the first time, it feels as if I can meaningfully reassure them that I am going to be fine. Our initial conversation is difficult. My adrenalin is pumping and I can see how hard it is for them to imagine chemo woven into the skein of our lives. I write to my daughter when I perceive her distress at the thought of her bald mum:

Darling Kats

I want to say a few things to you at this moment. The first is that I am so sorry that our family is facing this enormous challenge – yet again. It is such a horrible time, with Josh writing matric and you starting at a new school. It is especially hard for you as you are at that moment in life when you are just establishing your independence, separate from your parents. It is so important that you keep on with that journey and that you don't ever feel like you have to behave differently because of my cancer. I have some specific things to say:

1. *When you hear difficult stuff about the chemo – like my hair falling out – it is totally understandable that you want to run away. I get that. I also want to run a million miles away a lot of the time.*
2. *What I am learning though, is that speaking aloud some of my worst terrors helps. The words seem to release the fears and the sadness that I feel.*
3. *There are many different people to speak to. It doesn't have to be your parents or your friends. I have told your teachers and they are all offering support.*

4. *We can also arrange that you speak to a therapist although I know how opposed you are to this course of action.*
5. *Don't ever think that because I might be having a hard time, that I am not able to look after you. I am your mom, through thick and thin.*
6. *You have triumphed over so many challenges of your own. Don't worry if life isn't perfect. It is not meant to be.*
7. *I know that this challenge will not fell your indomitable spirit.*
8. *I know it will make us stronger as a family.*
9. *I love you very, very much.*

Where Things Stand

15 JULY 2014

Breaking the gridlock with my family helps me to reach out to my wider community. I send this email:

On 15 Jul 2014, at 7:02 AM,
Lauren Segal <laurensegal3@gmail.com> wrote:

Dear nearest and dearest

Please forgive my lack of returning of calls and SMS etc. This has been a really tough week. FUCCCK!!! I have been coming to terms with having to start chemo, speaking to people who have gone through it (very helpful), telling my kids (traumatic) and also trying to get work out of the way (way too much of it, needless to say). The hormone treatment that they put me on to bring about menopause already makes me a bit tired and nauseous. At some point, I just run out of steam and energy to talk, unusual as that may be. Just to let you know where things stand:

> 10. *It is certain I have to have chemo over and above the hormone treatment in order to shrink the tumour faster.*
> 11. *The doctors are not in agreement about which chemo regime I need – there is one particularly nasty variety (the Red Devil). Some think I need to have it, others don't.*
> 12. *We are waiting for genetic test results from overseas that might help determine which is the right intervention.*
> 13. *So I don't know when the treatment will start although it is very clear now that it is the way to go. (Please start sending me great hats.)*
> 14. *The treatment will continue for six months in all likelihood.*
> 15. *My operation will be next year and then radiation follows.*
> 16. *The prognosis is very good.*
>
>   *Happy 2015.*
>
> *It feels like I am about to run a marathon so I am trying to garner the strength and resources to do so. I know you will all help me do it. I love it when you say things like, 'We will get through it'. It feels right that I have you all by my side. I will have to play a lot of online scrabble whilst in the lazy-boy chair in the chemo room. It's such a frightful place. No point in being upbeat about it. But apparently the conversations that go on there are good!*

Yet again, the responses I receive build another layer of fortification around me and I appreciate being praised for my fortitude:

> *The litany of frustrations and anxieties continue to be more than offset by your determination to look forward rather than back, by your courage and wisdom and by the knowledge and insight that you have. Not to mention the team of family and friends lined up behind you – and some even in front of you – ready to stare down dragons on your behalf … Love Graeme*

Some wise counselling arrives from Paul:

It is also important not to be trapped into always being strong and brave – least of all by the imagined expectations of others. In addition to marvelling at your fortitude and loving your reflection through all of this, the truth is, we all also share your sense of trepidation and anxiety, your occasional anger and sense of complete injustice.

You will come out of this bruised, tired, but ready to take life by the balls as you always do. I can't imagine why you are being tested like this, but I do know that you have the right stuff and the strongest of personalities to deal with it.

My house opens up to the world outside again. Friends arrive, brave soldiers who come to wage war for me. And these kind souls bring with them resources that very few armies have at their disposal. They give me meditation cushions, books and recordings on mindfulness, Buddhist writings, aromatherapy oils, giant homegrown roses, poems, boxes of cake. They bring sorrow and support in their eyes. I am grateful for every gesture that reminds me again and again that I am not alone.

Project Everlasting

My jauntiness is paper-thin. I struggle to hold on to all this goodness. There are many times when it slips through my internal safety net and the invisible seams holding me together are torn asunder. This yo-yoing of emotions is exhausting. I wish that I was compelled to work more consistently, and had an office to go to each day. My freedom to choose when and how I work allows me too much time for my mind to run amok. But I know better than to let myself plunge into unrelenting despair.

I call Marissa twice a week. I pay heed to how she encourages me to face my situation with bravery rather than fear. 'The circumstances we find ourselves in are the curriculum of life. They can either undermine us, or we can use them to grow.'

I stammer: 'What must I do with my immense fears that burst through my defences?'

'Stop and notice them,' she implores, 'but don't let them be your guide. Use the vision that you wrote to lead the way. Your life is going to be so much greater if you can find the meaning and positive convictions in this situation. You are now on the road of Project Everlasting.'

I liked the word 'everlasting'. It contrasts starkly with my own constricted sense of time. My internal chronometer constantly needs readjusting.

Marissa re-emphasises her message from our initial session: 'Remember Lauren. We are all energy. As we know from science, energy is malleable. That is a fact. We can use our perceptions to alter our energy and change our circumstances. We choose our thoughts. We can refuse certain of them. We have the power to create our future. We don't want to plant a home in a state of victimhood.' She makes me repeat a series of affirmations which focus on acknowledging my power and learning to love and accept myself. I hear myself saying: "I am not a victim. I grasp my power and will use it wisely to heal myself. I deeply accept who I am. I love myself."

The promises that I make to myself radiate a soft blue light that counters my inner darkness.

Marissa ends the conversation by urging me to read Bernie Siegel's *Love, Medicine and Miracles*. 'It will change your view on being a patient,' she promises.

I download the book immediately. Siegel, a surgeon, tells how he suffers a career crisis after he realises that he can longer provide proper care to patients unless he treats them holistically. He starts running groups with his cancer patients and becomes interested in why some of his patients survive their cancer while others die, despite having a better prognosis. He reaches the conclusion that patient empowerment, the power of the mind to heal, and the mind-body connection are crucial to healing. 'Those who survive,' he says, 'don't allow their diagnosis to dictate how they are going to live.' He names them his 'exceptional patients'. I recite the 10 key characteristics of these patients to Jonny just before we retire:

1. *Employed*
2. *Receptive and creative*
3. *Strong egos with high self-esteem*
4. *Strong sense of reality*
5. *Rarely docile*
6. *Self-reliant but value interactions*
7. *Non-conformists*
8. *Solution seekers*
9. *See problems as opportunities not failure*
10. *In participatory relations with the doctor*

I go on reading the book long into the night, and scribble down some phrases that strike me as most relevant: 'Pessimism is a luxury you cannot afford.' 'In the face of uncertainty, why not hope?' 'Use your tumour as psychological food for your own growth.' I eventually fall asleep with Siegel's four-worded mantra for cancer patients whirling through my exhausted brain: 'Forgiveness. Acceptance. Peace. Love.'

Becoming an Exceptional Patient

The next day, I wake up inspired to become an 'exceptional patient'. It is such a relief to have a goalpost to strive for. It strips me of my wintry bleakness and helps me to regain some of my old energy and drive. I am going to save my body from its deadly incursion. I am not going to take this cancer personally. I am going to learn to befriend my thoughts and embrace my inner turbulence rather than letting it imprison me. In essence, I am going to jump off my self-destructive path.

I reflect on how, after my double mastectomy, no deep inner transformation was necessary. Despite suffering real physical distortions, my life required no fundamental adaptions or adaptations.

I only experienced amplifications. I increased the intensity of being alive without altering the texture of life. I did not manufacture the tools to take charge of my fears.

Now, the cliché of 'the journey' that is taken by the ill starts to resonate. It is a prerequisite of my survival. Like those characters in fiction that have the ability to take another form, I too have to 'shape-shift'. If I had a choice, I would want the powers of a magical being so I could wave my magic wand and wish away this disease. But I do not have that option. I have to become a chemo patient. That is my task, the new curriculum of my life. Embracing this identity as a part of who I am is the only life raft that will ensure my 'exceptional' status. There is no option for a spiritual or emotional bypass. Awareness has to become my new teacher and liberator.

I once read that Fred Astaire critiqued his own performances in the third person. This mesmerising dancer evaluated his errors by saying things like, 'He needs to up the tempo'. I try to step into this third-person role. I come up with four immediate hurdles, some more complex than others. Each relies on the lifting of my internal drawbridges.

1. Losing my hair

This has been too difficult to contemplate. It is only now, in my new frame of mind, that I have the courage to phone my hairdresser. 'Come and fetch me tomorrow and I will take you to a great wig shop. I am booking off my afternoon,' Candice tells me. This is another example of the many acts of kindness coming my way.

The wig shop is a world so far beyond my own – one I would never have discovered in the ordinary course of life. The small sliver of a space is covered with wigs of every shade and style. It is a veritable hive of activity frequented not only by cancer patients like myself, but by gay men, by straight men who are balding prematurely, by those just looking for a change of image. The assistants seem matter-of-fact about their job. When it is my turn, a heavily bearded man with kind eyes says to me, 'There are a range of potential styles that might suit you.'

Candice puts a stocking on my head and then she hands me

one wig after another to fit. Almost forgetting the reason for this exercise, I manage to enjoy the radically new versions of myself that appear in quick succession in the mirror. The dead straight bob in the Raquel Welch range is my favourite. Its coppery colour is not so far from my own, and I have always wanted straight silky hair, the Uma Thurman's 'Kill Bill' look. Besides, the curly wigs that would mimic my own curls look ridiculous.

After at least an hour of trying on a variety of styles, I order the straight wig and buy a few soft and hard hats for everyday wear. In gratitude to my hairdresser, I buy her a long platinum blonde hairpiece that makes her look like Marilyn Monroe. I see now how this gesture might have been my way of affirming that it is not just the imperative of cancer that brings one here.

As we drive away, I tell Candice, 'I never could have done this alone. Thank you so much.' Inside, I am beaming at having taken an important first step in becoming an exceptional patient.

2. Chronicling My Future

My second task is easier. I become intentional about keeping a journal, and I buy a deep blue leather notebook in which to jot down my thoughts. It works as a catalyst. My writing takes on a new intensity, and I experience an even deeper pleasure in condensing my daily exploits into words on a page. The act gives me focus and courage and helps me to understand that my illness is an act of invention in much the same way as a hairstyle is. It helps me to locate my blind spots.

In my journal, I plot new strategies and new ways of being. I start using new words that have been unnecessary before now – words that speak of sadness, vulnerability and pain, but also of courage, resilience, fortitude, awareness, stability, intentionality, resolve, sturdiness and finding succour. I want to now believe that these are all attainable states of being.

I jot down notes from endless books about the drama of human experience, how to overcome adversity, and how the body communicates hidden traumas. There is no exact science, an 'X factor', in this journey that I can discern except for a belief in a positive outcome. I look at drawings of bodies in captivity; the diseased body; medical bodies besieged by contagion; demonic beings. A new mode of seeing and of listening trickles in.

I start to understand how my previous cancer episodes have amplified the vexed relationship between my body and mind that I am now experiencing. I understand how they contaminated both my present and my past. I read about insidious trauma – that which is not visible to the eye but is trauma of the spirit and soul. I see how my previous traumas are echoed in me. Betrayal. Passivity. Perfidy. Despondency. These have all contributed to continuous traumatic stress.

I paste in poems of hope as a ballast to these negative forces. Emily Dickinson's simple poem of the persistent and unconscious nature of hope during the most difficult times is one of my favourites:

"Hope" is the thing with feathers –
That perches in the soul –
And sings the tune without the words –
And never stops – at all –

And sweetest – in the Gale – is heard –
And sore must be the storm –
That could abash the little Bird
That kept so many warm –

I've heard it in the chillest land –
And on the strangest Sea –
Yet – never – in Extremity,
It asked a crumb – of me.

Her simple words and those of other writers draw protective boundaries against the clutches of darkness. I rejoice in their capacity to name the unnamable and to conjure possibilities for optimism when my own strong gale is blowing. I love that they make visible my 'shadow life' in a way that leaves me exclaiming: 'Oh, this must have been written for me.'

Empowering Myself

The next important task involves reclaiming my power. I have to say, 'No!' to the brooding and shrivelled person inside of me. I have to try to cultivate something of the Buddhist state of wakefulness by freeing myself from suffering. I need to calibrate my mind much like I would a bathroom scale. To this end, I write three emails in quick succession. The first is to Jonny to explain my need to take charge of the medical realm and not to succumb to my 'default setting'; the second is to my children asking for a new kind of awareness between us; and the third is to my friends and family, conscripting them as my emotional bodyguards.

On 17 July 2014, 8:12 AM,
Lauren Segal <laurensegal3@gmail.com> wrote:

To Darling Jonny

I am coming to recognise my 'deer in the headlight' moments when I turn firmly into myself, battling to work this all out and feeling like I am moving in a bubble, far away from the world. Last time this happened, the news of the chemo treatment had melted my resolve and weakened my capacity to connect.

While now I am in a completely different space, I still have to stay by myself for a while. The most powerful thing I have learnt from Bernie Siegel's book is the need for us cancer patients to own our treatment and feel positive about the route of healing we are journeying along. This is the distinguisher of the 'exceptional patient'.

You and I have a complex relationship with health and medicine. It is your greatest area of strength and empowerment and my weakest. During my mastectomy, I willingly handed over the reins to you. I chose the most unconscious route to the finish line, waking up only when everything was done and dusted. It worked. I came through feeling emboldened. Most importantly, I have never missed my breasts, thanks in no small part to how you have related to me.

*This time, I **have** to take charge. There is no way under, over or around chemo. I have to go through it. I need full resolve and consciousness to get through the slog. You know more than anyone that I am not a marathon runner. I hate the idea of 18 weeks of putting 'one foot in front of the other'. I hate the interventions that are about to happen. Somehow, I have to find the strength to embrace them.*

*We **have** to discuss how we can rebalance the forces between us so that I feel more empowered. Of course, you will never stop being the person with the medical knowledge and understanding and I will keep on utterly relying on you. BUT I also have to feel in charge.*

Together, we have to make the call about when the treatment starts. Monday does not feel right. We have to talk about Thursday or Friday as an alternative.

I would love you to help me to shift the way things happen this time round.

Empowering myself also means empowering my children. If they are to report to therapists later in their lives, I would rather it is about too much being said than too little. This doesn't mean sharing with them every shred of information about my disease. But it does mean confronting the elephant in the room, those feelings that remain shrouded despite their weighty presence.

On 17 July 2014, 8:37 AM,
Lauren Segal <laurensegal3@gmail.com> wrote:

Darling Kats and Josh

Dad and I meant what we said a few weeks ago – that my cancer diagnosis does not mean that you have to change your behaviour. We are just the same people as we were a few weeks back. So of course if you are angry or irritated, you need to be able to express that.

At the same time, I would like us to remember the importance of kindness and gentleness at this time. We are all stressed for different reasons in our lives outside of the cancer. BUT, we are also all stressed because we share this diagnosis. It is happening to the family and not just to me. I cannot do anything without the three of you right by my side.

It is easier to be angry and aggressive than express love and vulnerability. We all need to learn to show our weaknesses a bit more regularly and learn to be honest about our feelings.

I really believe that this difficult and challenging path ahead is also an opportunity for our family to learn new things together and apart. We will become even stronger than we already are.

In the end, each of us can only change ourselves but we can also help to shape each other by how we treat one another.

I love you both very much.

Mum

I pen the third and last email to friends after Jonny calls with the preliminary results of my genetic testing.

On 17 July 2014, 2:15 PM,
Lauren Segal <laurensegal3@gmail.com> *wrote:*

Dear All

Through Jonny's unbelievable persistence with the overseas lab, I have received my genetic test results earlier than expected. The 'excellent news' is that I do not have to endure the 'Red Devil' chemo as it is shown as being not effective on my kind of tumour. Thank goodness I waited for the results of this test. It is one of those tiny victories in a long string of defeats of my body and mind.

Jonny called with this news as I was reading the first pages of Viktor Frankl's book, 'Man's Search for Meaning'. I kept reading and re-reading a line on the first page which is Frankl's most enduring insight into how people survived a Nazi concentration camp: 'Forces beyond your control can take away everything you possess except one thing – your freedom to choose how you will respond to the situation.'

I cannot pretend to feel it is okay that my radiologist missed spotting a 6.5 cm malignant tumour repeatedly over the last two years. It's a gross medical injustice. BUT I am refocusing my energies and summoning the courage (which you have all so kindly refracted back to me in multiple ways through the last weeks and years) in order to face this (nightmarish) situation.

I start weekly chemo next week Friday. I don't know how long it will last yet. But 'one step at a time' is my new mantra.

At the end of all of this, I hope I will come out with as much hope for life as Viktor Frankl so eloquently expresses in a situation so much bleaker than my own.

All that I know right now is that my beloved husband and children, my unbelievable mom, brothers, sisters, extended family and my deeply caring community are the key source of my strength to take on this fight.

Luckily, I already know we will win.

Tears flow freely as I read the emails that I receive, and I carefully file each one in recognition of the strength that the words provide me at such a desperate time. It is my archive of love. Carol, who was the first to take my hand one day on the playground when we entered primary school in 1974, writes:

I am struck again and again by what you said about this being a lonely marathon. All I can tell you is how much I love you and rely on your presence in my life, which is almost as old as my very first conscious memories. Your place in my daughter's life is also central and irreplaceable. Your survival feels like my survival … I also have absolute faith in your ability to choose to respond to these terrible forces in an extraordinary way – the honest, emotionally tuned and amazingly resilient way you have. The other thing Frankl said was that the people who survived the devastation of the camps and the total loss of family best were the people who had a sense of their own lovability and worth. You have that in spades. And we will be there to remind you of how deeply you are loved.

3. Facing the Needles

My fourth and biggest task is to face my needle phobia, which has been embossed on my life for the last 49 years. It has frightened me more than any of my childhood terrors of snakes, scorpions and the ghastly image of the 'cat burglar' that stalked our suburbs.

In my virtual investigations on the matter, I am amazed to discover that needle phobia is a defined medical condition that affects roughly 20 per cent of the adult population. I am relieved that there is a large constellation of human beings similar to me. I am also surprised and relieved to learn that avoidance of medical care puts needle phobia among the world's leading causes of premature death. My own avoidance of a biopsy as a result of my needle phobia appears more reasonable.

One of the websites states: 'Telling a patient to get over a needle phobia is as inexcusable as telling a depressed person that they should "just cheer up".' The phobia requires serious attention – so much so that US health insurers have assigned a medical code to this condition. This is empowering to know but I still have no clue how I am going to deal with chemo. I copy down one clear message in my journal: 'The initiative for treating needle phobia must come from the patient.'

I call Susie to an emergency meeting down the road where I cry copiously into my tea: 'I don't know how I will do it,' I say. My friend tries to shift me from the physical into the psychological realm. 'Your fear probably results from traumatic experiences with needle procedures when you were very young. Think back to your early associations with needles,' she entreats.

An operation I had when I was four years old to remove some of my molar teeth comes to mind. I can remember screaming and screaming into a void as I was wheeled into the operating theatre with no memory of being consoled. I can also still conjure the god-awful fear I experienced when a school nurse came to give us kids a measles vaccine. I kicked up such a fuss that I never got vaccinated. After listening to these stories, Susie suggests that the phobia may be a way of managing unbearable emotional experiences: 'A phobia concretely excludes things from your world that remind you of things that are too painful to bear.'

I don't entirely grasp these words, but Susie communicates something else to me during this conversation. By listening and engaging with my phobia in a serious way, she reinforces the idea that it isn't just about me being histrionic. She points to the complexity of phobias and how they are caused by myriad psychological events that crystalise together and need to be unwound. My challenge is to unpack the millions of strands.

I value these insights enormously, but time is running out. Right now, I need to find more immediate ways to cope.

As I am walking back home, I am struck by a memory of a lecture on 'flooding' that I attended as part of a first-year Behavioral Psychology course. It was one of the few 8 am lectures that I woke up for. I can still hear the lecturer's booming voice: 'Is it true or false that it would help a person afraid of snakes to be thrown into a pit full of these slithery creatures?' Of course the correct answer is that it is true. He explained that 'flooding' is a way of unlearning fear by exposing yourself to the thing you fear most.

This memory switches on a light for me. Acupuncture is my answer. Close friends of mine go to a Chinese healer who is also a doctor, Dr E. They have always told me how 'The "E bed" can take you to the most astonishing places'. I call the doctor right away. She listens to my tale of woe and says, 'Come and see me at 4 pm today.'

Dr E has a calm and laconic presence. Like others, she finds my medical history of three primary tumours before the age of 50 rather 'unusual'. She says, 'We need to work out why your body is working against itself.' She adds, 'It's not that you are doing something wrong but we have to find your blockages. What we are really treating here is fear.'

She examines me simply by feeling my pulse and looking at my tongue. 'Your liver is the home of your entrapment,' she pronounces. And then continues in her absolutely straightforward manner: 'In Chinese medicine, this organ is the force of creativity.

You are a creative free spirit who hates being told what to do. You are railing against obstacles that are being placed in your path.' I listen in rapt attention. These words resonate. How is she able to discern my constitution through such a simple examination? Things go downhill from there.

Dr E leads me into the treatment room and ignores my writhing as she inserts her long needles into the palms of my hands, feet and – wait for it – the top of my head. I dare not cry out, desperate not to show my fear. Dr E then leaves the room. As the minutes tick by, a weird tingling sensation spreads through my body. The feeling intensifies and I become panicked. 'Dr E,' I call out.

I can hear her in the next-door room talking to another patient, but she fails to respond. My cries of distress become increasingly plaintive. Something dreadful is happening to me and my initial enchantment with Dr E and the 3000-year-old practice of acupuncture whittles away entirely.

I am now feral with fear and anger. I am here precisely because of my needle phobia. Surely, if a doctor is going to do something that they know is traumatic for a patient, they should not leave a patient on their own like this? My amygdala that regulates my fear-based reactions is in overdrive. It becomes hard to reach for my adult, thinking mind.

When Dr E calmly saunters into the room to remove the needles, I am so overcome that I remain silent. She can see my anguish, however, and says to me, 'You are a mother to your body and mothers don't run away from a child in pain. They pay attention to their child and try and fix it. The pain you experienced while I was gone is telling you that there is something wrong with your liver and spleen. We need to work on that.'

What a cheek, I silently rail. She is the one who has just abandoned me. I came here precisely to learn how to become a mother to myself in relation to my needle phobia. 'You are the emotionally unavailable mother who did not manage my trauma.' I want to scream. 'You should have hung around to see what I was able to bear. That way you might have been able to pre-empt my fears, calm me down and extend my capacity to manage. Instead you abandoned me.' I flee back home and pour out my confusion and rage in an email to Carol and Sue:

> *I actually don't know if I have strength for all of this right now. I am very weepy. I know that I have to conquer my needle phobia but this flooding business was too much for my fragile psyche. It was Dr E's job to think this through and she failed.*

A Breakthrough

That evening, I have my scheduled call with Marissa. She is furious about my experience. 'Trust your intuition, the voice in your heart and not in your head. That doctor was not listening to you. She might be a great healer but she didn't get your needs.' She carries on: 'She was cruel and unprofessional. This is a great learning opportunity for you to be clear about what you need.'

It is a relief that Marissa shares my anger. She helps me to understand how this experiment has played right into my feeling of not being properly listened to when I was vulnerable as a child. 'Let's try a different approach to the needles,' Marissa says. She gets me to recite my intentions for overcoming my phobia. I begin:

1. *I don't want to feel terrified for hours before an injection.*
2. *I don't want to feel faint and sweaty as I enter the rooms.*
3. *I don't want to pull away from the nurse.*
4. *I don't want to feel powerful.*

My voice stops dead as I utter the last sentence. I had meant to say, 'I don't want to feel powerless'. The Freudian slip is a therapist's dream-come-true, my unconscious revealing itself. Marissa doesn't miss a beat. 'Why is it so dangerous for you to feel powerful?' she inquires. 'Try to connect with your small child inside and ask her why she is so frightened of her power? This is a highly self-limiting belief.'

After a long pause, I tell my coach who is thousands of miles away: 'My own power was very frightening. It seemed to tear at the fabric of my family.' We carry on untangling this revelation. Towards the end of the session, Marissa changes tack. 'Try to step out of your relationship to a needle as you know it. Think of new associations with this thin object. You can make meaning in any way you choose.' Again, I recite some possible associations:

1. *They bring relief to millions of sick people.*
2. *They deliver much-needed drugs.*
3. *They are used to create beautiful things.*

As I speak the last sentence, I have another 'aha' moment. I tell Marissa: 'For many months now I have been working with a group of women in Boipatong. This is a poor and forsaken township where a terrible massacre occurred during our country's transition to democracy in 1992. The Boipatong community have been too traumatised to tell their stories until now.' I can hear Marissa listening intently: 'A team of us are creating a new memorial centre in the middle of the township. My colleague has trained a group of women, who lost their loved ones in the massacre, to do needlework. Each day they gather to stitch their pain into the fabric we have supplied to them.'

Over the last months, I have observed how their small squares of cloth have become a form of witness and hope. The threading action allows them to revisit and record their memories, linking their history to healing. A light switches on. Needles are a form of empowerment.

I retrieve an image for Marissa of these women with their arms in the air after they had first joined together their sewn testimonies.

Marissa is deeply moved by this story. 'You are already in close contact with the enormous power of the needle in bringing about healing. Your task now is to welcome the needle into your own body and create a safe environment for it,' she says. 'Now is a perfect moment to heal the wounds of childhood.'

Marissa implores me to let go of my anxiety: 'The universe

doesn't want you to play small. It needs you to bring to it your special gifts.' She makes me repeat these sentences:

1. *I am willing to release the pattern within me that has created my condition of deep fear of injections.*
2. *I am stepping out of the victim role.*
3. *I am no longer helpless.*
4. *I acknowledge my own power and choose to use it positively.*

Then she makes me write down my new positive associations with needles:

1. *Women with hands in the air in a genuine gesture of joy.*
2. *Trees with needle-like leaves bringing shade.*
3. *Quilts of great beauty.*
4. *The power of needles to heal.*

The Boipatong women, who live so far from my own world, have unknowingly become partners in my journey. Their bravery has forced a small chink in my impenetrable armour of fear.

As I click off from the Skype conversation with Marissa, I call my friend Shireen. She had given Katya the most beautiful embroidery as a gift for her Bat Mitzvah two years before. She had stitched the trunks and branches of a tree with the names of several strong women who have stood up against the tide of history.

'Would you start a sewing group with me?' I ask her. She doesn't understand the question at first, but is delighted after I explain my need to create a positive relationship with needles before chemo starts. I add: 'I failed home economics at school but this is not about high art!'

We invite five friends whom we have in common to join the group. A few days later, they arrive at our home with heartfelt love and openness. Shireen is carrying a large wicker basket filled with skeins of coloured threads beautifully arranged in different shades.

The mood is solemn at first. I talk about my phobia and my hope of transforming the meaning of these sharp objects that have caused me so much woe. Through my veil of tears, I observe how my friends are grateful to have a concrete way to accompany me into Chemoland. The light filters gently into the room, casting a warm glow on the table where we work. They all hold me in my zone of pain.

We decide that we will each stitch a 30 by 30 centimetre square in a pattern of our choice over the next weeks. At the end of chemotherapy, we will turn our squares into a tapestry. We discuss what to stitch. Lynn decides on an African healing doll; Mandi likes the idea of foot prints on a beach; Karien wants to create a mandala with the circles made of leaves. Shireen settles on a series of tiny symbols that will create a peace sign; Janine chooses to sew leaves filled with words of love and life. Being the least talented sewer in the room, I decide to stitch a series of red buttons onto my square and see where this leads me.

Although my husband and kids make fun of me each time the sewing circle arrives at my house, this group turns into something way beyond what I initially imagined. A radiant light continues to guide our sessions. Our chatter creates a circle of love. Together, we fashion positive associations with the needle that I carry forward with me over the months to come.

I never discover a talent for sewing. I don't learn a single formal stitch. Yet threading my needle and guiding it in and out of the cloth provides me with a fierce determination to dull my blinding panic. It is not simply another device. I begin to believe in Marissa's statement that the universe acts in intelligent ways, and that we attract the energy that gives power to our dreams. The collective act of threading becomes a symbolic act that helps me to join the disparate pieces of my being and make them feel whole.

Taking action in these four ways is a potent enabler and takes me a significant way along the path to becoming an exceptional patient. I record my new lessons in my journal:

1. *Listen carefully to your needs.*
2. *Let others in.*
3. *Take as much help as possible if it serves you.*
4. *Reject being around anyone who is negative.*
5. *Allow for surprises.*

One Size Does Not Fit All

21 JULY 2014

Jonny and I return to Dr G's office at 7 pm for a follow-up discussion on my chemo regime. My efforts to become an exceptional patient have fortified me since we were last here. My body is less rigid, and my mind less blind with fear.

Jonny has also been fortified. His research over the last weeks, specifically on the study of the genetics of tumours, has exposed him to the enormous strides being made in the management of breast cancer. He excitedly explains to me: 'We are on the threshold of an age of miracles with potential breakthroughs for an eventual cure. Gene sequencing is rapidly leading to an era of personalised medicine in which every cancer patient's treatment will be bespoke.' He tells me that I am caught in a moment when the prevailing science is still driven by evidence based on large trials: 'There is no evidence as yet to support using different types of chemotherapy for different types of breast cancer, such as for your lobular breast cancer. The volume of evidence is not available, but it soon will be.'

I learn how powerful computers, machine-learning algorithms and the wonderfully named technique of 'bioinformatic spelunking' will produce mountains of data that will hopefully lead to all cancers being 'druggable'. The new cancer story emerging from breast cells being studied in petri dishes in labs all over the world combines with the increasingly intimate understanding of individual genomes.

Jonny also learnt more about the significant risks and severe side effects of the 'Red Devil', including possible heart damage. Many women do just fine on the treatment and many may read this and think, 'Why all the fuss?' I ask Jonny, 'Are we just dancing on the head of a pin?' His response is emphatic: 'You do not want to be exposed to the risks of this drug if there is no upside.'

Jonny presents the case to Dr G for going against the one-size-fits-all approach. In his concise but humble manner, he reports what the genetic screening of my tumour – with a supercomputer sifting through a mass of my genetic data – seems to suggest:

1. *Lauren's specific tumour might not be all that responsive to the 'Red Devil'.*
2. *In any event, the 'Red Devil' seems to confer only about a 4% improvement in long-term results on average.*
3. *Her unique tumour does appear to be responsive to Taxol (a chemo agent with fewer side effects).*

Jonny ends off: 'Taking this all together, my sense is that the potential benefits of the "Red Devil" don't justify the side effects and the risks. So perhaps Lauren can start with Taxol, and then we can assess her response.'

Dr G tells us that the doctors in the team looking after me had already debated this at their weekly meeting. Some had supported this approach while she herself is not entirely happy: 'I will remove the "Red Devil" from the chemo cocktail but I insist that we add in another drug, Gemzar, and that Lauren have 18 rounds of treatment.' Then she warns, 'I want you both to know that I have not taken this route before and I have no evidence of its efficacy. It has never been trialed.'

There should be a word that describes the moment of a patient taking a decision against the wishes of her doctor. The notion of 'patient empowerment' does not quite reflect the element of risk involved, or the levels of pressure that the patient is under.

Any slight sense of victory I may have felt by eliminating the 'Red Devil' is undermined by Dr G's insistence on 18 treatments. 'Are you serious?' I ask her. 'Eighteen chemo sessions? I have never heard of a person having so many treatments.' She insists: 'That is my compromise for going this alternative route.'

Our drive home is subdued but not quite in the same way as the first time we left Dr G's office. I have won one battle but the thought of 18 sessions leaves me radically concertinaed. I don't, however, ask Jonny to circumnavigate our house. My email to my family and friends doesn't reflect my anxiety. It is simple and to the point:

On 21 July 2014, 22:10 PM,
Lauren Segal <laurensegal3@gmail.com> wrote:

Confirmed NO 'Red Devil'.
Chemo treatment starts this Thursday at 8.30 am
Weekly for 18 weeks.
2–3 hour sessions.
No total hair loss just thinning.
Some undesirable symptoms but I prefer not to think about them.
No brave words.
Just a relief that the countdown begins.

A wise friend, David, from London, responds to this email immediately: 'Remember that the number 18 is a "lucky" number in the Jewish religion and has great spiritual significance. The letters of the Hebrew word, *chai*, (meaning life) add up to 18. You should see your 18 treatments as life-giving.'

It is comforting to be reminded of this. Later, when I take a course on Mysticism and Kabbalah, a form of secret knowledge in Judaism, I learn that the number '18' also corresponds to the power of '*ratzon*' that roughly translates as 'will in the soul'. At this moment, however, the number 18 means:

1. *At least 18 blood tests – one before each chemo session (to check my white blood cell count).*
2. *Eighteen intravenous chemotherapy infusions.*
3. *At least six injections to reduce my oestrogen levels and keep me in menopause.*
4. *An unknown number of injections to boost white blood cell count.*

The thought of a minimum of 42 jabs turns me cold. In the meantime, I have 72 hours to ready myself.

Preparing for a Marathon

Now that my treatment path is clear, I start to make final preparations for the new life ahead. Our local pharmacist arranges a meeting for me with her homeopath. Together, they make me a pledge: 'We promise to keep your immune system strong for the next six months. Here are our suggestions for various vitamins and immune boosters.' Another set of angels joins my circle.

Jonny looks askew at the packet full of alternative medicines on the kitchen counter. I know that he is worried that I am turning into Gwyneth Paltrow with her 'shoo wah wah' penchant for all alternative forms of living. Wisely, he says nothing as I later carefully divide the pills of every shape, colour and form into small daily containers. Jonny's skepticism doesn't bother me. His medical training made no space for alternative methods of healing. Ordering these pills in this way contains me and signals a form of control in an otherwise borderless universe. My battle plans are falling into place.

Other layers of love are built around me. A group of six women, dubbed the 'coffee girls' because of their daily early morning coffee gathering, decide that their task over the next six months is to make me laugh. In this week before chemo and on the day of every subsequent chemo session, they deliver a package of goodies to my door. Frivolity is hard to pull off in the face of a serious cancer, but they triumph every week.

There are many other gestures by friends and acquaintances that constantly remind me that I am not embarking on this journey alone. Anne, a doctor and poetry enthusiast, pops a poem into my postbox before every chemo session for the next six months. She understands all too well the rhythms of my journey as she herself has had her stomach removed because of a genetic predisposition towards stomach cancer. She also understands the power of poetry to speak what there are no words to say. It is uncanny how the poems she chooses so often describe my states of bewilderment, anger, hope.

I like the first poem she chooses called 'Bad Year' by Jane Hirshfield, which says that even in a bad year the apples grow heavy and round. Hirshfield, who spent eight years living as a Zen Buddhist monk, gives me a way of seeing how even grief has its own beauty.

Two other foot soldiers – my sister-in-law's mother, Shirley, and her aunt, Cynthia, deliver several large containers of food. Every dish has love as the key ingredient. Their deliveries also become a weekly affair and I come to savour the thick creamy corn pie, the richly coloured stewed fruit, the delicious fish cakes and other delights. This home cooking is exactly what my taste buds long for.

Other kinds of packages arrive at my door. Books full of the wisdom of life and bunches of flowers festoon the kitchen counter. I am amazed at the love that is beamed into my house from friends across the globe as well as from all my close family in Israel, London, Toronto and Montreal.

The vast kindness that envelops me fortifies the spinal column of my existence. I am being shepherded into the centre of a fairy ring as I prepare for that which I have dreaded most in the world.

Three tableaus are imprinted on my mind from these few days before chemo. The first is the Friday night Shabbat dinner when my mother, my daughter and I cup our hands over the candles and say an ancient Hebraic prayer that is intended to spread light across the world. A single tear runs down my mother's cheek. We are all aware that tonight we are praying for light for our family. I can see that my mother is most lost in the anguish of the moment.

In that split second, I realise how deeply my mother's love is inside of me, how our differences evaporate in the face of our pain. This thought takes me back to the day of my wedding when my mother and I were standing in front of the mirror just before I walked down the aisle. As our reflections stare back at us, she says: 'This is your day. You look so beautiful inside and out.' With these generous words, she releases me into my adult life. Tonight, she stands beside me as I am about to start the fight for that life.

The second tableau is captured in a photo that Janine takes of me at the end of the evening. It is something of a lie. I am smiling at a pink feather fan that the coffee girls have sent me. It is a clever present for someone who has been precipitously delivered into menopause and is about to start chemotherapy. The broad smile, however, masks the deep feelings of utter dread that have possessed me for the past three weeks. It is a brave attempt to paper over the cracks that have opened up in my heart and to create edges to my world. This momentary sense of mirth is nonetheless good for me.

The third tableau is of the moon. As Susie and I walk down the mountain on our farm that weekend, we see an extraordinary orange disc rise through the trees. It is dazzling in its size and brightness. Susie turns to me and says, 'The moon is beaming down to guide you on your journey.' We have in fact witnessed a 'super moon', a rare occurrence when a full moon is closest to the earth on its elliptical orbit. It seems like a good omen. Susie frames the photos that we take that night and, to this day, the image of the moon in its rare glowing state amidst the trees sits on my bathroom window ledge.

The night before chemo, I call Marissa. At the end of our session, she says, 'Have fun.' Her words astonish me. Surely this is taking the 'gladness' not 'sadness' philosophy of illness too far?

I am, however, relieved in the sense that starting heralds the possibility of an ending. Finishing is the only thing that sounds good right now.

PART THREE

Chemoland

Chemo One – Terror

24 JULY 2014

What does one do on the morning of one's first session of chemotherapy? My D-Day is a freezing winter morning with a thin layer of frost still covering the ground. The garden is bleached of all colour as if to mimic the ashen state of my interior landscape. My kids have gone to school knowing, but not quite understanding, where their parents are off to today. I don't quite understand it myself. There is still an hour before I am due at the treatment rooms and Jonny and I decide to meditate, something we learnt to do together after my mastectomy. The experience of sitting side by side in silence binds us and focuses us for what lies ahead.

When it is time to get ready, I listen to the advice of other cancer patients to dress up 'as if I am about to attend a cocktail party'. My efforts make me think of a woman I recently bumped into while huffing and puffing up a steep set of stairs near my house. She was wearing a totally outrageous pair of gold climbing boots and when I admired them she told me, 'I am about to climb Kilimanjaro. If I am going into hell, I might as well look good.'

What sartorial choice should I make to enter my own version of hell? I choose a soft blue jumper that shows off my blue eyes, a pair of tapered jeans and blue high-heeled boots that I seldom wear. I take extra care with my makeup. 'How do I look?' I ask Jonny as I try to apply an earthy shade of lipstick that I have borrowed from Katya. Jonny, who is getting edgy, is not invested in my camouflage and leaves me to approve of the last image I have of my pre-chemo self.

My bag is packed from the night before. The water bottle, a gift from a fellow traveller, is filled with hot water. The fennel tea from the coffee girls is in the flask. The gemstones that I carried in my bag throughout the time of Katya's operation jangle in a small box alongside magic potions sent by my four-year-old niece and a lucky seed from a friend from Mozambique. It is made heavier by anticipation and fear.

I grab the two wild bunches of purple and pink flowers on my kitchen counter for the oncologist and the nurse, a tip I got from Bernie Siegel's lecture on preparing for chemotherapy. They create a misplaced cheer in the house.

Although this day is different from all others before it, leaving home follows my usual pattern. I am always ready until I am in the car and I remember something vital that I have left behind. Today, I have forgotten my lip ice and blanket, both essential items. 'Do I *really* have to leave home and make *this* particular journey?' today's run back inside seems to suggest.

Unlike most journeys, when leaving and returning home does not mark a monumental shift in one's consciousness or bodily experience, I know that today when I return home, the edges of my world will have shifted entirely. On the short drive to the centre, I sob as I read Jonny the text messages popping up on my phone:

You are attaching your Wings of Victory and beginning your journey. So from a fellow flyer I am sending you so much love and peace and rest. Sue

I will be right with you, just quietly sitting next to you at 8.30, my La. Jess

Sizo indlela ndawonye (We will journey together) – Ngezinyawo (On foot). Fiona

Time to turn it inwards and beat this thing! We are all praying for your quick recovery. Paul

Know that you are in my thoughts and in my heart. You are brave and wonderful. Keep that in mind. Tana

The waiting room is jam-packed. Tens of patients and their loved ones sit on every available surface. The patients are easy to spot as they are either bald or are in wigs and hats of every variety. Some are physically wasted, mere bone and sinew or 'cachectic', another medical term that I learn in the world of cancer. My heart is screeching, 'I don't belong here. This is a club I didn't ask to be part of. Please refuse my membership.'

It is totally obvious that I am the new kid on the block. While others laugh and chat, looking quite relaxed, I plant my noise-cancelling headphones firmly on my head and I cling to Jonny's hand. On another day, I know that I would have nattered to the woman with an inviting face who sits opposite us. I am not ready to enter into this kind of interaction. John Lennon's voice calms my jangling nerves. After a long while, Jonny gently lifts off one of my headphones and says: 'They have called your name. It's our turn to go in.'

We cross the threshold into the infusion room together. A teeny step but a firm line of demarcation for us both. In that crossing, I am instantaneously drafted into the ranks of the sick. It is now impossible to resist the identity as a chemo patient. My psychic surrender has begun. Although we take this step together, and I am so grateful to have Jonny by my side, I am to become acutely aware of how alone I actually am.

The Treatment Room

The air in the room feels thin. Like an astronaut exiting her spacecraft and stepping onto a new planet, I tell myself over and over again, 'I have to learn to breathe and trust myself here. I have to embrace the laws of gravity in this new galaxy.'

The room is much more boisterous than I had anticipated despite the languor and varying state of health of the patients. For a start, a lot of people are crammed into a relatively small space. It is surprisingly free of the septic smell of most hospital wards.

The first issue I confront is where to sit. The lazy boys – which have previously conjured up images of afternoon siestas, comfortable conversations, reading a book, reclining and relaxing – are mainly occupied. My gaze falls on an empty chair closest to the nurses' station. Perhaps I choose this one because of its proximity to these saints of the cancer world. Or perhaps, from here, I can look into the courtyard where I imagine that the souls of those who do not make it through this god-awful treatment are hovering. I sit down gingerly and avert my gaze.

1. *I don't want to catch sight of the people who are already hooked up.*
2. *I don't want to watch those who are having their needles inserted.*
3. *I don't want to imbibe the cozy chaos and camaraderie of the room.*
4. *I don't want to hear the chatter between the nurses.*
5. *I do not want to hear the exchanges between those who are bringing food to their loved ones who are pinned to the spot by their drips.*

Once again, I plant my earphones firmly on my head and so I don't hear the 'Hello,' of a nurse with a most dazzling smile. This is Nurse Julian. Her inner light draws me in from the first second I lay eyes on her, as does her musical laugh and her charm and confidence. She is to become my guardian angel, the person I rely on over the next months for comfort and support, especially in dealing with the needles. She sees my terror and reassures me: 'I promise that you will be fine. The first time is always the hardest. I am not going to hurt you.'

I feign a smile and weakly reply: 'Please forgive me. I am utterly terrified of drips and needles. I promise that I have been working hard to overcome myself!'

Nurse Julian assures me, 'You are not the first basket case to sit in front of me.' There is a moment, as she takes my right hand and places my arm on the chair and covers it with a hot silicon bag to open up my veins, that I catch my husband's eye.

I am so sad that he is with me in this place, that it is *his* wife becoming a member of *this* club. I also feel a deep sense of shame and humiliation. Jonny did his medical internship in an oncology ward so this is a familiar space for him. It is totally different when the patient in one of the chairs is your wife. I am remorseful that I have dragged him here. His eyes are so full of sorrow. His lips are drawn and pale, and his beautiful olive skin has temporarily lost its glow.

There is no doubt that it is harder for the person standing by. We patients feel every part of the hours to come through our veins. Those beside us can only look on, wishing, as I know that Jonny is right now, that he could take my place on the black chair.

Before any more of these thoughts have time to take form, Nurse Julian instructs me to breathe deeply. I shut my eyes and turn up the music. The needle pierces my skin and I let out a startled, involuntary cry similar to that of a baby's as she enters the world. Mine too is a new beginning, a first breath of a kind. The only difference is that it is mingled with despair.

After that, it isn't easy to settle into the chair. My body is fidgety and my mind is on high alert, watching as Nurse Julian switches one bag after another on the drip stand. The first bag contains an antihistamine to counter any allergic reaction I may have to the drugs; the second bag has something to prevent nausea; the third bag has a drug to strengthen my bones. The last two bags contain the chemotherapy agents. Taxol, which is made from the bark of a Pacific yew tree, is an irritant that can cause inflammation of the vein through which it is given. It is important for the drip to run slowly this first time so that Nurse Julian can monitor my reaction to the drug. The other chemo drug that flows through me is Gemzar, made in a laboratory, and which too has potentially damaging side effects.

While these drugs are flowing into me, and as the minutes drag on, my curatorial instinct kicks in. I decide that the photos that have been so haphazardly stuck to the glass wall of the nurse's station are in desperate need of rearranging. The mounds of paper that flow from the badly stacked credenza just next to the pharmacist's window can do with some serious ordering. A calmer colour should replace the dreadful yellow on the wall. As for the television set, it should definitely be moved somewhere less central. Who in this room wants to stare at bodies in a state of extreme health on the sports channel? The tacky curtains that surround the beds for those patients who are too sick to sit, definitely need to go.

Why has no one paid attention to any of these spatial arrangements, I wonder? Surely in this kind of space, the *feng shui* is more important than ever.

A few hours into the treatment, Penny, who is starting chemotherapy the following week for a recurrent breast cancer arrives at my side. She hands me a jar of 18 marbles: 'Congratulates for starting the countdown,' she says. What a luminous gift, so typical of an insider who knows the ropes. The incandescent streaks in the coloured marbles are mesmerising. I stare at each of the 18 balls that hold within them the hours of treatment that lie ahead.

The First Marble

I arrive home without a memory of how chemo ended, or of the drive back. All the new drugs circulating in my bloodstream must have wiped out my mind. I do, however, remember taking my first marble out of the jar and how this was a genuine act of joy. Josh will take out the remaining 17 marbles while Katya is assigned the job of rewriting the new number of remaining sessions on the blackboard patch of the jar.

Instead of answering the myriad text messages asking about my wellbeing, I write this email:

On 24 July 2014, 13:22 PM,
Lauren Segal <laurensegal3@gmail.com> wrote:

Dearest friends
One down. Seventeen to go.

Your prayers and messages and love swept me into the room this morning. I swear it. I just couldn't have got there without feeling so held, loved and contained.

I am just back an hour ago. It was LOOOONG. Nearly four hours from start to finish.

Not sure yet how to write about the experience. Very different challenges from what I imagined. The room is enormously friendly and congenial. Everyone else seems surprisingly cheery under the circumstances. I am by far the least brave person there.

The nurses are saints. The injections were nothing for me. Almost besides the point! Hard to believe given my phobia, but it's true.

Two surprises: having to wear gloves and shoes of ice during the Taxol chemo drug to reduce the risk of damage to my peripheral nerves. Thank god for the water bottle and blanket – they were ingenious gifts from a fellow traveller.

The other chemo drug was actually painful in my veins. I did a guided meditation through a pair of spanking new headphones (called beats) that literally deliver sound into your soul. I can't recommend them enough as a natural tranquiliser.

My overwhelming sense is that this is going to be relentless. I was eventually quite sleepy but it's hard just to relax and drift away. My best analogy is trying to sleep on a long haul flight. It's impossible to get comfy and there is a bit too much going on to pass out despite a deeply desperate desire to do so. I also feel the need to be present – just in case of engine failure!

The only thing missing was a good bowl of chicken soup. Talk about a deep and coded response to difficult situations!

I feel stoned right now, that feeling one gets on a Myprodol too many. BUT mostly, I feel immensely relieved.

This is a whole new world that has opened, not to be ordered but certainly not to be feared in the way I had constructed it.

I ramble.

Looking back, I am as surprised by this email as my friends are. Like the rollercoaster ride that is to come, my burst of energetic writing is followed by a deep sleep. I am to learn that the antihistamine administered in the drip is responsible for the state of utter oblivion.

I awake with a feeling of extreme haziness. It is hard to move from my recumbent position until I realise that, in less than an hour, Josh is leaving home for debating training for the whole of the next week. My son is a very serious debater and as the captain of the team, he is determined to lead South Africa to victory in the world championship about to take place in Thailand. This is a big moment. It is also a big moment for a mother-with-cancer.

Illness forces definition on the previously unquestioned identity of mother. Now is my first test and I quickly look at my journal where I have written a list of the qualities that I wish to retain:

1. *I will remain available to my children at all times.*
2. *I will remain robust and absorb the teenage jibes and criticisms that come my way.*
3. *I will remain the creator of their home and their world.*
4. *I will express my love readily and bountifully.*

The strength of my maternal fiber is immediately put to the test as I dart out of bed and enter into the last minute fluster of my son packing. Even though Josh doesn't strictly need me to help him, my presence indicates 'I am here'. As it happens, I am greeted with a barrage of questions: 'Did you get the ten exam pads I asked for?' (Isn't ten overkill?) 'Are there extra South African flags for the other teams?' (No. Sorry.) 'Can I borrow your credit card just in case I run out of money?' (You can have anything that you want right now.)

Josh gives me an extra long hug before he leaves. His squeeze is filled with so much that is unsaid between us. Tears quietly roll down my cheeks as I watch him set off on his own formidable journey.

As Josh exits, Katya enters the frame and a new mothering challenge presents itself. My daughter, who has an Afrikaans exam the next day, declares that she cannot remember a thing of what she has learnt. My fierce determination to uphold my maternal obligations overcomes my extreme lassitude. 'Let me test you,' I offer.

'Let's start with *trappe van vergelyking* (degrees of comparison)':

'*Dik*?' I ask. I am met with a blank stare.
'*Dik, dikker, dikste*' I remind her. (Thick, thicker, thickest)
'*Maklik*?' Another blank stare.
'*Maklik, makliker, maklikste*' I say. (Easy, easier, easiest)

At this point, the full might of her teenage angst erupts. Katya flings her cue cards down and rants, 'I don't see the point of learning this language'. In this complex and tangled moment, I want to say to Katya, 'This situation has little to do with the Afrikaans'. But it's difficult to talk about 'unconscious defence mechanisms' to a 13-year-old. I try my best: 'Kats, don't worry about the exam,' I gently proffer. 'Life is not normal. Even though I am the one having the chemo, it is happening to you too. You might not understand that right now, but it's okay if you collapse a bit too.' I add: 'You don't have to write the exam if you don't want to.'

She dismisses my attempt at containment and support as 'psychobabble'. Our only point of agreement is that she will go straight to sleep and then wake up early to study. I am wracked with guilt. My daughter is at the age where she needs an expansive mother figure rather than one truncated by illness.

In this desiccated moment, I decide that it is my job to find a way for Katya to defer the exam. Jonny agrees. So at 10:30 pm, on the night of my first chemo and despite a deep aching to go to sleep, I find myself phoning around to get the number of the grade head at Katya's school. I am successful and shoot off an email to him to describe our plight.

Plummeting

25 JULY 2014

At 5 am the next morning, my maternal instincts again overcome the deep leaden feeling in my body. I drag myself out of bed and tell

Katya: 'I have just got a response from your grade head and he is more than happy to defer your exam.' She rejects this offer outright. I am stumped. Why would anyone say no? With my mother superego on high alert I say, 'Well then, let's go over the *trappe van vergelyking* again'. And so I find myself lying on Kat's bed while the sun is not yet up on an utterly freezing morning, chanting:

> *'Min, minder, minste'* (few, fewer, fewest).
> *'Siek, sieker, siekste'* (sick, sicker, sickest).

These darn *trappe van vergelyking* spin around in my head for the next hours and are a prelude to my sharp descent into hell. This downward spiral begins during an unannounced visit of a friend who has come to deliver the most beautiful bunch of poppies from her garden. Lynn is to bring a bunch of these flowers every week for the next six months. Tears well in both of our eyes as we talk about my treatment.

And then, without warning, something starts to happen to my body. My leg muscles go into spasm. My feet and hands start to tingle. My skin begins to crawl. Streaks of colour dart in front of my eyes. Sue, my friend who has been through chemo herself, arrives at the moment that the room starts to spin. She is here to do yoga with me. Lynn hurries away and I collapse onto a mat. 'Something is horribly wrong,' I tell Sue in a panic. 'Could this be a toxic reaction to the chemo?'

Sue massages me, trying to cajole the terror out of my body. For over an hour, she kneads and rolls my shaking muscles. There is some relief. Janine arrives. Together, they put me to bed with cushions carefully positioned under my legs and feet and water bottles on my stomach and back to soothe my aching body.

Tears form rivulets down my cheeks. The vessel I once inhabited is suddenly and irrevocably gone. Those words in every self-help book that tell you repeatedly how important it is 'to stay positive' are a lie. How is it possible to smile while I am curled up in a ball of pain? How dare all of those women tell me that chemo is not nearly so bad?

At this moment, chemo and life appear entirely incompatible. They are oil and water. Israel and Palestine. Poison and an elixir. More tears. More self-pity. An email to Susie and Paul. Paul is a psychiatrist and, being HIV positive, has lived close to his own mortality for many years now. This has added to his special qualities as a healer. Unfortunately, he lives in New York and so I have to write to him:

> *I read and reread the lines of your last mail where you advise me that I don't always have to be brave. So I thought I would write to you in my very un-brave state. I have been working so hard to overcome my fears that today I am collapsed. I am wondering how I will get through another 17 of these treatments. I am tingling all over and am wracked by terrible images of my body being at the top of a tall slope tumbling down. This is not flying long haul. This is a crash landing. Could this be a kind of PTSD (post traumatic syndrome)? Thank you for receiving this email that can be sent to very few.*

Paul responds in a matter of minutes:

> *I don't think it is PTSD, though it is very traumatic of course. I think it's physical ... Your body goes through a lot with chemo and the steroids feel great at first but then there's a crash. This is not a sprint, it's a marathon, and you will learn to ride the waves of up and down. Self-care is vital!!*

Susie arrives at my bedside as I am reading this. She is worried by my mail and I am intensely relieved to see her. She agrees with Paul: 'Your body is in shock. But your mind is also preying on itself at this moment.'

When Jonny arrives home, he assures me that my symptoms are a common side effect of the Taxol. He has already researched possible relief and brought me a vitamin powder to try. This is an extremely kind act but to both of our dismay I shout at him: 'I want you to be my husband, not my doctor! Can't you see my distress? You can't fix everything. Sometimes, I just need you next to me.'

I am to discover that my needs in times of deep anguish are always going to be hard for Jonny to meet. My challenge is not to punish my husband's deep desire to take away my pain. He has to learn that he can't fix everything despite his heartfelt wish to do so. I have to learn to tolerate my painful feelings. We both realise how much we still have to navigate through the travails of a serious illness.

That night, I send my family off to Neil's birthday dinner. I cannot possibly make it out of my bedroom. In the stillness of an empty house, I mould my body into different yoga positions. This attempt to take charge of my flesh and bones is only partially successful and I take myself to bed with the internal fires still raging. I feel so alone. This is my first experience of what Virginia Woolf calls 'the daily drama of the body' and how the 'ill go alone, and like it better so'.

By the next morning, the tingling – or neuropathy as I learn it is called – has subsided slightly. But the email message from my oncologist in response to my appeal for her guidance is not at all reassuring:

> *It's not common that the neuropathy is so pronounced already. We usually find that it starts after six to seven doses of the chemo but of course each person's metabolism is different. I would have expected some sensitivity in the joints and possibly a pulling type of feeling in the muscles at this point. There is, however, no reason that you can't start using the glutamine, but please also be sure to use vitamin B especially pyridoxine (B6). Thank you again for the beautiful flowers.*

Another stroke of bad luck. Why am I the one to have such an unusual and instantaneous reaction to the chemo? I quickly book a massage in terror that the spasm will return. I also reluctantly agree to start on a small dose of anti-depressants. Besides reducing anxiety, this particular drug is meant to offset the side effects of the chemo and the hot flushes from the menopause. I need all the help I can get.

Defeated bodies create paranoid minds. My unconscious runs rampant. That night, I dream that I am being hijacked. As I am getting out of my car outside a yoga class, two young, innocent-looking boys point a gun in my face. I manage to stay remarkably calm and give them my car and my bag while managing to keep my computer. It has my journal and there is no way that I am letting it go. I walk into yoga but don't tell anyone that I have just been hijacked.

These unconscious images are undoubtedly an echo of the depth of the assault that I am experiencing. The cancer/chemo is the loaded gun pointed in my face. My state of aloneness is encapsulated in my silence despite the presence of others. My ability in the dream to safeguard my computer while relinquishing those things that are easier to replace, like a car and a bag, injects a sense of hope that I am anchored in some small way.

Three days later, there is a single moment when I start to feel physically better. I am to learn that this sudden transformation is one of the features of Chemoland. The change is as dramatic as a Shakespearean character swallowing a magic potion and being completely transformed. Instead of simulating death, as I might have done in *Romeo and Juliet*, or falling in love with an ass, as I might have in *A Midsummer Night's Dream*, the miasma in my brain evaporates and my hands and feet no longer tingle. I return to the person I know. The scorching winds that have swept through my body temporarily cease to blow.

Paper-thin

Just as one kind of hell recedes, another looms. This time, my challenges are psychological. My next chemo is only 48 hours away. The thought of the blood tests, the sea of faces in the waiting room, the needles, all begin to crowd my mind. The world feels paper-thin.

I grasp for the wisdom of others yet again. In Bernie Siegel's book, *Faith, Hope and Healing,* I listen to stories of different people's experiences of cancer treatment as I walk through the streets of my suburb. It is helpful to hear a woman describe her tumour as 'a series of breadcrumbs' and the chemo as 'a beautiful flock of birds eating them up'. Another man says his tumour is a block of ice that chemo is melting away.

The image of chemo that comes to my mind is that of a matador. During a bullfight I once reluctantly attended, I was transfixed in horror as the matador gradually subdued the imperturbably arrogant bull. He taunted this powerful beast, first with his pink and yellow cloak and then eventually with a red flag, before killing him with a single powerful stab in the back of its neck.

My tumour is more languorous than that energetic bull that ran into the ring, but I like the idea that it is being attacked matadorial style. My matador has no dazzling sequined outfit or long decorative spears. The chemo fight is much longer, the moves less balletic. There are no cheers from the crowd. And, of course, there is no certainty of the outcome. The tumour may or may not be finished off with a final blow. But the fight is equally cruel, and I pray for a triumphant outcome.

That afternoon, I enlist another source of help. Carina, a beloved colleague, offers to take me to her mindfulness coach and I readily agree. I have read much about mindfulness and cancer treatment, and I am grateful that there is a practitioner close by. Lucy is a beautiful woman with bright blue eyes and an angelically calm demeanour. While sitting on a mat in her soothing space, my floodgates open once again. 'Can you put words to your fears?' she asks.

'I know that I am meant to let the chemo in,' I say, 'but it is terrifying to imagine living with the physical symptoms I experienced for the next six months.'

She listens with heartfelt compassion. She talks about the techniques of mindfulness. 'They are deceptively simple but difficult to use. *Sati*, which has come to be translated as "mindfulness", also means "remembering". We have to remind ourselves to cultivate mindfulness and breath practices. We have to learn to stay with our experiences as they are rather than forcing everything to be different. We have to learn to be in a state of ease.'

She takes Carina and me through an extraordinary set of *ujjayi* breathing exercises. This ancient yogic breathing technique has been used for centuries to bring balance and tranquility to the mind and body. I see why the technique is also known as 'victorious' or 'ocean' breathing. New waves of calm douse my raging inner fires and sooth my nervous system as I take deep breaths in, and express a loud 'Aaah' on the exhalation. She also leads me through some movement practices where she encourages me, 'to re-befriend your body after it has seemingly let you down'.

Lucy ends the session with a hug and some anchoring advice: 'You are being brave and true to yourself by crying. Don't panic. You will learn to stay centred.' Carina and I agree that we will return together each week. I am happy to be Lucy's new disciple.

Michelle, a friend with green fingers and an expansive heart, arrives with a striking bunch of roses from her garden. I am struck by Jonny's vigilance as Michelle tries to approach me for a hug. 'Please don't touch Lauren,' he implores. 'She must avoid any risk of infection.' He is right of course, but it proves hard to push someone with outstretched arms away so harshly. I am to get used to this.

Josh arrives home for a few hours from his debating training. His team is setting off to Thailand the next day. We have a rowdy supper with his girlfriend, my mom and Phil. We get embroiled in the ins and outs of Israel's action in the Gaza Strip, fervently debating our responsibility as Jews. There is nothing like a real war to take one's mind off one's own war raging inside. Little do I know of how this discussion will resonate in the weeks ahead.

That night, I continue to listen to Pema Chodron. This Buddhist teacher's voice alone is a great salve. So is her message about how everything is impermanent and morphing all the time. It is our minds that keep everything solid, she says. We ourselves can ensure that our experiences are fluid and dynamic. She urges us to stay with the rawness of our experiences.

Her words open up the vast blue sky.

Chemo Two – Betrayal

1 AUGUST 2014

I start off chemo session two surprisingly calm. I am relaxed during the blood test to check if the chemo toxins have lowered my immunity. As we walk into Dr G's office, I know instantly that something is wrong. It's written in my oncologist's eyes. 'Your white cell count is unusually low,' Dr G announces. She may as well have said, 'Your body is yet again betraying you'. I am devastated.

'There are a couple of options,' she continues. 'You can skip chemo this week so that your white blood cells can recover ... Or I can give you an injection to bring up the white blood cell count and we can go ahead.'

Skipping chemo is not an option given the gargantuan effort it's taken to get here this week. I *have* to take another marble out of the jar. Despite my needle phobia, I opt for the injection. Somehow, I just manage the very large syringe that is inserted into my stomach. I lose my power to stay positive once back in the waiting room. The thought that my blood cell count is so low after just one round of chemo catapults me into a state of anxiety. My inner voice chides, 'You are failing yourself, your family and your friends'.

This sense of betrayal mounts as I wait for my drugs to be mixed – a process that can take anything from one to two hours. What starts as a storm in my head becomes a raging tempest. How will my body make it through another 17 of these sessions? Will chemo fail? Will I succumb to my disease? My attempts at the *ujjyi* breathing technique fail. I am too churned up to exhale steadily through my nose. Instead, I turn up the music really loud. I read the poem 'Things to do in the Belly of a Whale' by Dan Albergotti that Anne popped in my postbox for this week's session.

It is while pondering the 'dim glow of light' that I am called in for treatment. As luck would have it, Jonny can't stay with me today. He just has time to install me in one of the black lazy boy chairs. We share a light moment before he leaves.

There is a private joke in my family referred to as 'the Jew in the restaurant syndrome' which describes how Jews are likely to walk into any restaurant and move tables at least four times before they settle down for the meal. There can be any number of reasons for this: the first table could be too near to the entrance, exposing us to a small and uncomfortable draft; the second table could be too near the kitchen making the clank of dishes intrusive; the third is too close to the air conditioner vent; the forth table is claustrophobic with the arm of the person at the next table poking into you.

I suffer from this syndrome in restaurants and in hotels too. If the room is too near the lift, or the window is facing a brick wall or the position of the bed is wrong, I am quick to ask for a new room. My family simply wait with the luggage in the lobby while I find my place of peace. Today Jonny discovers that my syndrome extends to the oncology treatment ward. I describe it to my friends later as such:

> *Most people arrive in the treatment room carrying their handbag and a small bag of food. My dear husband has to make three trips to and from the car to get me into the room.*
>
> *I have brought along cushions and blankets to try to overcome the restless and uncomfortable long haul flight feeling of the week before; a large bag of ice packs to augment the freezing of my hands and feet to prevent the neuropathy; water bottles and huggies to warm up my body from the aforementioned ice packs and to ease the tension; an amazing photo album that Janine had brought the day before to take my mind off the experience at hand; different kinds of foods for different taste inclinations that may arise*

including the chicken soup I had dreamed of last time; the usual bag with books and the talismanic symbols of good luck from friends and family.

Jonny asks me simply, 'Where should I put all of this stuff?' (Un)fortunately the room is quite empty and I have the pick of the lazy boy. A circus dance results that can only be described as comical as I sit in at least five different chairs before I find the right one.

Jonny turns to me and says, 'I had no idea that one day you would become the Jew in the Chemo room'. We both laugh. (My all too witty friend, Jess, later responds, 'Like I always said, you'd be so bad in a pogrom, La!')

The laughter of that moment doesn't last. As I sit down on the chair I have finally settled on, I start to gasp for air. Annette, who replaces Jonny as my companion, tries to help me to breathe. Just the day before, I had visited her in her beautifully calm therapy room to warn her of my potential state of panic. She had recently lost her father and together we had cried and weaved together our different realities through listening and holding each other's pain. It was a wonderful hour together.

Now, she looks at me kindly and squeezes my hand while poor Nurse Julian battles to put up the drip. My body is in rebellion and I keep pulling away. I am in the grip of needle phobia again. Julian's beautiful dark face is pale by the time I open my eyes and the drip is up. Annette looks equally shattered.

A fellow patient who has witnessed this mini-drama comes up and says, 'You really don't have to endure this each week. I am in my fourth year of chemo and had a port inserted some time ago. You should try it out.'

We wrestle with this option for the next 16 sessions. Nurse Julian thinks that a port is the answer to my struggles. Dr G remains firmly opposed. So does Jonny. They both think that the risk of infection is too high. It is hard to know the answer. So I stay on path, trying to slay my demons.

I am bedeviled as to how I will get through another 16 rounds of chemo after the disastrous second session. Marissa and Lucy may have given me some tools to deal with my nerves, but I see gaping holes in my psyche related to my needle phobia.

I remember Vicki, the woman who taught Jonny and me to meditate. We both loved the calm that meditation introduced to our lives. We have both since lapsed from our daily practice, but this seems like the right time for me to return.

I realise that I am collecting healers like others collect stamps, but these are desperate times – my life is at stake. My anxieties are not going to be quelled with a single shot of emotional Panado. This is a complex malaise and I'm not afraid of having a revolving door of healing figures. My internal reckoning suggests, 'I am willing to try anything; the more the better.'

Walking into the Meditation Centre immediately calms me. Vicki's intense but incandescent presence casts a soothing spell over me. In her office, so full of her positive energy, we talk through my carousel of fears. We discuss how meditation and hypnotherapy might help to break my paranoia over needles. She issues me a simple instruction: 'At this moment, you need to look after yourself more than ever before. This is your time, Lauren. The outside world and its pressures should be completely secondary.' She continues: 'Together we are going to work out how you can prioritise your own needs and create complete calm around yourself.'

We agree that I will benefit from weekly sessions. I am happy to add another hour of beautiful calm to my week. Vicki also invites me to return that night for a group mediation session. I leave in the thrall of this new pillar of support. But like everything in Chemoland, the crashes are blinding and come as suddenly as the winds that blow from beneath the earth in the desert.

This time, the crash happens as I am driving to fetch Katya from school. I run my hand through my hair only to find that a substantial number of golden strands stick to my fingers. At the next traffic light, I frantically look at myself in the mirror. There are several long golden curls lying on the collar of my jacket. A couple more strands dance on the steering wheel.

My blood runs cold. Has the moment I've been utterly dreading arrived? Dr G has explained to me how the chemo drugs that kill the fast-dividing cancer cells also kill other fast-growing cells in the body which includes one's hair and nails. She has told me that with a bit of luck, the drugs I am on might not lead to hair loss. This appears not to be the case.

My eyes blur. I don't feel safe behind the wheel of the car, so I pull over into the emergency lane. 'Breathe slowly in. Hold. Breath slowly out,' I try to calm myself. Cars whizz past me down the busy three-lane road. While repeating this exercise, I run my hands through my hair again to see if I haven't been imagining the hair loss. More strands rest on my open palms.

It's getting late and so I force myself to take control of the fear threading through me. By the time I reach school, I have managed to put on a mask of 'everything is normal'. The three young people who bundle into my car don't suspect anything. We have a rowdy and cheerful drive back home. My heart is racing.

As soon as we are home, I make a mad dash into my bathroom and lock the door. The hair that has come out has not changed my overall appearance. I am to learn that a human head has on average over one hundred thousand strands of hair and that it takes a while before hair loss is noticeable to the point where it erases one's identity. I don't know this then.

૭

While I am wholly preoccupied with my appearance, an entirely different kind of storm is brewing. The first inkling I have of the gathering clouds is when Janine calls me – I erroneously think it's to make plans to take me to chemo the next day. Instead, I hear her asking: 'Have you been following the madness on Facebook involving your son?' I am taken aback by what I hear next: 'There is a photo of Josh, Sam and Saul wearing Keffiyehs (Palestinian scarves) at the opening ceremony of the World

Debating Championship. Josh's classmates at King David are going ballistic.'

For the second time that day, my blood runs cold. My son is the deputy head boy of a Jewish day school. The Israeli Palestinian issue is a real hot potato at the school and his community does not always share Josh's forthright views. We have found ourselves in the principal's office on numerous occasions defending our son's right to speak out against the prevailing views at the school. Right now, a war is raging in Israel and there is a groundswell of loyalty among Jews all over the world towards the Jewish homeland. For many Jews, this is not the time to criticise the Israeli state.

Janine reads me some of the rabid comments as well as other young people's messages who are rushing to Josh's defence. In response to the idiocy of those attacking his oldest friend, Neville's post reads, 'Just shut up!' Exasperation is quickly mounting on both sides of the debate. My mother arrives in my kitchen soon after I put down the phone. Through her own extensive networks in the Jewish community, and as president of the Union of Jewish Women, she already knows about the photo.

She is not supportive of her grandson's actions and speaks of her 'disappointment' – a word that is a red flag to a bull in the lexicon of child–parent relations. As it turns out, the word arouses deep anger not only in me, but in my very vocal daughter.

I flee the house to go to a group meditation session while Katya lambasts her granny – whom she loves very dearly – for not showing solidarity with Josh. As I close the kitchen door, Katya fires off a salvo about the 'closed-minded Jewish community' while she and her friend put the final touches on iced cookies for their Alice in Wonderland tea party at school the next day.

It is difficult to quiet my mind but I try desperately to imbibe some of the gentle karmic energy of my fellow meditators. When I arrive home, Jonny and I chat briefly about the photo. We guess that this storm will blow over soon enough. My mind is now on getting ready for round three of chemo.

During fits of wakefulness that night, I notice a new involuntary action of mine that involves pulling at my hair to see if any strands come out. In the morning, tens of golden locks are strewn on my pillow. With a pounding heart, I squash them into a tiny ball and keep them under the basin in my bathroom. A keepsake of my identity. It is a strange coincidence that the word on the daily website that I follow, is 'ecdysis' which means shedding or molting from the Greek *ekdysis* (casting off).

Chemo Three – Madness

8 AUGUST 2014

Despite the despair caused by my impending hair loss, this chemo session is altogether better. My bloods are back in the normal range, and I take in the chemo with a gentleness and ease that surprises me. My outstretched arm doesn't flinch as the needle goes in.

The usual malaise sets in once home. After I come out of a deep sleep, I send this email:

> *On 8 August 2014, 16:12 PM,*
> *Lauren Segal <laurensegal3@gmail.com> wrote:*
>
> *I have now completed the first cycle of chemo. Three treatments down. Fifteen to go. I actually prefer to think of it as one cycle down, five to go. The numbers are easier on the mind.*
>
> *Many of you have been asking me what I feel like. If I have to draw a picture of my experience so far, it would show me travelling into the centre of the earth. Chemoland is very dark and misty, and things move more slowly than they do in the real world. The quality of the light is neither that of night nor day. It is more like permanent winter twilight. It is a quiet place with little chatter. One's body feels very heavy. Then after about three days there, the fog suddenly lifts. There are glimmers of sunshine. The impact is immediate and extraordinary, and the world as I know it returns.*

Luckily, since the first treatment, which was very rough on my body and mind, the symptoms have not been as pronounced. The neuralgia I first experienced is more under control. I am not nauseous. I walk every day and have carried on with yoga and pilates, albeit in a new way. I am managing to work on the three good days.

It has been a bit of a roller coaster emotionally. But I am learning to meet my monsters on this journey. I am 'leaning into the sharp points' (Pema Chodron's words), rather than running away from them with a lot of help from life coaches, mindfulness teachers, music, meditation. I am reading amazing new literature about life.

Jonny and Kats are doing well. They might even like me requesting to watch so much more television than usual. Josh is still in Thailand. The team is doing great. They have caused a mini furor by wearing Palestinian scarves in the first-team photo of the tournament. That is a story all on its own and requires its own email. Let me just say it's been a diversion from the world of cancer.

As I press send, I notice an unusually large number of missed calls and text messages on my phone. While I was asleep, it appears that the Jewish community of Jo'burg has joined in the clamour of voices against my son. I phone Jonny immediately. He tells me that an online petition in the name of 'Concerned Zionists' has been set up calling for, 'The removal of the deputy head boy of King David High School from all leadership positions and having his honours revoked.'

There are several missed calls on my phone to find out if it is our son being referred to in the petition that's gone viral. This is a question we are to answer many times over the next days. In my chemo haze, I go online and am stunned by the vitriolic comments being posted. One comment calls for my son to be hanged. I then understand that another kind of war has been declared on my family.

I am consumed with anger and despair. How can grown adults hurl this kind of abuse at a 17-year-old boy? I wonder then, as I do many times thereafter, if these people would have behaved this way if they knew what we are going through. How can defending the state of Israel take on such an ugly form?

At the same time, the number of emails and messages of support at Josh's actions that we receive is astonishing. The initial frustration I felt towards Josh for creating this storm at this moment in our lives has completely dissipated. We are both so proud of how he has responded to the eruption of this unintended war. We are also proud of his sister who is his staunchest defender on the social media front. Even in our precarious familial state, our instinct is to stand united and I am so grateful for that.

The next morning, a chemo-induced thick torpor overcomes my brain. There is no time to wallow in the haze, however. Jonny shows me a post by Josh on Facebook in response to the outbreak of vicious attacks against him. We have not spoken to Josh yet – Thailand is eight hours ahead of us and we do not know how he is responding to the clamour. A great pride wells up in me as I read Josh's powerful attempt to communicate his beliefs: 'I am proud to be a South African Jew, and am proud to attend a Jewish Day School. I am also a Zionist. I believe in Israel's right to exist, and her right to defend herself ... We took a stand for the thousands without a voice but we do not for a second condone any violence whatsoever. We stand for peace.'

We hope that this brave and articulate clarification will help to calm things down. By chance, we are due at a Bat Mitzvah for Orenna's daughter in a nearby synagogue that morning. I welcome the idea of sitting in this progressive community and listening to a beautiful choir. We need to be reminded of all that is good about our religion so as to counter some of the rancour we are witnessing. As I sit with my husband and daughter on either side of me, with likeminded friends in the rows in front of and behind us, I am bathed in the best of what religion has to offer – community solidarity and the age-old ritual surrounding a young person's passage into adulthood. The spiritual cadences of the Hebrew prayers are a balm.

I long for home when the service is over, to give in to the miasma that has settled in my brain. As I put my feet up, my mom calls: 'Turn on the radio,' she urges. 'Josh's story is the first item on the news.' Jonny and I stare at each other in disbelief. Caught between the gravitational pull of my body and the fever pitch of the world around me, there is no way I can lie down, let alone sleep. Josh's story is the headline item on the news throughout the day.

By the afternoon, the story is on the television news as well. The stakes are now so high that I have to stave off all craving to retreat into a chemo bubble. I fail dismally to obey Vicki's injunction that I must not stress under any circumstances. There is just too much going on. Two counter petitions spring up online by that evening.

The second of these petitions is created by past head girls and head boys from Josh's school. The signatories grow to 14 ex-heads of the school by Sunday. The power of this petition is that it comes from within the very community that is turning against Josh. I read the petition entitled, 'Defend Freedom of Expression in the Jewish Community', through a veil of tears.

Instead of going straight to sleep as my body so desperately wants, I stay up watching the signatories roll in for the petition in support of Josh.

All hopes to wake up and to return to the world of cancer are dashed again the next day. The next morning, our cellphones buzz ceaselessly again. Other news stations are onto the story and want us to comment. The community of flag-bearers that has formed to support me through the cancer is being matched by a whole new community coalescing around Josh's battle.

We take calls from vice chancellors of universities, leading figures in the Jewish and Muslim communities, business people, teachers, public intellectuals all commending Josh's courageous stand. We receive messages that would make any parent proud.

Under any other circumstances, I would be buoyed by the furious buzz that persists in our house. Phones ringing. Computers pinging. Doorbell going. But my brain is on fire and my nerves are jangling. It is day two after chemo when my symptoms are at their worst. Where to escape to? I need a sanctuary. I lack imagination right now and the best place I can come up with is to take Katya and myself to a nail bar and meet Josh's girlfriend, Tali, for lunch. 'Why are you laughing?' asks Katya as we drive off. How can I explain the absurdity of this refuge at this moment? I don't try and simply resort to the cliché, 'Laughter is the best medicine in times of distress'.

We return home to the same frenzy as when we left. As I lie supine on the couch with my body stretched to breaking point, Jonny tells me that the body that runs the King David Schools is going to make a public statement to try to put an end to the furore. They would like our input.

I can no longer keep up the relentless pace being imposed on our lives by this saga. I have become Dr Doolittle's push-me-pull-you, cleaved in two diametrically opposing directions. Chemo coaxes me inwards and dematerialises my world. Defending our son takes me right out into the middle of the fray and requires an exterior stamina and focus. This schism is too stressful a place for my body and mind. Peace. Rest. Meditation. These have all but evaporated.

The statement ends up causing an outcry. Those baying for Josh's blood strongly oppose the resolution that Josh will retain his position as deputy head. Some of his school mates say that if there are no rules for our son, then they won't obey the school's rules either.

These reactions create deep gashes in my heart. At this point, I fear for Josh's safe return to school. 'Why we are being tested in this way?' I ask no one in particular. Thankfully my post-chemo symptoms start to subside and I am entering a break week. Despite having no chemo session this week, my mind and body are screeching, 'Please stop the stress'. My only hope is to flee home as much as I can. I call Lucy for an emergency mindfulness session. Lucy listens to the week's goings on with a look of shock on her face. 'Let go of the cruelty you have experienced and let's reflect instead on the many kind acts coming your way,' she says.

A penny drops for me with this simple suggestion. Until now, I have not paid much attention to this four-letter word – K-I-N-D. I tell Lucy: 'Kindness has become an active force in my life, a shadow and constant companion.' It doesn't take me long to come up with a list of the many kindnesses coming our way right now:

1. *The coffee girls' 'packets of kindness' that arrive in my kitchen each week.*
2. *Tens of emails written to us to lend solidarity and support to Josh.*
3. *An equal number of emails written to me to find out how I am coping.*
4. *Calls asking for my Hebrew name so that it can be read out as is the custom during the Friday night shul service when the cantor recites a special blessing for the complete recovery of the sick.*

Back home, I Google the word kindness. I am intrigued to learn how much has been written about the concept from so many different perspectives. Aristotle claims that it is the highest of all virtues precisely because it requires one to be 'helpful towards someone in need, not in return for anything'. His insight of 'no advantage for the helper, only the person helped' sharpens my appreciation of the kindness coming our way.

Then I read the Buddhist parable on kindness: Devadutta, jealous of Buddha and wanting to hurt him, sends the angry philosopher, Nalagiri, to confront Buddha and his colleagues. But Buddha's loving kindness and friendliness tames Nalagiri. This suggests how pure kindness can tame even the wildest of mighty beasts.

I also look at the writings of psychoanalysts on the subject. They point out that humans are the only animals that can share the plight and sufferings of another whom they can't see or touch. 'Real kindness changes people in the doing of it, often in unpredictable ways. Real kindness is an exchange with essentially unpredictable consequences.'

Scientists are equally enthusiastic about the physical effects of this emotion. Research has shown how when a person displays kindness there is an increase of dopamine to the brain.

It is the words of a 'wandering poet', Naomi Shihab Nye, whose father is a Palestinian refugee and her mother an American of European origins, that I jot down in my journal. I like the way she captures the complexity of kindness that so echoes my reality of this moment:

> *Before you know what kindness really is you must lose things, feel the future dissolve in a moment like salt in a weakened broth. What you held in your hand, what you counted and carefully saved, all this must go so you know how desolate the landscape can be between the regions of kindness ... Before you know kindness as the deepest thing inside, you must know sorrow as the other deepest thing. You must wake up with sorrow. You must speak to it till your voice catches the thread of all sorrows and you see the size of the cloth ...*

The unexpected consequence of my disease is that it has brought me closer than ever before to showing and being shown kindness. The fragility wrought by cancer has allowed me to focus on this virtue rather than being preoccupied with the mad events going on around me. Kindness now seems indispensable to my state of being. I fervently hope that Josh will imbibe all the kindness that he has been shown by so many, rather than the hate.

Josh Returns/I Lose my Hair

I let out a deep sigh as Josh's plane touches down at Oliver Tambo. My son is safely at home. On the advice of others, Josh, Sam and Saul are shepherded by a special protection service through the back corridors of the airport. Many strangers have called our house to ask when the boys will be coming home, and we are scared of untoward confrontations in the arrival hall. I wait in anxious anticipation with Sandy, Saul and Sam's mother, and a second mom to Josh. We have shared many trials and tribulations as mothers but this is something completely different.

When Josh steps into in our arms, we are flooded with relief. Odd as it sounds, part of my relief is also that I still look the same. I desperately did not want Josh to have to confront a mother without hair on top of all else. As it turns out, his arrival is in the nick of time.

The next day, we flee to our farm in the Magaliesberg for the weekend with the Van der Spuy family. At last, Josh is in the loving care of his friends and family. My delight at being reunited with my son, however, is undermined by the tug of war between my identity as mother and as cancer patient.

I am possessed with the sensation of my hair having started to coagulate. I cannot think of anything else. Every few minutes, I excuse myself and rush into the bedroom so that I can stare in the mirror. My soft curly golden locks that have earned me the title of 'Goldilocks' for most of my life have taken on the appearance of overcooked Chinese noodles. The few remaining softer patches more closely resemble bits of shredded cabbage.

In my parallel universe, even the contours of this tract of land that I love have flattened and the warm sun that beats down on the red earth has lost its shine.

Besides the increasingly odd appearance of the mop on my head, my hair is also falling out at a rapid rate. Instead of leaving behind me a Hansel and Gretel trail of breadcrumbs, I am shedding my curly golden locks wherever I go. My scarfs and shirt collars bear the telltale signs of my hair loss. It is driving me utterly insane.

Nobody besides Jonny knows the depths of my despair. Others may observe the debris of my hair I leave behind on a cushion cover but I still look relatively normal so the import of these signs is not obvious.

The time has come to cut off my hair. It is the only way to survive the internal distress that haunts my every waking hour. It is time to turn back to being a cancer patient and to leave Josh's saga behind me. Because my hairdresser doesn't work on a Monday, I am forced to wait another 24 hours to cross this frontier.

In the meantime, I prepare my husband and my kids. I am especially anxious about my kids' responses as I try on my new wig for them. Teenagers tell it like it is and my kids are no exception. You can imagine my relief when my son declares my straight new bob a 'good look' and my daughter's main complaint is that I went to the wig shop and chose the wig without her. Sweet girl.

The Dreaded Moment

My hands are shaking when I call my hairdresser first thing on Tuesday morning. I am reassured the minute that I step into the salon. Candice gives me a big hug, and I feel her compassion immediately. She ushers me into the back room. Under different circumstances, I could have been having a private hair styling session or getting one of those make overs that I have witnessed countless times in glossy magazines. Instead, I am a sheep, waiting to be shorn.

Candice is very calm as I lift my cap. I am embarrassed by what is revealed. This is not just a 'bad hair day'. It is a disastrous hair day, a shambolic situation. Dreadlocks appear to have formed overnight. My hair stands out from my head at right angles. Candice carefully begins to run her comb through the tangle. My hair comes away so effortlessly at the roots. I hate the sensation.

By the end of the exercise, huge chunks of hair lie on the floor all around me. I am now better suited to a flock of bald-headed eagles than to the breed of fellow compatriots sitting in the salon next door.

I ask Candice, 'What should I do?' Without hesitation, she says: 'You have to cut your hair off. That way, you won't feel the desperation as it falls out strand by strand.'

She is right. I have to cut off the red curly locks that, for my whole life, have been my physical and emotional shield. They've been my 'signature', the foremost part of my identity, something that other people have commented on every day of my life since I was born. My heart is in tatters. I am crossing my own Rubicon.

Candice's palms rest lightly on my shoulders. She gives me a slight squeeze. My head is bowed. My submission is complete.

She takes out a large pair of scissors from a container of blue antiseptic liquid that stands in front of the mirror. The blades' malevolent gleam plunge into my heart. My mind is racing.

I hear the snip, snip as the edges of the blades meet my entangled mass. My eyes sting with tears. I try to force them back. I have to stay strong even just for this moment.

Snip. Snip. Snip.

I stare into the mirror as my hair tumbles to the floor and amasses in small feathery balls all around me.

Snip. Snip. Snip.

A series of longer curls descend. Should I gather them up and keep them? Is it possible to reattach them? I can no longer bear to watch. I squeeze my eyes tightly closed.

Snip. Snip. Snip.

After just a few minutes, I sense that we are reaching the end as I can feel the cold metal of the scissors against the base of my skull. The breeze from the window tickles my newly naked neck. A cold shiver runs down my spine. Candice's hands still. She quietly entices me to take a look.

I do not know or recognise the person who stares out from the mirror. The Lauren I know has been erased.

In a mere 300 or so seconds, I have become a cancer patient. A sick person. A person everyone looks at sympathetically in the street. A person that is offered help. I feel vulnerable.

Candice encourages me to look again. 'You have a beautifully shaped head', she says. 'Your eyes are gleaming. You have a strong jaw line.'

My terror slightly relinquishes its hold over me. I try to reframe my gaze. I try to see things positively. The image of the beautiful bald singer, Sinead O'Connor, floats into my mind. 'Hold onto her strong visage,' I tell myself.

I am now being true to my situation. I have fully entered the world of cancer. My inside and outside are drawing closer. I am declaring my illness to the world.

Later, I learn not to feel sorry for myself. I enjoy being free of the burden of that mass of hair that no longer belongs on my head. This is not a capitulation so much as a gentleman's agreement with the disease. So long as the disease is in me, this is how I will look. Unexpectedly, my transformation feels a bit better.

This does not mean that I am ready to walk out into the world. But I am able to acknowledge that a new phase is upon me in my inexorable march to being a fully fledged chemo patient.

In that moment, it is apparent that nothing forges or re-forges one's identity like the disease of cancer. 'Your hair is so beautiful. Is that your real colour? Are those your real curls?' Will I ever have to answer these questions again?

In the 19th century it was common for friends to exchange locks of hair as tokens of affection. After death, these became precious keepsakes or, if from a famous head, prized relics. Later I am to visit the house in Rome where Keats died, and I get to see the locks that were cut off after his death. I wish that I had kept my locks as my own private keepsake.

Candice holds up a mirror so that I can see the back of my head. Neither the reflection from the back nor the front mirror are recognisable. The two images splinter and refuse to form a new whole. From each direction, I am but a feint reproduction of myself. The configuration of my musculature is no longer familiar without my curly hair as its framing device. I am no longer I. Candice gently places the wig on my head, sensing perhaps my urgent need to reconfigure my face into something more familiar.

She leans in and tells me again, 'You look beautiful. I am going to cut your wig now and you will look really funky.'

When I get home, I make a list of the things that I have lost in my life:

1. *My keys (every day).*
2. *My passport just before an international flight.*
3. *My mother's favourite jumper.*
4. *My car in an underground parking lot.*
5. *My dad.*
6. *And now my hair.*

All Eyes on Me

It is more shocking than I ever could have imagined confronting the world without my hair. My journal records my first two public appearances. The first is a ceremony to mark the end of my mother's term as President of the Union of Jewish Women. The timing is most unfortunate. It is a real baptism of fire to attend such a large event the day after I am bald.

My mother is already on the podium as Katya and I take our seats. I see my mother do a double take as she sees me in my straight-haired wig. Why have I not warned her, I wonder? Is it to protect us both from a situation too hard to bear? Or is it a cowardly act borne of the shame of the disease? Or is it simply that I have not had time to internalise what has happened to me?

My mother comes off the stage amidst applause and makes a beeline for me: 'You look like your dad's sister,' she says. It is hard to interpret this comment. Is it my father when he was dying from cancer that she is really seeing? I cannot imagine her pain that must be mingled in with the compliments that flow for her excellent performance.

After this difficult encounter, I face the rest of the room. All eyes appear to be boring into me. Some people rush over and tell me, 'You look so good'. Regardless of whether this assurance is sincere or not, it is profoundly welcome. The less gushy responses are more resonate with my inside, however. Amidst the words of praise for my mother and her final private speech of farewell at the lunch that follows, I long for the quietude of being a cancer patient readying myself for chemo the following day.

My second public appearance starts off before my mirror in my bathroom.

My reflection is very frightening. It captures the hiatus of my being, the suspension of all known boundaries of the person I have inhabited for the past 49 years. My smile is the last vestige of the known and is therefore important to me, the knower.

I test out various caps, hats and bandanas. Each time I catch a glimpse of my bald head, distress enters my heart. I am not a vain person but my eyes cannot adjust to what they see. I eventually settle on a black *'doek'* (scarf) which frames my face well and shows off my blue eyes.

I walk down to the local shops with my new accoutrement on my head. The Parkview strip is thronging with life. The pavements are packed with bead makers and wire artists selling their wares. Women sit in groups on downturned buckets crocheting blankets and table cloths for sale; the flower arrangers wrap huge bunches of flowers that spill out onto the pavements from the local fruit and veg shop; the broom sellers' eyes dart around, desperate for a quick sale. The smell of the bread from the local bakery perfumes the air.

A trip down to our local high street is usually a lengthy affair. It is punctuated by conversations with friends or colleagues that range from the merits of the local school to the virtues of a collaboration on one or other work project.

Today is completely different. As I open my mouth to say, 'Hello,' to an old acquaintance, he walks straight past me. The broom seller does not rush up to greet me with her usual glee. The café owner looks right through me. No one recognises me without my mop of curly red hair. I am shattered. 'Why', I ask myself, 'did I not anticipate my invisibility?' It is hard to know the answer. All I know is that I feel overwhelmed and vulnerable, crushed and inadequate.

Later, I come to enjoy my new identity and the anonymity it brings. It unshackles me from the burden of small talk and allows me to walk down the aisles of *naartjies* and oranges unnoticed. For now, a knife has been plunged into my heart. The incision is swift. 'You are nothing without your hair,' an inner voice cackles. I flee back home without making a single purchase, unwilling to linger in this new theatre of war. I am amazed at the extent to which I define myself through the presence of others.

Over the next months, my invisibility leads me through a maze of emotions which fluctuate wildly between a sense of liberation and sheer pain at not being recognised, of being isolated from the larger group. I try to accept the challenge and move forward. I start to introduce myself to people in advance as a way to avoid the blankness on their faces. Sometimes I explain my cancer guise, often I don't.

This chimerical state continues to be a feature of Chemoland but nothing upsets me as much as this first time. After that, I embrace my growing resilience. I choose break-through rather than break-down in the face of my new identity.

Chemo Four – Desolation

21 AUGUST 2015

It is hard to anticipate the new frontiers that Chemoland presents each and every day. They require a neuroplasticity, the formation of new neural pathways in the brain. There are no straight lines anymore. Life is a rugged landscape with huge peaks and troughs. The moral complexity of the last weeks of the Josh saga echoes the complexity of my own internal world. I am living without logic or rationality. There are just the rapid oscillations along a continuum with foreboding and happiness as the outer points. My return to normality after 'scarfgate' means a return to chemo.

Today, I arrive with a headscarf on for the first time. This is not strange in a room where I am surrounded by women who look just like me. But there is irony in the fact that my son and I have both donned a scarf and crossed such an enormous Rubicon at around the same time. The journalist's reference to Josh's affair as 'scarfgate' applies to his mother too.

I have joined the army of bald cancer patients, the final outward transformation in this journey. There is nothing simple about leaving the known self behind and I should have guessed that this session of chemo was not going to be easy.

It starts off with a reminder of the push-me-pull-you life I have been living, located between chemotherapy and Zionist fury. Jonny is pacing around the waiting room on a call when I see him gesticulating wildly for me to come and look at the TV. These bold gestures are out of character for Jonny, especially in front of a full waiting room. The reason for his behaviour becomes clear when I see Josh, Sam and Saul on the television screen. They were filmed in the television studio the day before, but we had no idea when the interview would be shown. It makes me proud to see how these three young men talk passionately about the power of free speech while avoiding the details of the controversy. They have been warned against mentioning Israel.

When I am called into treatment, tears well up in my eyes. The radical diversion from cancer over these last two weeks makes it really hard to be here again. Tears continue to slide down my cheeks as Julian struggles to find a vein. It's as if I am starting this journey anew. Jonny tries to calm me without success. 'Please come back in a bit,' I whisper to him. I need to be left alone in my struggle to offer myself up again for treatment.

What is the route back of fear into my psyche? There is no map for where it is stored. The absence of markers makes it hard to know how to quarantine it. When it seizes hold of me, I inevitably capitulate.

Once, in a hot air balloon, I was amazed at how gentle and peaceful it felt to soar up one thousand feet from the earth. The pilot explained to me that the ease of passage comes from flying with the wind. 'Anything is possible,' he said, 'when you travel in the same direction as the wind.' My challenge is to go with my own head winds that are tearing across my landscape.

Nurse Julian stands by patiently as I try to fly in tandem with her. After a bit, she tries the other arm. My tears become sobs. After what seems like eternity, she finds a vein. The marble for chemo number four can be taken out of the jar. After yet another harrowing experience, I come home and list the perilous contortions that poison my mind in Chemoland. I dub them my 'chemonoia':

Chemonoia 1: 'Will I cope with the needles?'
Chemonoia 2: 'Will Julian find a good vein?'
Chemonoia 3: 'Will my white blood cell count remain high enough to continue treatment?'
Chemonoia 4: 'Will my neuropathy become more serious?'
Chemonoia 5: 'Will I be able to live with all the not knowing?'

This list makes me realise that this journey never ends and that it is extremely difficult to change our inner realities. Just as I conquer one set of physical feelings and I start to discern a pattern, there is something new to worry about. I am literally building my own world brick by brick each week.

Chemo Five – Equilibrium

THURSDAY 28 AUGUST

Life regains its rather strange equilibrium. I attend a daylong meditation, chanting and yoga workshop to counter the weeks of stress. In my pre-chemo life, I never would have invested this time in nurturing myself. The seismic shift in my circumstance allows me to relax into the eight-hour course with 20 other people all seeking healing of a kind. We don't talk. But the energy in the room is one of generosity and caring. This collective consciousness allows me to feel like a thick blanket has been thrown over my

Arctic storm. There is also a deep sense of replenishment that comes from relinquishing the tyranny of time. It allows my outer world to blur and my inner world to become more defined.

The benefits of this are obvious over the next days. Fiona, my long-time friend and gym buddy, takes me on our usual route and I easily climb a hill that I haven't attempted since starting chemo. Another friend sends Hilde, a talented and beautiful Pilates teacher, to my house and we start sessions – that continue to this day – to stretch and build my muscles. We laugh copiously while I attempt to strengthen my inner core, both physical and metaphysical. My energy is back.

I accept an invitation to a work party in a distant suburb of Jo'burg. I travel there with Nicola who has just lost her mother and we commit to having a good time despite our immediate troubles. We take a selfie of 'the chemo gal and the bereaved' and send it off to close friends.

Jessica, a professor at an English university, calls me the next day to say, 'My student said you look like Maxine Peak in the photo which I pinned to my wall. The student can't write for toffee but she's still gonna get a first from me.' I beam when I learn that Maxine Peak is a well-known British actress and is something of a looker. Who could have anticipated the unforeseen advantages of my hair loss and a good wig? Maybe I am a little vain after all.

Another new frontier opens in the self-help department. My needle phobia is still troubling me and Vicki suggests that she try a hypnotherapy session with me: 'This route is a very effective way of reaching parts of the unconscious mind that can be stubbornly inaccessible. It can create new responses and alters behaviour patterns.'

I know very little about hypnotherapy other than from friends who were taught this therapeutic modality to help them in childbirth and found it effective. I have nothing to lose though and so I embark on yet another adventure to reduce my unwanted symptoms. Some months later I learn that the clinical applications of hypnotherapy have become widespread including it being used to reduce pain and treat habit disorders so this route isn't quite as offbeat as my description may seem.

Vicki asks me to lie down on a bed. Despite my skepticism, I succumb to her calm voice saying: 'Feel yourself going down a long flight of stairs. As you descend, you will go deeper and deeper into a state of complete relaxation.' As Vicki counts down, 'Ten, nine, eight, seven …' I feel my body getting heavier. I am conscious of Vicki's presence and the instructions she gives me but it is as if a thick veil has descended over my supine form. I enter a hypnotic state.

At some point, Vicki places a teddy on my chest. 'This is a stand-in for your inner child. Give her an age.' Almost instantly, I say, 'Three'. But then I struggle to follow the instruction to embrace her. Why is it so difficult to wrap my arms around the 'three-year-old me' and say, 'It's all right,' as I have been instructed to do?

When I came out of the hypnosis, Vicki confirms my intuition: 'The adult part of you is so well developed but there is a vulnerable little girl inside that needs love. Get a photo of yourself at the age of three and talk to her gently over the course of the next week.' I carry out this instruction.

Once again, I need to add to my 'Who I am' list – I have an inner child who is forlorn and abandoned. I try to find the words to tell this three-year-old me the many reasons why she is worthy of being loved. 'What has overwhelmed you?', I find myself asking her. 'Can you unlearn your responses to fear and rage that are so frightening for you?'

While this session with Vicki takes me back to my childhood, my life coach in America spools me forward. 'Try to imagine where you will be a year from now,' she says. Just as it isn't easy to embrace my inner child, nor is it easy to imagine my life in 365 days' time. Marissa encourages me to drill down and concretely describe what I will be doing in August 2015.

It takes a while before I am I able to tell her: 'I will be finishing my book. It will be called *Moving Mountains – A Journey from*

Fear to Hope.' Marissa interjects: 'Think about the word hope and what it implies. To hope is to wish for something to happen and encompasses the possibility that it may not happen. Try and find a word for the title that is more enduring and finite.' The word 'faith' comes to mind although I resist its religious connotations. I take the point though.

'What else will you be doing?' Marissa asks. I describe the garden I am busy planting: 'By next year, it will be a meadow, full of colour, unstructured and joyful.' I tell her how my friend Roz and my work partner, Clive, are helping me in my garden quest.

Marissa points out the connection between this garden that I envision and the internal garden that I am learning to grow and nurture. Our session ends with her reading from Louise Hay: 'All disease comes from a state of "unforgiveness" and whenever we are ill, we need to look around to see who it is that we need to forgive. The very person you find it hardest to forgive is the one you need to let go of the most. Forgiveness means letting go ...' These thoughts lingers with me as I renew my commitment to my inner and outer garden and to writing this book. I need to 'stamp-in' these patches of green and colour into my consciousness.

Chemo Six – Renewal

4 SEPTEMBER 2014

It is officially spring, and the whispers of rebirth are scattered across the city. This is by far my favourite time of the year. Blossoms of every colour emerge all around. The sweet fragrance of jasmine scents the air and mingles with that of the magnolias that are starting to bloom. The weavers return to construct their nests on the palm leaves above our pool. I marvel at how the male bird painstakingly and lovingly creates a home for his lifelong mate again and again until she grants her approval.

These glimmers of new life sweep me into the chemo room this week, and session number six carries with it a sense of rebirth. I do not drag half the world into the treatment room. I leave my water bottles and blankets at home along with other of my daily concerns. The promise of a new season brings with it a determination to be the captain of my own space ship, propelling myself towards new emotional planets.

My body plays along. My white cell count is normal. Dr G palpates my tumour and tells me that it has visibly shrunken. We are overjoyed. As Dr G writes the script for my infusions, I pluck up the courage to ask her: 'Given that the tumour is responding so well, can we reduce the number of my chemo sessions?' The two doctors in the room – one the oncologist and the other my husband – only laugh. 'It is precisely when the tumour responds that one carries on the treatments at full tilt,' says the oncologist. Jonny adds: 'Isn't this a sign to actually increase the number of doses?' I glare daggers at Jonny and a small fracas follows. This is a good sign. The withered persona that sat in this chair a few weeks ago bears no resemblance to the person in the room today.

News of my shrinking lump makes me realise how my tumour – the main character of this story – has been so sorrowfully neglected. My needle phobia and other anxieties have ironically pushed fear of mortality to the periphery of my vision.

Throughout chemo session six, I wonder if other cancer patients have anxieties that trump their cancer, or if their rapidly dividing cells are constantly in the spotlight.

I look around me. The other patients come from every walk of life; young and old, black and white, South Africa's 'Rainbow Nation' that Nelson Mandela so vividly invoked in the early days of our democracy. Many are asleep with their heads tilted at odd angles. Some are just resting. Others are eating and chatting and could be mistaken for customers in a cafeteria on a high street were it not for the IV lines snaking up from their arms. What reckoning has each of these people made with their mortality? Do they speak to their loved ones of living or dying?

As the toxic poisons enter my veins, I come to understand why mortality has not been my most immediate fear. The prodding, the pricking, the insistent identity of 'patient' that cancer thrusts upon one, have been my preoccupations. The all-encompassing nature of the physical has overwhelmed the metaphysical.

The long hours on the chair also allow me to ponder the benefits of this ordeal. Out of the chrysalis of my chemo cocoon, I see some of the new attributes that are emerging for the 'Who Am I' list:

1. *I am quieter, kinder and more at ease than before.*
2. *I want less of others and the world and more of myself.*
3. *I seek new kinds of experiences that focus inwards.*
4. *I embrace a sense of aloneness and apart-ness.*
5. *I would answer, 'No' to the proverbial question in the self-help literature – 'If a fairy godmother offered to take away your cancer, would you want that?'*

The last point requires some clarification. I am not romanticising cancer. I would never wish this disease on my worst enemy or myself but, for the very first time, I can see why people sometimes call it a 'gift'. There are many insights that I would not have gained without this harrowing experience. If I am an iceberg, a much greater proportion of my bulk is now above the water and is directing my new conduct in the world. It is in this spirit that I pen an update to my family and friends:

On 4 September 2014, 8:21 PM,
Lauren Segal <laurensegal3@gmail.com> wrote:

It is hard to believe that I am at the end of another cycle of treatment. Two cycles down, four to go or six treatments down, 12 more to go. I haven't been able to be in touch with all of you over these last weeks, so I thought I would send my update.

I look back at the last email that I wrote after the end of the first cycle and I have to chuckle. My last sentence read: 'Josh's is in Thailand. His team has caused a mini furor by wearing a Palestinian scarf in the first-team photo of the tournament. That is a story all on its own and requires its own email.'

Little did I know that an international social media storm would erupt and that Josh's brave act would require an entire book of its own! It has proved a difficult diversion from the world of cancer as it felt like our family had jumped involuntarily onto a small raft that was being belted through a class five rapid with the Victoria Falls up ahead and hippopotami all around. Life at home became worlds away from the quiet, calm and ordered space that I was supposed to inhabit.

BUT since then, over the last three sessions of chemo, I can see that I am making some sort of progress:

1. *I no longer feel like an alien that has landed in the chemo room.*
2. *It is 'me' in there and I am no longer the new kid on the block.*
3. *I don't faint from the needles.*
4. *I have discovered amazing chanting that calms my nerves as the drip goes in.*
5. *I do not take most of the contents of my bedroom or the fridge with me.*
6. *Jonny now has to make only one trip from the car to get me inside the chemo room.*
7. *I have lightened up literally and metaphorically.*
8. *I am not in search of the perfect seat.*
9. *I am not suffering from bad symptoms.*
10. *I am spending hours on the Internet looking for an alternative house to buy with a north-facing bedroom.*

I continue to draw strength from all of you. And I thank you for staying the mile. This is indeed proving to be a marathon. I am still wondering how I will do another four of these cycles. But I am learning to slowly put one foot in front of the other and spend as much time as possible in the present.

The next day, Jonny and I meet Katya at the airport. She is returning from a week with friends in Mozambique. I am eternally grateful to Janine, Mandi, Naomi and Nicola – who have taken over our role at a time when we are unable to think of going on a holiday. Each photo I receive of my daughter frolicking in the waves with her friends makes me again relish the community of mothers that surround us.

The poem that arrives in my inbox this week called 'The Unprofessionals' by UA Fanthorpe serendipitously describes these women. My favourite line of the poem is 'They come'. With such economy, these two words describe the solace I imbibe from those who console me and my family without being solicited to do so.

Chemo Seven – Acceptance

11 SEPTEMBER 2014

When I enter the chemo room for the seventh time, I am truly different. My fears seem to be forgetting themselves, and my body has a newfound confidence that it can handle the treatment. Chemo has now acquired a formulaic repetitiveness:

1. *Blood test*
2. *Results*
3. *Consultation with Dr G*
4. *Long wait for chemo drugs to be mixed*
5. *Insertion of the drip*
6. *Infusions for three or four hours*
7. *Ice packs during the Taxol*
8. *Warm pads that ease the pain of the Gemzar*
9. *Toilet visits with the IV pole in tow*
10. *Rejoicing the final drips of the chemo medicine*
11. *Home*
12. *Deep sleep*
13. *Adrenalin rush from the steroids*
14. *Side effects for the next three days*

Being in a calmer state allows me to observe Jonny more carefully. During stages 1–4 above, he is a caged lion, pacing up and down on his phone and then stopping to type on his iPad which rests on the reception counter. During stages 5–10, Jonny turns chemotherapy into a turbo-charged affair. When the nurses aren't looking, he opens the drip so that the poisons can enter my bloodstream more quickly. I read this as his way of lessening my torture and of taking a semblance of control. 'Thank you for finding new ways to care for me,' I whisper to my husband.

When work meetings force Jonny to leave early, he issues strict instructions to friends who are his proxy. 'Don't let Lauren take off the ice gloves. It is critical they stay on so she doesn't suffer from neuropathy.' Today, Sharon, a friend who secretly wishes she were a doctor rather than a writer, receives these instructions. We are working together on a book about detentions in the apartheid era and, when she watches in slight horror as I grimace my way through the hour of ice gloves, she jokes: 'The security police should have used these ice packs as a form of torture.' Nonetheless, she strictly administers the gloves and ensures that they stay on.

Opposite, a young girl who is having the same chemo drug is less disciplined. 'Keep them on,' I urge her. How far a journey I have travelled in my inner and outer world.

With my newfound confidence, I attend a birthday party for my godson that night, and then continue the merriment the next day. I lunch with Graeme who is visiting from abroad, and then go to Lula's birthday party in the early evening.

By the time I get home, I feel like a snail that's been crushed underfoot. Layers of concrete have replaced my bones and muscles, while the epidermal layer of my skin is crawling. My anxiety feels trapped in the electro-chemical chatter of my billions of nerve cells. The chemo devil cackles: 'You are paying the price for thinking that life can just go on as usual.'

When Jonny arrives home I wail, 'I cannot move!' He assures me that these symptoms too shall pass, but there is a whiff of chastisement in his question: 'Have you pushed yourself too far today?' Physical distress along with self-admonishment for my hubris keeps me awake long into the night.

By the next morning, new symptoms appear. I feel like a frozen lake in the Russian tundra. 'There's ice in my veins,' I cry and then add to the drama: 'I wish the sound in my head was the quiet emptiness Buddhists aspire to … Instead it is the persistent sound of cleats on a locker room floor.' I'm submerged in a dense mist, the kind that would prevent a small plane from taking off or landing.

These unexpected symptoms are a cruel betrayal. Despite trying so hard to make friends with my cancer, I am suffering. Again, the all-encompassing nature of the disease hits home. Cancer cannot be overcome. It grips your body and mind; it intrudes into your world; it inhabits your heart and soul. Life must go into quarantine. There is no 'business as usual', however tempting that may be. It requires multiple strengths to counter its forceful hold.

In a desperate attempt to transition from a minor to a major key, I phone Janine and ask her to take me for a massage. For that brief hour and a half when we lie side by side at the Thai spa, my positive life force prevails. I am rejuvenated. It doesn't last long.

When my brother calls later and asks simply, 'How are you feeling?' my floodgates open yet again. The strong new me from just a few days before has faded from view, buried under the salvos of this chemo offensive. I am the pile of rubble left after a bombardment. My evolving consciousness is spooling backwards.

That night, I have a powerful dream. I encounter a young child who is lost and doesn't know how to get home. She is utterly forlorn. 'Don't worry,' I tell her. 'I will take you to find your family.' We set off on a long and complex journey down the main arterial road of Johannesburg. There are multiple obstacles along the way. In the end, I get her home safely. This dream assures me that I have the capacity to bring the vulnerable part of myself back to a place of safety. I am grateful to my unconscious for alerting me to this strength in the midst of such despair.

A few days later, I say to Marissa, 'Surely it's normal to fall apart like this?' She shares her special brand of wisdom with me: 'You are entitled to break down. But you should ask yourself what you might do differently in that state. Do you want your symptoms to be magnified? Or do you want to acknowledge your fears but counter them with higher order feelings? By sequestering your fearful thoughts, you will diminish them.'

Together we create a list of statements for me to say to myself when these painful feelings recur:

1. *I see the symptoms but I choose not to focus on them negatively.*
2. *I choose instead to send positive images of heat to my frozen cells.*
3. *I bring a warm light to transform the energy of my feelings.*
4. *It's in my power to turn my sense of betrayal into something more positive.*
5. *I have tools and resources to conquer my distress.*
6. *It's in the trying and staying with the pain that learning is revealed.*
7. *Everything is ever changing. Nothing stays the same.*

She ends by explaining that, 'Our subconscious doesn't know the difference between imagination and reality. In a scary movie, our bodies experience the same metabolic changes that they do in real life. We can always change the channel though and allow something more positive to enter into the unconscious mind.'

This advice gives me the courage to attend my goddaughter's Bat Mitzvah that weekend. Along with other special people in her life, I give Ella a blessing in front of a community of friends and strangers. It is a beautiful occasion even though it is hard for me to appear in a large crowd with a wig on.

The next day, Carol reflects: 'I am taken by how changed you are. Your being is very different in a positive and extraordinary way. The existential reckoning you have done and are doing is profoundly part of your face and body and manner. This new dimension is hard to describe. With the slowing down and conserving of energy is a wisdom and maturity and compassion and insight. It's really very beautiful.'

I am so grateful for these words.

Chemo Eight – Wisdom

18 SEPTEMBER 2014

Chemo not only puts you in a new relationship with yourself. It changes your relationship with the world around you. Everything is renegotiated to accord with the new landscapes that spring up in one's soul. The holy day of Rosh Hashanah, the Jewish New year, a time of visiting the graves of ancestors, asking for forgiveness and fasting, is no exception.

Our family is wholly secular but these holidays hold a special significance for me. Most of all, I love the ritual of a predictable group of family and friends coming together for a meal to celebrate the promise of a new year. But I have never had a Rosh Hashanah with cancer before and this requires something new of me. What exactly does this season of prayer and repentance mean this year, I wonder. Is this a time for me to pray? And if so, to whom? Would I be enriched if I followed Jewish rituals more closely?

If I were religious, I might have turned to a Rabbi for answers. Instead, I search for commentaries on this High Holy Day online. I find one of the key liturgies for Rosh Hashanah, *Unetaneh Tokef*. The passage starts with a description of God opening the Book of Remembrances and inscribing in it people's fates for the next year. It lists the decisions God must take. It says: On Rosh Hashanah will be inscribed and on Yom Kippur will be sealed ...

Who will live and who will die –
Who at his time, and who before his time –
Who by water and who by fire ...
Who will rest and who will wander;
Who will live in harmony and who will be buffeted;
Who will enjoy tranquility and who will suffer;
Who will be impoverished and who enriched;
Who will be degraded and who exalted.
But repentance and prayer and charity will make the Decree less bad.

The first line is obviously the most eye-catching in my circumstance. The last line, however, really calls out to me. The liturgy tells us that while the future is not in our hands, we can control how the future controls *us*. A commentator on this passage believes that the prayer suggests that we have the power and choice to experience bad things as being *less bad*. Life will throw lemons at us but we can avoid being hurt and can even make lemonade.

This religious liturgy is an echo of Victor Frankl, Louise Hay and other spiritual writers whom I have been reading so voraciously these last months. Perhaps it is no wonder. Despite not believing in God, I am delighted to have discovered a meaningful association with the religious holiday.

I step into the New Year dinner at my mother's house holding this meaning of the night in the front of my mind. When my mother says to me with great irritation, 'You are spreading the herring on the wrong side of the *kichel* (sugary cracker),' I am stung. How dare she focus on something so insignificant at a time like this? My internal voice is booming: 'Flee. Go back to the safety of your home. It is taking too much strength to be here with a wig on your head and chemo's fires still coursing through your veins.'

I choose to ignore this voice. I listen instead to what my heart knows. My mom shows her deep care in so many ways but seldom uses words. I can't always make sense of the pain she is feeling around my cancer and this is hard for me, but I have to hold on to the fact that she is hardwired to worry about the small stuff, and that focusing on the right side of the *kiegel* is, for her, a return to the safe.

Rosh Hashanah's promise of a sweet and happy new year is not safe, not for my mother, not for my family, not for me. We have all lost the certainty that comes with this occasion. This is why my mother worries about the *kiegel* and why it is important for me to remember that each of us battles in our own ways to make things 'less bad'. We all wish to be inscribed in the Book of Life in a way that ensures our sanctity. Whatever our decree, we can work towards it being the least bad year possible.

Chemo Nine – Joy & Trepidation

2 October 2014

Halfway. The word has never sounded more beautiful. Each letter is perfectly positioned, its cadence melodic. I walk into the oncologist's office with a grin on my face. 'Nine down,' I proclaim as I take my seat to be examined. Dr G's fingers move deftly over my tumour. She exclaims. 'Oh Lauren. It is shrinking. It's much smaller than I ever could have imagined.' My grin extends from ear to ear.

'I couldn't be happier,' she tells me and Jonny. 'Given that we are at the half-way mark I want you to go to Dr P so that she can measure the tumour's exact size.'

I freeze. I haven't seen the radiologist since she gave Jonny the news that the mass she was so certain was not cancer was in fact a large malignant tumour. This unfortunate error is still a smoking gun. How am I to contain my anger or stop invectives from shooting out of my mouth when I see Dr P?

In Henry Marsh's book about his life as a brain surgeon, I read and reread the paragraph where he talks about a catastrophic operation in which a young girl dies unexpectedly on the operating table. He reflects on the mistakes doctors make in a lecture called 'All my worst mistakes'. He surprises a group of medical students when he tells them that doctors need to be held accountable since their 'power corrupts'. His reasoning is that if doctors don't hide or deny any mistakes when things go wrong and their patients and their families know of the doctor's distress, the doctor might be lucky enough to receive the precious gift of forgiveness.

I can imagine that Dr P is deeply distressed by her mistake and yet I am not ready to forgive. 'Can I go to another radiologist?' I ask. Dr G is aware of why I ask this question. After all, she and my radiologist must discuss my case at the shockingly named weekly 'morbidity and mortality' meetings. Dr G explains why I shouldn't change: 'She is the only person who has seen this tumour, the only one who will have a perspective on how it has changed.'

I go into the chemo room mulling over my predicament. The

scan brings a black cloud onto an otherwise shiny halfway horizon. But ending my ninth chemo infusion wipes out any shadows. I am euphoric. Nine out of 18. I never imagined that I would reach this point and still be standing. My joy is evident in the email I send out:

On 2 October 2014, 10:16 PM,
Lauren Segal <laurensegal3@gmail.com> wrote:

Half way. I feel tentatively elated. The same stretch of road may lie ahead but psychologically, I feel like I am standing at the top of Everest looking down instead of being at Base Camp wondering if I will summit.

Most importantly, the oncologist says that 'the tumour is melting away'. The chemo is working. So there was hope hovering in the room today, inflating my lungs.

I deliberately sat in the same seat in the waiting room as I did on that day of my first treatment. Nothing looked or felt the same. There was an incredible moment that illustrated this. I spotted a woman across the room who was clearly there for the first time. It was so easy to tell. Despite her huge round glasses, I could see that she had on the same mask of fear on that I had worn three months ago. I went to give her a quick hug and was still sitting with her and her family an hour later. She told me she had a needle phobia and I smiled in empathy. I recounted all of the ways that I have been dealing with my own fears. By the time she was called to see the doctor, I felt like I had briefly become a counsellor rather than simply a mirror of this women's terrified self.

I loved this encounter and that it happened today. It helped me to believe in the impermanence of the world and confirmed the sense of 'boundless possibility' that I so often read about in Bhuddist texts. There are many other ways that I know that I am not quite the same person that sat in that chair three months ago:

1. *I am learning to enjoy the space that comes with paring down one's life.*

2. *I am learning the joy of being single-tasked.*
3. *I am learning to enjoy the clarity that comes with having no hair.*
4. *I am learning to trust and befriend my body even though it has let me down.*
5. *I am learning to enjoy buying hats nearly as much as I enjoy buying shoes.*

The only thing that never changes for me is that each day I am sustained by drinking in the kindness that you all provide. It makes the roof, floor and walls of my dwelling in Chemoland. It is the blanket I wear each time in my chemo chair. And it is undoubtedly the thing that has allowed me to feel that I have been bumped to business class on my long haul flight. The next time I write, I will have six more. I love the sound of that.

The responses I receive are as edifying as ever. There is one image I love in particular from my cousin, Keith: 'Truly, you are a breath of fresh air, a gust that lifts hats off heads and makes people run laughing after them, a breeze that holds kites in the sky.'

A Shadow of Its Former Self

My appointment with Dr P is deliberately scheduled in the early morning before the hordes of other patients arrive. As we walk into the ultrasound room, Dr P looks at me with the gentleness of one who has done much reckoning: 'I am not the same person that you knew. I have thought of you every day since I discovered that your lump was a tumour.'

Just writing this sentence makes me cry. Unexpectedly, her candidness, vulnerability and remorse call forth my own vulnerability. My vocal cords are too twisted to say, 'It's okay,' but she registers how my body softens. I am so overcome that I don't feel the gel being smeared onto my chest. It is only when

I see Jonny anxiously peering at the monitor that I realise the ultrasound is underway.

Dr P says quietly: 'The "thing" that I thought was scar tissue is a shadow of its former self. It now resembles Emmental cheese.' She marks the edges of the tumour with green crosses and then joins them with a dotted line. 'The tumour now measures just over two centimetres. It has reduced by more than 70 per cent! I am really amazed.' Dr P confesses: 'Lobular cancers are just not that responsive to chemo.'

My mind is dancing all over as we leave her rooms. I feel lighter, both because of the news that my tumour is smaller than could have been hoped for but also because of the nature of my encounter with Dr P. She is not the ogre I had turned her into. The 'precious gift of forgiveness' has overcome my anger.

I understand fully for the first time how holding onto my negative emotions would only damage myself. By letting them go, I have created an opportunity for learning about making mistakes. Ironically, I have also potentially helped other women – Dr P will never again make the assumption that scar tissue is not a tumour. She will insist on a biopsy. This acknowledged error reminds me of what the well-known analyst D.W. Winnicott said about the difference between good and bad mothers – it is not the commission of errors that divides them. Rather, it is what they do with their errors. Dr P has done all she can do to correct her mistake.

Once in the car, I dial my breast surgeon to tell her the news. Dr Benn is delighted and says, 'Come to my office immediately'. As she examines the tumour, I watch for her response. She is equally shocked at how my invader has all but disappeared. We hug. I am so elated that I don't hear her telling me about the next steps. All I hear her say is, 'The new size of your tumour makes your operation a much simpler procedure as I can now take a wider margin around it.'

Until this point, the operation has been far from my mind. Like everything on this journey, the good and the bad are tightly intertwined. The reminder that in a mere three weeks after chemo ends I will be back in the hospital punctures the joy over my shrunken tumour. 'Day by day,' I say to myself.

Not Quite a Holiday

I arrange a trip with Jonny for a four-day 'half-way celebration'. It is the first time that I am venturing away from home and having a respite from the gruelling chemo routine. Despite doing hundreds of domestic flights before, I am thrilled to find myself at the security check-in point in the cavernous hall at Oliver Tambo Airport. It is as if I have been let out of prison or picked up one of those cards on the monopoly board that says, 'Pass begin and collect R200'.

As I hand over my ticket, I realise the extent to which Chemoland has restricted my boundaries and closed in my walls. All my work travel plans have been cancelled; all holidays put on hold. When I walk through the X-ray machines, I grin broadly at no one and nothing in particular. The smile expresses a soaring inside my soul. At that moment, I am not a chemo patient. Rather, I am on a journey, going to meet my husband in Durban, moving through the crowds of people who are all on journeys of their own.

My sense of revelry is interrupted when a young girl asks if she can join me at my table at a café in the departure's hall. A rather rude intrusion, I think, but I perk up when she tells me that I look very stylish. She then asks, 'Are you having chemo?' With that simple question, my fantasy that I can look and act normal, is completely erased.

The woman turns out to be a blogger for a breast cancer advocacy organisation that is pressurising the government to develop a more progressive breast cancer policy. She tells me, 'I am motivated by the poet, Lord Byron, who says that "a single stroke of ink can change a million lives".' I soften. She is trying to reach out and make the world a slightly better place. I open to her presence.

'What is wrong with the existing policy?' I enquire. She tells me that one in eight women in South Africa get breast cancer. Sixty per cent of women who arrive at public hospitals already have a metastasised cancer as opposed to 20 per cent in private hospitals.' I wince at the thought of my own privilege. She continues: 'Women in the public hospital system die every day because of the time that passes between diagnosis and treatment.' This is horrifying to hear.

She explains that because the drugs to treat TB and AIDS are so much cheaper than those used for cancer, 'breast cancer treatment lags far behind. We need to speed up the government's fight against the disease.' Before long, we are exchanging details. Yet I can only take on the reality of how extremely privileged I am when my own struggle to survive is over. It is only then that I learn of the extent of the problems surrounding breast cancer for most South African women and that I can add my voice to the campaigns for early detection of the disease. At this point, while living in Chemoland, my focus is on another powerful lesson for myself – despite feeling empowered inside, I cannot pretend that I am not a chemo patient.

The exhilarating edge that has started the day erodes further during the plane ride. Jonny has reassured me a hundred times that I will not suffer an embolism as a result of my medication but I am anxious from the minute I sit down on the plane. There is an empty seat between the passenger on the aisle and myself. When I steel a glance at his book, I am relieved to see it is J.M. Coetzee's *Youth*. I imagine that his literary tastes, together with his kind eyes, mean that he will not mind if he has to resuscitate me during the flight.

A few minutes after take-off, I remove my shoes to wiggle my toes around and then rotate my feet vigorously in balletic circles. Panic mounts especially as I experience shooting pains in my feet and as my brain adjusts to the high decibels of background noise. The man-reading-Coetzee-with-the-kind-eyes gives me a sideways glance. He is probably making up his own story about who I am, why my hat is so firmly planted on my head in an airplane, and why I don't stop moving my darn feet! I order a tomato juice as is my habit on a plane. I read somewhere that it is the umami flavour in the juice that creates this appeal. There is great relief when the wheels of the plane touch the tarmac in Durban.

The wild swings between elation and despair on the journey down continue all through my mid-way celebration. A walk on a coastal path so close to the sea allows me to feel as if I am flying. Watching the herds of animals roam in an expansive landscape the next day reminds me of the remarkable natural cycles of life and death.

My inner terror, however, keeps chasing me down, reminding me that I have no right to happiness. At a beautiful candlelit dinner table that night, I am suddenly overwhelmed. Once the tears start, they don't stop. The raw cauliflower salad on the plate remains untouched. I am totally baffled. Here I am sitting with Jonny, the torque of my soul, in one of the most beautiful settings on earth during a much-anticipated celebration. Instead of feeling unencumbered, I am a prisoner of my lugubrious fate. My unexpected outburst and my tearstained face equally bewilders Jonny.

The toilet cubicle is once again my refuge. 'What is happening to me?' I type frantically to Susie. 'Utterly forlorn and hopeless. Can't stop weeping.' A response comes back within a few seconds. As always, her wisdom is so containing: 'My darling La. My heart goes out to you. It's called post-traumatic stress. You have found a way to manage the nightmare of the cancer and incorporate it into your life. It's hard to suddenly be confronted with pleasure and beauty and "all is well". It's not all well, you are still in the middle of it and you cannot quite enjoy the break.'

The email exchange goes back and forth across the miles until I calm down a bit. I return to the table to find a magnificent stack of aubergines and mozzarella cheese with layers of basil. Through my red eyes, I smile at Jonny. We drain our glasses of wine, hold hands across the table and eat in silence. He gets it. Even when a fire goes out, the logs continue to burn. My cancer and I are entwined right now. There is no possibility of artistic distance, studied remoteness or willed detachment.

The next day, I am as suffocated by the openness of the game reserve as I am hungry for it. We travel home with all the complexity of a holiday in external paradise while existing in a pocket of internal hell.

Chemo Ten – Envy

14 OCTOBER 2014

Going back to chemo proves as hard as being away from it. My short-lived encounter with the outside world has been disorientating. In order to inhabit Chemoland, one has to succumb to its specificity. Strangely, I am ready to return to illness and all its preoccupations.

It is significant that I go to first double-digit chemo alone this week. Enough chemo weeks have passed for me to manage. Besides, I wish to tell Dr G that I do not want to increase my chemo dose. I have decided that there is no need to put my body under more duress.

Dr G pushes back. 'Given that you are coping so well,' she says to me, 'it's better to up the fight. The more the better.' In the end, we agree that we will not increase the dosage today but will talk again next week. I leave her office victorious. Even if it's an illusion, I feel like I have taken control of the situation. This is so important when everything else is so out of control.

When I sit down for my first double-digit session, I am sitting next to an elderly woman who is having her last treatment. I have not seen her before. She is so happy about the end, and we discuss how she might celebrate. I pass on my enthusiasm and my unending desire to mark important events. We come up with an elaborate plan.

I confess, deep down I feel an inexplicable envy when I see her walking out through the doors. Shame overwhelms me. The fatigue of the long-distance runner has set in. Watching someone else cross the finish line while you have miles to go is both an incentive and a cruelty.

When I arrive home, I try to take charge and plot my finishing date. My calendar is blank before me. For my whole life, I have lived by the markers of a 24-hour day and measured success by how much I can pack into these hours. For the moment, a daily diary has lost all relevance. Chronology has unravelled. In this Dali-esque world with watches melting over the branches of a tree, the days are without form and the hours without meaning.

In my surreal state of being, chemo demands that I invent new units of time. My new marker is the number of chemo sessions I have left. Yes, I have finished the uphill climb. Yes, I am able to see the finish line. But there are still eight more sessions to get through. With two weeks of break time, this means 11 more weeks of chemo blur, 1 848 more hours in which I have to conjure energy and positivity.

I pour over the calendar to find a way to finish chemo within this year. I cannot possibly start 2015 with a marathon still to run. I hatch a plan to skip my break weeks between my three remaining cycles of chemo. This way, I can end my treatment on 15 December – a day before the national Day of Reconciliation that traditionally marks the end of the year for many working South Africans. It seems auspicious that the public holiday, which was known as the Day of the Vow under apartheid, is to become my own personal day of freedom.

Giving up my break week will be hard for my body to endure, but not as hard as the waves of agonising thoughts that I will have to continue my hell into the new year.

In the midst of this planning exercise, I realise how unthinkingly we live our normal lives. I have never before thought how I would like time to work for me. I have always worked for time.

Chemo Eleven – Self-Reproach

21 October 2014

Sometimes, significant events in the outside world penetrate the Chemoland bubble. Today, as I walk into the rooms, the televisions are turned up higher than usual so that patients and nurses alike can watch the final moments of the Oscar Pistorius murder trial that has transfixed our country and the world for the past six months.

This is the day of sentencing. After 36 weeks of incessant broadcasts and debate about whether the disabled athlete deliberately killed his girlfriend, Reeva Steenkamp, behind a closed bathroom door or thought she was an intruder. The case has aroused strong sentiments for and against Pistorious. For his supporters he is a victim; for his detractors, a ruthless killer. Now South Africa's 'trial of the century' is drawing to a close.

The judge reads her arguments from an endless ream of notes. She eventually announces a sentence of a mere five years in prison. The room is abuzz. Most of us waiting for chemo that day believe that Pistorius killed his girlfriend and that the judge should have handed down a life sentence. The conversation that threads through the waiting room focuses on the shamefully high levels of violence against women and children in our country, and how this lenient sentence is sure to send the wrong message.

As the chatter subsides, my head switches from the Oscar trial to my own inner trial. When I walk into Dr G's office, I am hell-bent on telling her that I do not want an increased dosage of the chemo drugs. I have rehearsed my argument with Vicki the day before. We prepared this mantra: 'I am intuitive with my body. I know what is best for me. This is my decision.'

Why I am so fixated on this extra 140 grams of the Gemzar is hard to decipher. It may have to do with the paradoxical nature of chemotherapy – how something that potentially cures you can also kill you. Dr G's insistence on more chemo feels like both an act of concern and a form of sadism. Such is the complex nature of the care that oncologists provide.

Dr G listens to my prepared arguments. She nods when I express my main anxiety: 'The additional poison could push my body over the edge.' She sticks to her guns, however: 'Sorry Lauren. We need to increase the dose.' Jonny studiously looks down at his phone during our exchange. Of course he sides with Dr G but he knows better than to openly agree. In the face of my vociferous doctor and my silent husband, I lose my case. I acquiesce to having the extra dose. Oscar is victorious and I am a loser.

In retrospect I see that Dr G and I are both acting blindly. Neither of us knows what the extra dose will or won't achieve. She acts blindly in the name of science; I, in the name of fear.

Chemo Twelve – Fury

28 OCTOBER 2014

Maybe it is my defeat in clawing back some power that makes me so resentful of chemo number 12. I wake up with a rebellious soul. A demon has entered my being during the night. Silently, I rail against what is to come – the endless wait, the jabs, the drips. This is utterly self-defeating but still I set off to treatment with a black heart.

I become even more bellicose when I discover it is Breast Cancer Awareness Week. The waiting room is festooned with pink and red balloons. The enforced cheer sickens me. So does the table laden with the worst kind of pink and red junk goodies.

Surely the healthcare practitioners who provide the poison that enters our veins also know that sugar is our disease's number one dietary villain? Every website on cancer nutrition teaches us that cancer cells harness glucose to grow and spread. Eating sugar for us patients is like pouring gasoline on a fire.

My preoccupation with the junk food overwhelms all other thoughts. I fixate on creating an alternative offering for those of us who sit here with our incomplete lives. Watermelon, guavas, strawberries, ruby grapefruits, red apples, cherries, raspberries and cranberries would surely be better than the fizz bars, marshmallows and ghastly sorbet sticks. Or a more savoury offering of chopped Italian tomatoes and basil, tuna tartar with a red chilli salsa, red peppers with dips, shot glasses of gazpacho and sangria or a Satan's citrus cocktail? In my head, I rant to the doctors: 'Why can't you see us patients holistically? Why do you simply treat our 6.5 cm tumours and ignore the rest of our bodies?'

As if to echo my internal state, one thing after the other goes wrong today. The all-too-cheerful nurse misses my vein in my blood test and I am left with a big bruise on my arm. 'I am so sorry,' he says afterwards. Then Dr G announces that my white cell count is borderline. She agrees I can go ahead with the treatment, but there is an extra long wait for the chemo cocktails to be mixed and this gives me hours to get more anxious. Nurse Julian takes one look at me when I am eventually sitting in the chemo chair and asks, 'What's wrong?' My anger spills forth.

Julian confesses that she is also having a hard time: 'My daughter is being impossible,' she moans. 'Why?' I ask. 'Today is the fifth anniversary of my husband's death from stomach cancer. He was 35 years old.'

Our eyes fill with tears. I am astounded that this woman who treats cancer patients every day of her life with such *joie de vivre*, has lost her own husband to the disease. What a cruel twist of fate. My own anger takes on a new form. It is directed at this disease that inflicts such pain and hardship on so many. Today, everything feels particularly unjust.

Things don't improve when I arrive home. Catherine, our housekeeper and part of the scaffolding of my home life, is sitting in the kitchen looking grief-stricken. 'What's wrong?' I ask immediately. 'I have TB,' she replies. This is awful news and a shock to us both. Catherine is young and strong and never ill. Until recently, she has had no warning signs. 'What treatment is the doctor suggesting?' but Cath can't answer. The tears roll down her cheeks. I know this feeling of devastation all too well. My heart goes out to her.

As I start to talk to Cath about what I have learnt about the power of the positive mind to boost our immune systems, my children arrive home. They have learnt about TB in their life orientation classes and are both very distressed by the news. Josh also warns: 'TB is highly contagious. People with compromised immunities are the most likely to contract TB.' Before I can panic too dramatically, my ever prescient husband calls: 'I called Dr G and she reassures me that the chances of you getting TB are low. As a precaution though, she says you and Cath shouldn't have contact for the next three weeks.'

I wander around my garden, verdant and lush. My internal blackness smothers the colourful spring arrays. I rage to a friend on the phone: 'Why are we being tested in this way? Why yet another challenge for my family? Cancer and now TB.' I know all too well the shock Catherine is facing in receiving this diagnosis and that she too needs all the support she can get, but the small abandoned child in me rears her head and pleads, 'Please don't leave me alone now, Cath. I need you. My children need you.'

Back inside the house, the latest packet of goodies from the coffee group has arrived on the kitchen counter. The ghoulish Halloween paraphernalia make me laugh. As I don the Halloween hat and long black wig, it seems that no gift to date has better reflected my inner state of being.

'It's Not Fair'

Thankfully, Catherine successfully fought her TB and returned to work after three weeks. That first night, however, I don't anticipate this positive outcome and my tetchiness keeps me awake. As the hours tick by, the whisper 'it's not fair' becomes a roar. Sheer distress pulses through my 96 000 kilometres of blood vessels that are long enough to wind around the earth two and a half times.

Over the next week, my anger morphs into an all-devouring rage. All the work to stay positive evaporates. Whenever I am asked how I'm feeling, two words come out of my mouth: '*Gatvol* and *woes*'. These Afrikaans words roughly translate into 'enough' and 'mad with anger'.

Even the slightest mishap sends me spinning. I order my mother packing when she arrives to visit. There are midnight rants with a friend whose child I believe has hurt my daughter. I retreat to sleep on the couch out of fury. My inner lacerations are deepening. So are my external expressions of malice.

When I trawl through the utterances that have escaped my lips these last few days, I feel wretched. Gone is my newfound wisdom. Anger is leaking all over my life. I have travelled backwards to the emotional space of a forsaken child.

Roz tells me, 'It's the full moon causing your woes. It is characteristic of menopausal women to be unable to deal with anything inauthentic.' Is this an excuse for my perpetual low stooping behaviour? Surely menopausal women with cancer are a category all of their own?

The symphonic dissonance in my head gets louder as I learn of three cancer-related deaths in my immediate community. The most tragic of them is an 18-year-old boy who has died of brain cancer. My son's girlfriend comes to our house straight from the funeral, looking shattered.

These deaths add to my morbid state. 'Why should I be the lucky one?' is the question that casts a shadow over my days. Until now, I have been mostly certain that I will beat the odds. Now I have lost that conviction. I start to compose letters in my head to my husband and children, telling them how joyful they have made me. In these imaginary ramblings, I assure them that the large happiness quotient I have shared with them makes it easier for me to leave this world. My imaginary composition extends to assigning tasks to friends. I think of the person who will:

1. *Arrange meals for the family in the transition months after I am gone.*
2. *Accompany Jonny to the airport when Josh leaves to study abroad.*
3. *Shop with Katya for her dance dress.*
4. *Help organise my children's weddings.*
5. *Assist Jonny with my children's spiritual needs.*
6. *Provide emotional inspiration at times of difficulty.*

This list grows after I watch a webcast of the memorial service for my colleague who was diagnosed around the same time as I was. Gerald was a visionary philanthropist who funded many projects that I have worked on. It is impossible to fathom that he is gone. His memorial makes me think of:

1. *Who will organise my memorial service.*
2. *What photos I want to be shown on the screen.*
3. *What flowers I want in the vases.*
4. *Who will pay tribute to me.*

When I recount these self-pitying thoughts during my session with Vicki, she listens intensely. Without any special solemnity in her tone, she asks me, 'Would you like to talk more about how you think of your own death?'

I reel at Vicki's question. Despite the grisly images of violence and death that saturate our media, the subject of death is taboo in our culture, hidden in the tenebrous shadows of our lives. In medieval times, guides to *ars moreindi* (the art of dying) were extremely popular. These Latin texts, which were reprinted in more than a hundred editions across Europe, helped the dying to reaffirm their faith, repent their sins and let go of worldly possessions and desires. They also provided families with prayers and questions for the dying to help them through their final hours.

In Western society today, death is terrifying, something totally hidden. For us cancer patients undergoing chemotherapy there is also a twist – talking about our own death is very hard when we are so ferociously trying to stay attached to life.

Instead of answering Vicki, my mind lingers on the vivid images of the last moments at my father's bedside as he lay dying. He is the first and only person I have ever seen take a final breath. I was 41 years old. My brother, who lives in Canada, called to recite the *Shema* (the last prayers of the dying) and the prayers for forgiveness. Mark's breaking voice crossed the oceans as he stood in his home far away with his *tallit* (shawl) around his shoulders, holding his *siddur* (prayer book). My mother and I held my father's hand as the Hebraic words emanated from the receiver. At the moment my father drew his last rasping breath, and we realised that there were no more breaths to come, I cried out and wished him well on his journey.

I sat with his newly inert body while my mother and Jonny left the room to take care of the duties that accompany a death. My mother lit a candle. Jonny called the *Chevrah Kadisha*, the Jewish Burial Society that performs acts of practical assistance for bereaved families.

Jews believe that our *neshoma*, or soul, takes a long time to leave our body. This is why there is an injunction that the newly dead cannot be left alone. It is wise. As I lay next to my dead father, I experienced a moment of profound peace. I was relieved to think that my father had been released from the hell caused by his diseased brain. His expansive spirit still hovered in the room, shedding a primordial light. I clung to the image where I felt most alive with my father – at the back of his motorbike with my arms around his waist, belting down the highway with the wind and the canvas of the sky as our only companions.

Some time later, Carol, who knew my father since she was five, joined me. We sat together in silence, drinking in this intense moment and occasionally sharing memories of my father's generosity, his enthusiasm, and his radiant smile.

I didn't know then that my father's spirit would remain inside of me so that when the Burial Society arrived to take his body away, I cried convulsively. I hated the thought of my father being put into in a large black plastic bag. 'Please don't put him in there,' I remember screaming. Friends and family who had gathered at my parent's house tried to calm me. The image of that small white van driving away from my mother's house with my father in the back will be forever etched in my mind.

Some years later, it is a deep comfort for me to learn of the age-old Jewish rituals of *taharah* – the washing and dressing of the body of the deceased. I learn how my father's body would have been cleansed with warm water into which an egg is mixed as a symbol of life. How during this purification, all dirt would have been removed from behind his fingernails with a special silver instrument. How his hair would have been arranged with a beautiful silver comb. How, after his purified body was dried, he would have been dressed in a *kittel,* a loosely cut beautiful white shroud symbolic of humility. How he would have been wrapped in a *talit*, a prayer shawl from which one of the fringes is removed. How the prayers that accompanied the preparation of his body for burial all express faith in his ultimate resurrection.

Vicki's voice cuts into my thoughts, bringing me back into the room. 'Death,' she says, 'is something that we are all going to face. No one knows when it's their time. You have just been made to think about it earlier than most. There is something called a "good death".'

In the next hour, I struggle to articulate my beliefs on death. They are dark and muffled. I have a lifetime of vocabulary to describe hope and happiness. Few words for life's ending. My mind circles back to my family having to relearn their lives without me. Vicki gently cajoles me to give shape to my thoughts: 'I believe that my body will disintegrate but that my spirit will live on. It will hover above the earth keeping a watchful eye on the people that I love, especially Jonny and my children,' I begin.

'My spirit will enter the realm of the living on special occasions, just like my father comes into my world at important moments. He appeared in a dream just before my son's Bar Mitzvah. He would have so loved to see his beloved grandson, the light of his life, cross the threshold into manhood.'

Vicki reflects on the comfort that this dream brings. She encourages me to paint a picture of the world without me. 'My children will look just the same on the outside ...' I begin. 'Their grief will not lead them to turn to drugs or alcohol or other self-destructive behaviour. They will walk tall each day. But they will feel my absence acutely, especially as they get older and can articulate the gaps that I have left.'

After a long pause, I continue: 'They too might sit in a chair and struggle to give form to the silences and perforations in their soul. They will talk about the faint and not so faint scars that I have imprinted. They will find their own detours through life.'

The session ends, and I am lighter. Vicky has gently shown me the importance of preparing for death just like one prepares for life. I promise her that I will write letters to my friends to share my fears. A chink has opened in mortality's armour.

Is it a coincidence that I hear a song of Leonard Cohen's as I drive home? How the dice are loaded, the ship is sinking, how lovers cheat and the end is coming. Despite the pessimism of these words, I know from listening to this singing prophet throughout my life, that he offers redemption even while reminding us to steer our hearts towards our own mortality. He reminds us that it is only through the cracks that the light gets in. I am starting to experience the meaning of these observations in my soul.

Chemo Thirteen – Courage

4 NOVEMBER 2014

This is a significant week because, after this session, I can count the number of chemos left on one hand – *5-4-3-2-1*. Their dense presence still defines my life, but a future tense looks possible again. It is symbolic that Tali, herself a two-time cancer survivor and mother-to-a-daughter who had cancer at 17, is by my side. Both Tali and her daughter are living full and rich lives again. I am working with Tali on the exhibit at the Jo'burg Holocaust and Genocide Centre and although the material is grim, the project is engrossing. We have an animated conversation while the toxins enter my veins. My email update on my return home reflects a new optimism:

> *Five to go.*
> *Music to my ears.*
>
> *I am huffing and puffing on this last stretch – there are still some hilly bits.*
> *BUT the end is truly in sight.*
>
> *In real time, I can now count my chemo sessions on one hand.*
> *In chemo time, I now count:*
>
> *6 more weeks*
> *5 more blood tests*
> *10 more hours in the waiting room*
> *5 more needle drips*
> *900 more minutes in the chemo chair*
> *54 000 drips of medicine through my veins*
> *300 more minutes with Arctic ice packs on hands and feet*
> *15 more trips to the ladies with a drip stand*
> *25 more bowls of chicken soup*
> *250 more hours living with a chemo fog in my head*
> *5 more marbles in the jar*

63 more days of turbans (756 more hours)
An allowance of 15 more hours of tetchiness
1 more email to inform you of no more of any of the above ...

Except for:

Infinite hours of kindness from you all.
Infinite hours of gratitude in return.

You remain the wind in my back that propels me towards the finish line.

By chance, just as I press send, I receive an email from Carol in London in which she describes an anecdote about the persistent problem of the autumn leaves on the street that she lives on. Her partner spends ages trying to clear them with little success. One day, a neighbour says, 'Don't be discouraged. The way I think about it is when I have filled a bag of leaves and gotten rid of it, that particular bag is NEVER coming back!' 'La, count the chemo's that you have completed and that are NEVER COMING BACK. Looking backwards may have something more to offer than looking forwards,' she says. So simple. So profound. I feel compelled to rewrite my list:

Thirteen gone.
Music to my ears.

In real time, I can now count the chemo sessions I have had on both hands. In chemo time, I now count:

13 weeks gone
13 blood tests gone
26 hours in the waiting room gone
13 needle drips done
2 340 minutes in the chemo chair done
1 404 000 drips of medicine through my veins done

780 minutes with ice packs on hands and feet done
91 trips to the ladies with a drip stand done
91 bowls of chicken soup consumed
1 500 hours living with a chemo fog in my head done
13 marbles in the jar taken out
70 days of turbans worn
39 hours of tetchiness expressed
8 emails already written

That night I have a powerful dream. I am at an awards ceremony in a primary school hall. In reality, I hate these ceremonies. They make me anxious for the children who don't get awards, and equally anxious for those who get too many.

In my dream, I am one of the kids, anxiously sitting there, listening to the names of the people being called up. The time comes for the big award of the evening – the Gandhi prize for the display of inspirational behaviour. Suddenly, it strikes me that I may be eligible for the trophy and I list why I might stand a chance. Then everything slows down as I hear my name being called. The faces around me urge me onto the stage. The clapping seems sparse as I walk up, but I don't mind. I am bursting with pride, overflowing with a sense of achievement. I have done it. I have inspired others. What more could I possibly ask for?

I thank my unconscious for urging me on, telling me I can do this last stretch and that there will be rewards at the end of it all. And then I wake up to this mail from Phil that makes the planets feel aligned: *Last night I had a dream that you and I were on mountain bikes at the top of a mountian. You turned to me and said, 'I am taking off my helmet and I am going to cruise down and feel the wind in my hair.' You were smiling with such light and happiness in your eyes. You are an inspiration to us all – and you are almost there!*

The redemptive power of my relationships is clear.

Chemo Fourteen – Vulnerability

12 NOVEMBER 2014

During the night before my fifth-last session, a deep soaking rain settles in. Water buckets down hour upon hour. Our bed is a raft out at sea and the pounding sheets of water wake me repeatedly. In my restless state, I long for the stormy currents to wash me back into the chemo room so I can tick off another session.

Little do I know that the sodden weather signals the onset of yet another tempest. My inner winds start to howl when Dr G says to me with a degree of alarm that, 'Your white cell count is very low. You can continue with chemo but you will need a dose of Neupogen.' I collapse as the very long needle enters my fleshy stomach. Tears start and don't stop. My soul's complexion resembles the weather outside – damp and soggy.

'What is happening, La?' Jonny asks with deep compassion in his eyes. He witnessed my enthusiasm to come today and is taken aback at the sudden change of clime. 'I don't know,' I mutter. All I know is I am back in perilous waters. I try to assemble reasons for my rapid descent:

1. *I fear that my low white cell count is the chemo version of the telegraph punch, the one that knocks me over and leaves me whimpering in the ring.*
2. *I fear that the toxins are invading the good cells, secreting layer upon layer of 'unwellness'.*
3. *I fear that I have fallen prey to hubris by eliminating my break weeks so that I can finish chemo by 16 December.*
4. *I fear that I should submit to the process rather than the other way around.*
5. *I fear that I won't be able to attend Josh's 18th birthday party next week.*

While these thoughts wash through my mind, I see a chemo friend who has finished her treatment some time ago. She was my role model because she looked so beautiful each week when she came for her treatment. Her makeup was always immaculate, and her blue eyes twinkled. She wore large hoop earrings that swung from side to side as she walked around with her drip stand. She radiated wellness despite her bald head.

Today she is grey, bleached of all the sparkle that has been her signature. She tells me: 'My chemo has not worked. The tumour is back. It is the same size as before.' She stammers, 'I have to have another six months of treatment with an even more drastic cocktail. I haven't been able to eat anything since I started this new treatment, and I can no longer take care of my nine-year-old son.' She looks me straight in the eye and says: 'I can't face it all over again. I want to die.'

Her metamorphosis is shocking. There is little I can say in comfort. She is the mirror of my worst fears, the walking incarnation of what starts me off crying this morning in the first place – the sense that cancer is able to conquer all the will in the world.

I cry some more – for this young woman, for myself, and for everyone else who lives with this dreaded disease. Today, the question of 'Why me?' becomes 'Why won't it be me?' I am teetering. Michi, who joins me at my session today, tries valiantly to cheer me up. She is a magnificent presence by my side, but even her wit and charm don't overcome my bleakness.

In an email to Jess after my return home, I ask, 'Why the collapse now?' Her response is helpful: *Perhaps this is how the psyche works. It can only afford to express its fears when there is some space of liberation – of relatively good news – for it to do so. When all is black and dark, we have to shut it down. Every moment you have the courage to express all your deepest terrors is another moment of building up your emotional white cells.* She ends the email with one of her favourite letters by Rainer Maria Rilke to a young poet:

> *I beg you, to have patience with everything that remains unresolved in your heart and to try to love the questions themselves as if they were locked rooms and books written in a*

> *foreign language. Don't search for the answers ... Perhaps then, someday far in the future, you will gradually, without even noticing it, live your way into the answer, some distant day.*

Despite welcoming these thoughts, my thunderous internal storm won't abate. I am shocked by my state of dissolution at an event that Jonny and I attend. It is a conversation between a renowned artist and a renowned psychoanalyst about the intersections of their work. When the artist greets me in the lobby before the lecture, I start to cry. His daughter has been through chemo some years before. Something in the way he says, 'How are you?' and the kindness in his eyes sets me off. My eyes become sieves leaking water. This same tempest of emotions is repeated each time I say 'hello' to the many people that I know. I have no skin. In my shrunken state, I rush to find a seat in the distant corner of the auditorium.

The 'pre-chemo' me would never have sat in that place. She would have entered the room with gusto. She would have greeted everyone warmly. She would have connected easily with those she hadn't seen for a while. She would have chatted endlessly. The 'chemo me' is so different. Skulking in the corner, I long to go home and deal with my inner lashings. The agony of my situation is unbearable.

I drift in and out of hearing the conversation that is taking place on the stage. I am distracted by my sense of how suddenly and vastly my world has changed. Stripped of my usual mask of confidence, I am now open to the immediacy of my own pain and distress. It's as if I have been turned inside out with my vulnerability moving from my internal organs to my skin. I wish to ask the analyst and artist who sit before me if there is a way to map these internal shifts of our emotional geography on paper. 'Can you draw the skin dissolving? Can you draw my invulnerability as the seashore, and my vulnerability as a vessel out at sea?'

I ask Jonny to take me home before the end of the lecture so that I don't have to encounter anyone on the way out. This business of being so far out in stormy waters is proving too painful without an anchor on board. Back in the solitude of my own room, my mind searches for a way to understand what is happening to me. I wonder if I have reached that place of integration of opposing psychic forces, what in Vedic philosophy they call a 'unified field'. Could I be at that stage of integrating my cancer polarities?

I am neither vulnerable nor strong. I am both.
I am neither sick nor well. I am both.
I am neither invincible nor fallible. I am both.
I am neither happy nor unhappy. I am both.

If I can hold onto this cohesion, cancer will not be just an expression of malicious agencies; it will become a saviour of sorts. I can reach a state of transcendent, integrated and healing emotions. My subterranean gale starts to subside. Foul becomes fair.

Chemo Fifteen – Excitement

19 NOVEMBER 2014

My fourth last chemo session is on the morning that Josh turns 18. The day that I gave birth to my son feels so close, as if I can reach out and touch it. When my waters broke, I was lying in bed in our flat in Yeoville editing the final pages of a book I wrote on the history of Soweto. It was three weeks before my due date, and I panicked. Luckily, the gynaecologist told me my baby was not in distress. 'He is just impatient and ready to come into the world a little earlier than anticipated.' Impatience defines Josh's persona to this day.

Eighteen years later, I am in another kind of doctor's room waiting for another set of results. As if in honour of Josh's birthday, my white blood cell count has risen dramatically. My spirits soar.

Today, my oldest friend of 43 years is accompanying me, and Carol and I have an extraordinary session together. We discover we have both been repeatedly dreaming about ginger cats. In my dream, the cat keeps jumping on my bed, interrupting my sleep. In Carol's dream, the cat has run away and she is frantically trying to find her. Carol googles the symbolic meaning of these feline creatures, and distracts me from my chemo torture. She tells me that a cat holds many symbolic positions in the dream world. For some, they are omens of bad luck and are warnings of betrayal. For others, these slinky creatures denote sexual prowess, spirituality, instinct, femininity and power. 'When a cat comes into your dream, it is important to listen to what it's saying. It can be letting you know that you have the power and magic to create anything you want in your life right now,' Carol reads.

We continue exploring the layers of meaning in our respective dreams. At the end of the session, Carol says, 'I have not been able to understand your journey until today. I am grateful to have come so that I can understand how brutal it is. I am struck by how this is indeed a lone marathon, and how you are getting through it.'

I arrive home to find an especially good packet from the coffee girls. It has a kaleidoscope, frog pens and a 'pig popper' that sends balls flying out of its mouth. I tell my friends:

You have overturned a week of tears
And helped me to conquer my growing fears.
I am so happy that there are now just three more.
For me and for my famed esprit de corps *(that's you all)*
It means that the rhyming couplets will soon be at an end.
And I can become a plain old friend.

For the next two days, I am preoccupied with staying strong for Josh's 18th birthday celebration in two days time. This is usually when my chemo symptoms are at their most severe. 'No mists, no leaden feelings, no nausea', I plead with no one in particular. I walk for extra long in the hope that this will keep my symptoms at bay.

I am so relieved when Friday night comes and I feel vaguely normal. I take special care in applying my makeup to hide the fact that I no longer have eyebrows or eyelashes. Those went a while back, but it is tonight that I really miss them.

This special night is threaded with a particular emotional charge, but with no mention of cancer. It is a moment of reprieve and a celebration of Josh's life.

Chemo Sixteen – Kindness

1 DECEMBER 2015

Last week a friend emailed me on World Kindness Day. 'I want you to know that I am thinking of you today,' he wrote. 'Nations across the world are encouraged to make a declaration of kindness. I am declaring my admiration for you and the hundreds of other women with cancer.'

It is serendipitous to have received this message on the same day that we return to Josh's school for his valedictory service, the night after chemo 16. It is the first time that Jonny and I come face to face with the parents and kids who launched the vicious attacks on our son.

Despite my determination to be brave, I can't bear to face the assembled parents. My mother, Jonny, Katya and Tali, Josh's girlfriend, seat ourselves in the back row of the hall just seconds before the ceremony starts. My turban signals my vulnerability.

I cannot help but notice how many parents don't clap when my son goes onto the stage to receive several academic prizes and some of the 'character' awards too. The lump in my throat grows. Afterwards, a friend tells me that the woman sitting next to her – whose daughter wins the tolerance award – went ballistic when Josh's name was called out for the award for 'outstanding achievement and bringing honour to the school'. She wants to galvanise parents to lay a complaint against this 'outrage'. 'Let her try,' I tell Yda with fierce lioness-like protection of my son.

I rant to Jonny all the way home about the lack of sympathy for our family's difficult situation that I experienced from some in the hall tonight.

When I recount this narrative to Vicki the following day, she urges me to a higher order approach. 'Don't let these folks in. Rather think about how your own learnings can help you deal with your difficult feelings from last night. Let's list them.' And so together we write a list:

1. *Be kind to others and myself.*
2. *If I am not kind, the consequences can be serious.*
3. *Avoid situations that make me feel vulnerable.*
4. *Avoid stress.*
5. *Be more available to others and myself.*

Then we list all the things that I need to tell myself regularly:

1. *I am my own mother.*
2. *I am my own good parent to my child within.*
3. *I respect my mothering.*
4. *I can look after and trust myself.*
5. *I don't need to be sick to be loved.*
6. *I give myself permission to have more leisure time.*
7. *Do less.*
8. *Be more.*

This list clearly demonstrates how my priorities have changed over these last months. Atul Gawande's book *Being Mortal* provides concrete evidence of my own experience. A research study shows how it is often traumatic events like illness that most influence our attitudes to life.

A team of psychologists tracked the emotional experiences of 200 people over decades from multiple backgrounds, ranging in age from 18 to 95. The starting assumption was that people grow unhappier as they age, but the research revealed exactly the opposite. Rather than growing unhappier, people reported more positive emotions as they aged. Over time, they became less prone to anxiety, depression and anger. They found living to be a more emotionally satisfying and stable experience, even if old age narrowed the lives they led.

The lead psychologist on the experiment concluded that the change in needs and desires has nothing to do with age *per se*. It has to do with perspective – your personal sense of how finite your time in this world is. The findings sum up my life today – when your future becomes uncertain, your focus shifts to the here and now, to everyday pleasures, and the people closest to you.

Cancer has allowed me to reorder my life in a way that I could not have anticipated.

Chemo Seventeen – Triumph

8 DECEMBER 2014

Load shedding. This term entered my vocabulary in 2008, when South Africa faced an electricity crisis. The government explained to its citizens that there would be periods of 'load shedding' at a series of specified and unspecified times. And so the lights went out in our homes, sometimes for hours on end. A general panic set in after the first series of these bouts of darkness. For some reason, it is living without lights that symbolises the decline of our democracy.

Now, five years later, on the afternoon of my second last chemo, South Africa finds itself back in the dark. I arrive at my session at the usual time to discover an unusually large number of people in the queue for blood tests. The computer systems are down. Our records cannot be accessed. The labs that process the test results are not operational. People are not able to start chemo.

Unlike in the real world, where broken traffic lights create chaos and confusion, where people's tempers flare as shops close down, where households rush around to find candles, us patients do not complain. We have all put the whole day aside and the calmness and camaraderie among us is striking – particularly for me, an impatient, type A personality, who has struggled her whole life to wait for anything.

It is deeply gratifying to feel no inclination to be somewhere else or to shout at the receptionist. How ironic, I think, that it is 'chemo time' that has taught me to quiet the fires in my soul.

Hours later, it is my turn for my penultimate appointment with the oncologist. 'The tumour is now completely detached from your chest wall,' she says as her hands prod my chest. 'This is the best possible news. It will make the excision much easier.' I dance home that day and write a group email with a new sense of lightness:

On 8 Dec 2014, 13:15 PM,
Lauren Segal <laurensegal3@gmail.com> wrote:

I have entered the stadium. I see the finish line. It is really just ahead now. In chemo time it is 7 days, 1 blood test and 1 drip away. It is such a sweet moment that this is the perfect time to write my last update. There are not many words left. Just a sense of sheer joy and a wish to celebrate with those of you who have cheered for me from the sidelines for the last six months.

Someone asked me the other day, 'What do you want to keep from this unwanted experience?' It took a moment but the answer soon became clear. I want to keep the image I have of you all waiting for me at the end of the race with your arms open wide. In my mind's eye, these arms have held my vulnerability, worries and fears and have shown me the very best of what people are capable of. They are responsible for a precious new alchemy of give and take as I have plodded and sweated up and down some of the darker inclines. 'Thank you' is not an adequate acknowledgement of this gift but will have to do for now.

On the subject of darkness … I thought that I would be the one switching off the lights in the chemo room next week. But it appears that Eskom will beat me to it. Today the whole chemo session was in the dark and they warned that it may be the same again for my last session next week. The nurses had to hold up torches for each other when they were inserting the drips and finding the right medicine bags.

There was a sense of frenzy when we discovered I had someone else's medicine, but all of us on the lazy boy chairs were laughing and chatting more than usual today. It was nice. So between the marathon and load shedding, I think I have been given the perfect metaphorical ending for this part of the journey.

My operation is on 8 Jan. A new chapter of the race begins in 2015. I am grateful that I will be under anaesthetic for most of that one. I hope you all have a great, well-deserved break. I wish you peace and health for 2015.

My friends assure me they are waiting for me with their arms outstretched and with glass bottles charged with solar lights – the new essential accessory in our sometimes-dark country. As always, their encouragement ignites optimism in me. Then, Anne gives me this poem, 'If everything' by Margaita Aliger, and I include it in my journal as it so perfectly captures the essence of my gratitude.

A Green Turtle Day

My last hurdle for this week is an MRI and CT scan. The oncologist wants an accurate measure of how the tumour has responded to the chemo. As the bed moves in and out of the big spinning drum, I am issued instructions through an overhead speaker in the room. 'Stay still. Breath in deeply. Hold your breathe. Release *now*!' When the loudspeaker tells me, 'You will now feel a deep pressing sensation on your bladder, cold up your veins and hot flashes through your midriff,' I think of what my body has been subjected to over these last months. And I confess: I feel very sorry for myself. The tears roll down my cheeks. All of the humiliating medical experiences flash before me.

Jonny steps into the room just before I spiral downwards. The love and care on his face has got me through so much. Unfortunately, he cannot stay for my MRI procedure and I am left in the hands of yet another one of those nurses who remind me of Nurse Ratchet in *One Flew over the Cuckoo's Nest*. She straps me face down on the too narrow bed and instructs: 'If you move a muscle, you will simply have to return tomorrow.'

Lying in this state of induced paralysis with a loud and ominous hooter noise going off every minute or so, I start an involuntary chant. After all, the nurse did not prevent me from moving my lips. I chant my daughter's name over and over in honour of all that she survived as a baby. This reminder increases my own strength.

When I hear the nurse enter the room and say, 'It's over,' I want to scream at her, 'You punitive cow,' but instead I just glare.

As I am dressing in a tiny booth, the radiologist calls my name. It is impossible to tell from the expression on her face if she has good or bad news. I tremble inside. She calmly tells me, 'Nothing lit up on the scan'. I ask, 'What does this mean?'

'It means that your tumour has disappeared. We cannot see it on the MRI. The CT scan shows no cancer anywhere in your body.' In doctor speak I have achieved a PCR – a 'pathologic complete response'. The chemo has effectively killed the cancer cells prior to surgery. These words sing in my mind. I start to cry.

The doctor asks, 'Can I give you a hug?' I nod and reassure her, 'These are tears are sheer joy'. I immediately text Jonny the astonishing news. Then I text my kids and my mom. But it is only when I go home and hear myself speaking the words 'The tumour has gone. I am cancer free,' to Susie that the true import of these results hits home. I find myself sobbing into the phone. My dear friend is equally tearful. She has seen me through so much, and the victory is hers too. The same pattern continues throughout the afternoon. A phone call. My tears. The tears of others.

That evening, my husband, children, mother and I go out to celebrate. Prosecco has never tasted so sweet. Nor has the chinking of the glasses sounded so rich. Love entwines us. I look from one to the other and think how lucky we are to be in a position to celebrate. Many others who have sat next to me in the chemo room are not given this opportunity.

My phone pings and I read aloud this message from Janine in Mozambique that sums up this rapturous moment: *My beloved friend. I have no words. I am going to doll up, Tofu style, and go for a celebratory dinner with Clive to a wonderful restaurant called Green Turtle – they live forever and it feels so right!! Love you very much. xx*

Today is my 'green turtle' day. Living forever does sound just right.

Chemo Eighteen – Elation

15 DECEMBER 2014

The morning before my last chemo is a whirlwind. Both Josh and Katya are leaving for a debating tournament in Cape Town. Last-minute items have to be bought. Ties found. Suitcases packed. Quiet descends after the hurly burly of their departure. Jonny and I head to the farm to spend the day-before-the-last-chemo session at our favourite place on earth.

Jo'burg recedes and the spaces open up around us. We drink in the peace of our surroundings. As I plonk down on our balcony, I am dazzled by the brilliant greens of the rain-drenched trees, and I observe the spider webs dancing in the dappled light of the canopy created by the branches of a nearby tree.

On the day-of-my-last-chemo, the mountain in front of our house beckons. I have to be at chemo by noon so that gives me an hour to get to the top and back. The angle of the sun casts an elongated shadow of my body on the sandy road as I start the climb. 'There is soon to be a whole new me,' I tell this dark form as it follows me up and down the mountain. I take a selfie at the top with the world stretching out behind me.

A delicious breakfast awaits me on my return. Ruby has fashioned the chopped tomatoes and red pepper relish into a smile on my plate. As always, I am fortified by these gestures. The de Lanerolle family hug us tightly before our departure which today has a momentous feel.

The hour-and-a-half drive back into town is chaotic. Because it is the last working week of the year, the roads are choc-a-bloc. Our car weaves past heavy-loaded trucks, and the out of order traffic lights make it difficult to know whether to stop or go. 'This journey is here to remind us of our year – full of the unforeseen obstacles we have navigated,' I say to Jonny.

The chemo room is equally chaotic. Because the next day is a public holiday, there is double the number of people than usual. The mayhem in the waiting room passes me by. Nothing can rile me. This is my last of 18 chemo sessions, after all. It takes three hours before I am called into the treatment room.

Sadly, Nurse Julian, who has guided me through each of the last 17 sessions, has already gone on holiday. An equally kind nurse puts up the drip. For the first time, and only because it's the last time, I let myself feel the needle going in. I welcome the sensation. Not in my wildest dreams could I have imagined this moment. Jonny is also different today. Because the treatment room is so busy, he is edgy and changes my bags of medicine when the nurses don't arrive. This simple gesture is his way of alerting us that we are nearly back in control of our lives.

As my hands and feet slide into the ice gloves for the last time, I wince in pain. But we both watch the Taxol drip into my body with utter relish. When it is down to the last drops, I can't resist a countdown – ten, nine, eight, seven, six, five, four, three, two, one, ZERO. 'It's over,' I cry out.

Denise, my new chemo friend, and others around me, understand the significance of this moment. When the nurse takes out the drip, I fling my arms around my husband. He hugs me tight: 'Your ordeal is over.' We catch the moment in a photograph, but the smile on my face is not an adequate representation of what I feel inside. I am soaring.

My heart is still throbbing against my chest wall as I walk out of the oncology centre. It is such a sweet contrast to the first time. The unintelligibility of this inner war that I have being fighting, the immersive experience of chemo, the inscrutability of the pain it induces, has ended. My confinement is over. I will no longer be:

1. *Sealed off from the world outside.*
2. *Stripped of my identity.*
3. *A patient.*
4. *Restricted in movement.*
5. *Constricted in mind.*
6. *Counting weeks.*

Although in reality, the parking lot looks exactly the same as it always did, today I see a full-piece orchestra playing amidst the doctor's cars. Melodic tunes serenade us to our car. Strings of coloured bunting blow on the street poles. Roses sprout from the cracks in the hot tar. A perfect finale.

The 18th gift packet that awaits me is the most beautiful yet. The actual packet is a magnificent Indian spiral pattern print on a silky fabric. It has within it an ultra long thick beaded necklace which I love wearing to this day. Later that night, I send this mail to everyone who has accompanied me on my journey:

On 15 Dec 2014, 11:26 PM,
Lauren Segal <laurensegal3@gmail.com> wrote:

I am screaming hallelujah from the rooftops!!

Number of sessions left: zero
Size of tumour: zero centimetres
Man in photo on my right: my hero
Happiness factor: off the Richter scale

And then I paste the email, the photo of the packet and my final poem from my postbox, 'When It's All Over' by Myra Schneider, into my journal.

This poem, dripping with relief and sensuality, captures precisely how I feel. It's no wonder. Some years later, I learn that the poet herself is a breast cancer survivor and has thus experienced first hand both the darkness and the light of what this diagnosis brings.

She too has tasted the sweet sensations of release in the republic of a cancer patient's body when it's all over.

After Effects

16 DECEMBER 2014

The next day, Jonny and I fly to Cape Town where we will have a summer holiday with friends and family. The mountains look more pliable from the air today. Their ridges and bulk are more forgiving. While speeding through the clouds, I reflect on how so many of my initial fears of chemo never materialised:

1. *I did not get fat and bloated from the steroids.*
2. *I did not look disgusting without my hair.*
3. *My nails did not turn black or fall off.*
4. *My hands did not bloat.*
5. *My veins did not collapse.*
6. *I did not stop exercising.*
7. *I did not look too awful without eyebrows and lashes.*
8. *I did not feel like a shrivelled shadow of my former self.*

Many good and unexpected things happened, which I record in my journal:

1. *My skin became as soft as a baby's cheek.*
2. *I have learnt to experiment with my image.*
3. *I lost weight.*
4. *I learnt how to apply makeup.*
5. *I came to enjoy less hair.*
6. *I maintained my fitness.*

My list making is interrupted by our touch down in Cape Town. It is a champagne-perfect day. Each vista is sprinkled with a little bit more magic than usual. The steel blue sky has gossamer-thin wisps of white clouds. Table Mountain is bold against the horizon.

I cannot think or talk to Jonny about anything other than the chemo having ended and my tumour having disappeared.

We spend a glorious first day in the Cape Winelands. We have a delicious celebratory meal. We are happy to find ourselves in this new place, both physically and metaphorically. We are so blessed.

I should have known, however, that the transition would not be that easy. The next day I wake up in chemo hell. The mountains that looked so majestic just 12 hours before now seem to have taken occupation in my head. I am pinned down on the bed. I force myself up and try to act normal. Converse. Eat lunch. Laugh. While seemingly engaged in these ordinary daily rituals, I am floating in a world far away. Eventually, the heaviness in my body overwhelms me, and I am forced to return to our room. As I reach the bed, I succumb to my internal delirium.

My symptoms are far more severe than ever before. Streams of volcanic lava course through my veins. Trickles of sweat roll down by forehead and erupt in small bursts on my bald head. A crimson and blue lattice appears in my mind's eye. The patterns are fixed at first, and then they began to swirl around. Time becomes slippery, and I lose hold of the hours going by. A whole afternoon passes without my noticing that a measureless force has taken hold of me. I am spinning around an axis of reality. The cumulative effect is deeply enervating. My body is in extreme duress.

Jonny wanders in and out of my sight. He assures me, 'These symptoms are the accumulated effect of the chemo, but they too shall pass.' I cannot harness comfort from his presence or his promise. Desolation overwhelms me. I hover between reality and a dream-like state, my own 'bardo', the Tibetan Buddhist name for the state of consciousness between death and rebirth. In this lonely and forlorn place, I am still amazed that the fight against the mutation of a single strand of DNA can unleash such a storm.

As has been my salvation for the past six months, I eventually force myself to go for a walk. It is the very last thing I want to do. The sight of the sun twinkling along the rows of grape vines just beyond my window helps to drag myself outside. I plod through the perfectly formed rows of vines, noticing how the level of order and harmony is so at odds with my inner world.

Suddenly, as if I possess an internal windscreen wiper, the fog in my brain lifts slightly. My body loses its immense heaviness. My feet start to walk faster. There is no intimation that this will happen. It just does.

When I return to our room, Jonny immediately notices my metamorphosis: 'I am so relieved to have you back,' he says. As if to prove the point, we take a photo in front of the wall of sunflowers. Our happiness is half the truth as photos always are. The despair from the last chemo still lingers, although I feel the stirrings of a return of the elasticity of my body and mind.

We drive to Cape Town with hope in our hearts, but the first days remain hard. The long-term effects of the chemo prove obstinate and enduring. My ritual of climbing the mountain behind our apartment poses a real challenge. The incline is steep, and my legs are still heavy. As I huff and puff along the path, I have an image of years gone by when I leapt over the boulders with gusto. Over the next weeks, this climb is my barometer of my re-entry into the world. Each day, my legs lighten as the chemo poisons ebb out of my system. The incline becomes less daunting, and I am less tethered to the ground.

Each day, I am also a little less foggy as the interminable exhaustion starts to lift. One morning, I know the tiredness has truly evaporated when I open my eyes and they stay open. I choose to greet the day rather than retreat back into sleep, as I have over the past six months. This is an oblique hint of robustness returning.

The time in Cape Town is filled with meeting family and friends from all over the world. I have not seen many of them since chemo began. Imperceptible shifts have taken place across the ether. In particular, my vulnerability invites others to respond differently to me. Gentleness modulates each interaction. This is most marked with my brother. We don't discuss the ways in which our childhood entangled us in a web of anger and conflict. We simply move into the present, into a new relationship marked by tenderness, without the barriers that have kept us apart for as long as I can remember. I marvel at the ease with which we shed so many years of our fraught shared histories.

I am ever vigilant of the new microclimate of my emotions.

The Year of the Goat

1 JANUARY 2015

On New Year's Day 2015, my anxiety starts to bubble up again. Our summer holiday is drawing to a close, and there is now only a week left before my surgery. We head to the Cedarburg Mountains with my mother and Katya for a final few days of vacation. As our car twists and turns on the steep mountain road, I am relieved to be leaving behind the social whirl.

Our destination – a place called Kagga Kamma – is otherworldly. Clusters of rocks protrude from the earth to create the most wondrous sculptural arrangements. Big boulders balance precariously on their smaller relatives. Some of the rocks look as if they've been dripped onto the earth, a process that creates surreal ridges and patterns on their surface. Others are as smooth as marble, creating a stunning contrast to the crenulated surfaces around them. Strings of clouds arch across an inky blue canvas high above. This magical expanse looks as if it can hold the whole world. The effect is staggering.

The hotel is built in and amidst the boulders and our room is a cave. There is a spiritual energy that tugs me in. The stillness echoes a deep internal desire for silence. I am utterly compelled by this ancient and fugitive landscape.

We walk to rock paintings that are thousands of years old. It is a relief to view our mortality against this vast backdrop of human evolution. My time on earth is set against a much larger canvas. By chance, I am reading Rebecca Solnit's *The Faraway Nearby* in which she writes that we love places and that places love us back: 'They give us an expansive scale in which our troubles are set into context, in which the largeness of the world is a balm to loss, trouble and ugliness and distant places give us a refuge in territories where our own histories aren't so deeply entrenched and we can imagine other stories, other selves or just drink up the quiet and respite.'

This mystical place is a perfect respite from what lies ahead. I drink in the rocks and draw strength from their energy. This is a world where I can disappear. Sadly, this cloistered bliss must end. My health preoccupations trickle back the closer we get to back to Cape Town. The refuge of the boulders and the wide expanse are behind us. I can no longer banish the thoughts of the cuts and wounds that are soon to be inflicted on my body.

In particular, I start to fixate on how the plastic surgeon will fill the large cavity that is to be left on my chest wall. Dr J has explained to me how he will make a 'latissimus dorsi flap' which involves removing muscle from my back and bringing it round to fill the hole in my chest. He made it sound easy, like rearranging letters on a scrabble board. In my mind, I can't work out how he will accomplish this without cutting through important veins, arteries and nerves, and without scarring me terribly.

The possible complications of this three-and-a-half-hour procedure haunt me. The intraoperative pathologist needs to give the breast surgeon confirmation that there is a clear margin with no signs of malignant cells to avoid this happening. 'We need to hope that it is feasible to clear a large enough margin around the tumour without radical surgery to the chest wall,' Dr Benn has told me. 'Otherwise, I will have to call in a cardio thoracic surgeon.'

Tears flow readily now whenever people ask me how I am. The exuberant outward energy of Cape Town's sun no longer draws me in. Going back home means going into the operating theatre, ghastly drains, pain – becoming a patient again.

Before we leave, we spend a beautiful day with Paul and Simon – a true force of friendship – which distracts me. We eat, talk and laugh, as if the world is an ordinary place. Then I climb the mountain for the last time. I feel reinforced by its solidity, by the familiar edges of the rocky paths that I have walked and re-walked this last month, by the openness of the crystal blue heavens above. Getting to the top has become a synecdoche for my health and vitality and my ability to conquer the uphill battles of life. As I walk, my steps silently knit together the pain and joys of my cancer journey. I swim in the tidal pool for the last time, and feel bathed in the healing powers of the ocean.

The flight home is full of trepidation.

PART FOUR

My Second Cut

Please Use This Vein

8 JANUARY 2015

On the morning of my surgery, Jonny and I wake at around 6 am to the shrieks of the hadedas that drink water from our pool on hot summer days. I am often resentful of their intrusion but, on this morning, these prehistoric birds seem like a suitable alarm. A shaft of bright summer light filters into the room through a crack in the curtains, and I notice the flurry of dust particles that dance in its beam. The light is a good omen, and I have a deep sense of composure despite what the day holds for me. I observe my calm demeanour with some interest, as if it belongs to another person.

The hospital is a mere five-minute drive from home, and my arrival and the period spent waiting for the surgery are an immediate signal of how far I have travelled since my mastectomy. Whereas I was a bundle of nerves then, bordering on hysterical, I am fully sentient and calm this time around. In order to get through the dreadful wait, I do yoga in the small and awkward hospital room that is to be my home for the next few days. The hospital bed becomes my prop for all kinds of stretches as nurses wander in and out to take my blood pressure and dress me in one of those absurd surgical robes.

I focus on my still intact chest and back area that is about to be incised and gauged out. The yoga postures allow me to sense the connective tissues and muscles in the area between my shoulder blades. I am acutely aware of how, in a matter of hours, I will no longer be able to open these neural pathways for many months to come.

When the anaesthetist enters the room, I am in a downward hanging dog. He is momentarily taken aback but quickly regains his authoritative composure. 'When did you last do aerobic exercise?' he asks me. 'I climbed a mountain just two days ago,' I reply. He raises his eyebrows and says, 'Your heart will be just fine,' and then he promptly leaves the room.

Jonny responds to my puzzled look: 'There is a lot of evidence that shows that the stronger and healthier one is before an operation, the more confident one can be of a positive outcome. The anaesthetist's short consultation means that he isn't worried about you at all.' Given that I had finished 18 chemos just three weeks back, this interaction creates a small sense of victory.

When the nurse arrives to wheel me into the operating theatre, I place my trusty headphones over my ears, and play the chanting that got me through my 18 chemo sessions. The hypnotic and expansive voices of the monks have become a natural sedative. Again, this moment compares favourably to the one three years ago when I begged Jonny and Adam, 'Please make me unconscious,' on my way to my mastectomy.

The nurse pushing the gurney has a face full of compassion. She holds my hand as she guides me onto the cold steel operating table in the theatre. It is narrower than I had imagined. Clearly, an inert body doesn't require much space. Once in position, I notice a large cupboard directly ahead with boxes spilling out in a most disorderly fashion. The mess is a surprise. In my mind, an operating theatre is a pristine space. I start to rearrange the blue, red and green boxes into rows that neatly align. It's my attempt to grasp at the last vestiges of control just as I am about to lose it completely.

When the anaesthetist takes hold of my arm to put up the drip, I say, 'Please use this vein.' This four-word request astonishes me as much now as it did then. My radical transformation in relation to my needle phobia demonstrates what Marissa told me during our first call all those months ago – I will find a way to take charge. This Herculean accomplishment will be one of those handfuls of moments that come to define my life.

The far more courageous incarnation of myself that lies on the operating table at 12:10 pm on 8 January 2015 is a pleasure to behold. A year ago, I would have said it was an avatar speaking on my behalf. Yet I know that it is the person that I have become. With this newfound feeling running through my veins, the anaesthetist puts a mask over my mouth and nose and tells me to breathe deeply. There is a split second of awareness before darkness carries me away.

Four hours later, I faintly hear, 'Lauren, Lauren,' being called with some degree of urgency. The kind nurse's outline slowly comes back into focus. My first coherent thought is that I can feel no immediate pain. As my eyes grow accustomed to the light, Jonny and Susie emerge before me. Jonny takes my hand and says, 'The intraoperative pathology tests show no trace of malignant cells. They have managed to excise a wide margin around the original tumour.' Relief is etched on his face. In my groggy state, I only partially take in this good news.

Towards evening, the plastic surgeon, still clad in his blue scrubs, comes into my hospital room. Despite operating for many hours that day, he wears a broad grin and announces, 'Your operation went according to plan.' His impish countenance changes slightly as he continues: 'I was forced to change the prosthesis in your right breast to a smaller size in order to close the wound on your right chest wall.' I receive this information without flinching. Two differently sized breasts? Pah! Who cares? It's just another in the vast range of things that has happened to my body. All I feel is profound gratitude for my surgeon.

After he leaves the room, Jonny says with great tenderness, 'Don't give your differently sized implants another thought.' I trust fully that my newly re-arranged lopsided chest will not threaten our marriage.

There is yet more relief when I am told that I will not be in the high care ward that night as I had been after my mastectomy. I am so much calmer this time and feel less pain. I use very little of the morphine pack. This is not heroic. Even though I am harnessed to all kinds of apparatus and have a drain bag extruding from the site of my surgery, the discomfort is bearable. The rhythmic inhalation and exhalation of the blood pressure cuffs around my arms and calves – to prevent clotting – is strangely consoling. I play a game to arrange my breathing to correspond with their whirring inhales and exhales.

At 6 am the next morning, the night nurse who has the most angelic face I have ever seen, tells me, 'You have managed so well. You had a serious operation and the other patient like you has ended up in ICU.'

When she reminds me of the seriousness of my operation, I am also reminded of how well my mode of defence – to diminish an experience – serves me.

The next morning, I describe myself in texts to friends as 'demure'. The insane mania post my mastectomy is not a feature this time around. I don't want visits from friends. I crave solitude. This is also new.

Later that day, my daughter comes and gives me a makeover. She has a real flair for applying makeup and I am quite the challenge. She is not visibly perturbed by the drips and drains protruding from me, but nonetheless, my heart goes out to her. It cannot be easy to see your mother like this. I silently wrap my arms around her. She too is a brave warrior. Jonny and I take a selfie while the lipstick Katya has applied is still in place. Jonny is unusually playful and the photo is full of humour despite the setting on a hospital bed.

A specific incident throws me soon after. When the surgeon, who did my first surgery, pops in to see me, I pluck up the courage to ask him: 'How did you know that the angry lump on my chest wall was a malignant tumour when I first came to see you all those months ago?' He tells me that it was too far from the site where he had operated during my mastectomy to be ordinary scar tissue. My mind circles back to the radiologist assuring me that it was just that, to the irony of all my privilege, the irony of this happening to a doctor's wife, a category of patients usually treated with kid gloves.

'Don't go back there', something screams inside of me. It is hard not to imagine how different things would have been if I had discovered the tumour when it was much smaller.

Life makes no perfect offerings. There is a meant-to-be-ness in how this saga has unfolded. I tell myself, 'I may not have been ready for this ordeal two years ago even if the tumour was smaller. I needed to revel in life with a mind unfettered by cancer. I emphatically needed the time, even if it meant that a slow lobular beast was stealthily expanding itself along my chest wall.'

By Saturday morning, I am desperate to leave the hospital. It is a day earlier than planned, but I am free of the drips and there is no point in staying. Besides, it is our 23rd wedding anniversary, and the hospital is not an auspicious place to celebrate our Topaz year. The surgeon gives me the thumbs up to leave.

Once home, everything looks like new. The exuberant greens of the garden; the soft couches; the clutter of our lives; all loving expressions of my world without cancer. There is no more perfect place to celebrate two decades and three years of marriage. I descend onto a comfy chair and take joy in the birdsong and the sounds of urban life that mark the different hours of the day. Friends drop in with flowers, fresh bread, figs and custard pies. Kats and her friend make nectarine jam. I tuck in with relish, grateful for these simple pleasures.

That night, my dream feels significant. I am a child and my parents are moving house. (In reality, we moved home often; I lived in nine houses.) In this new house, there is no wall between my brother's room and mine. There are also no burglar bars or electric fencing. I panic at first. Us Jo'burgers are used to very high levels of security. I manage to drift off to sleep. I awake to an animal fair in the park across the street – dogs, lions, baby leopards and tigers are roaming freely in and out of our house. One particular puppy finds its way onto my bed. I know that this fat dog with its speckled belly is mine. I drift off to sleep again with this puppy nestled in the shape of my body.

On one level, the dream appears to be about my health. All the potential threats – the tigers and leopards – have been neutralised. Like the biblical tale of Daniel, I am saved from the lion's den – not by God but by my surgeons. On a deeper level, the dream is symbolic of my internal journey these last months. My defences – the walls and burglar bars – have been peeled away. The helpless puppy finding me suggests that I am now ready to take care of a vulnerable part of myself. The dream feels like a really good omen, as scales have fallen from my eyes.

Forty-Nine

14 JANUARY 2015

On the morning of my 49th birthday, Dr Benn arrives at my door with the final pathology report from my operation confirming the all clear. There are no more visible cancer cells in my body. I hug my surgeon with vast amounts of gratitude for what she has done for me. I will never be able to thank her adequately. What a birthday present. Susie and Annette take me out for champagne and a moist orange cake with a spun sugar topping. We toast life. That night, Nic and Indra cook a delicious Spanish dinner for my family. I am full in every sense of the word.

Back at home, I can't sleep. Is it the wine, the excitement of being home, or is it the strange tinges that appear down my right side that keep me awake? Not wanting to panic or to wake Jonny, I swallow a sleeping pill and find oblivion. A deep pain down my whole right side wakes me early. My chest is bloated and swollen. Tears roll down my cheeks.

Jonny takes one look at me when he wakes up and speeds me to the hospital. The sister on duty calls the surgeon. 'It's a seroma, a pocket of fluid in the wound that happens post-surgery. I have to do a needle aspiration,' he says. It's a ghastly procedure with Dr J inserting a long needle into my breast to remove the fluid. 'Enough!' I yell inside and out.

I arrive home and cancel the rest of my plans for the day. I long for an ordinary day that starts and ends the way I had planned. It has been nearly a year of waking up and never knowing exactly what to expect.

I have to repeat the needle aspiration several times before the seroma is properly drained. It is during these unexpected procedures that the laws of physics stop applying to me. Pain enters my body and does not relinquish its hold. It feels like I am sucked into a black hole where there is zero gravity to bolt me to the earth. My shoulder floats upwards and gets stuck somewhere near my ears. I can no longer use my smile as wallpaper to cover the cracks. In this astral wasteland, my navigation system keeps recalculating, never revealing the direction I should be travelling. There is no true north to be found. Time is again congealed.

Instead of forward movement, I circle back on myself. I am being white-anted, eaten from the inside out. The vultures are on stand-by, and I wonder if this feast on my own body will eventually cede to their relentless taunting presence. There is nothing more eviscerating than the sense of the betrayal of the self. How am I to stop the irregular mutant cells that have colonised my chest wall and caused this hell from winning this war? I am being derailed. I look like the vulture that I fear.

In this place of utter darkness, I force myself to focus on the flickers of light. My husband and my children are the fulcrums around which my body spins. They each emit rays of alternating shades of blue and green light that cast a soothing balm over my fragile existence. My mother, my family and friends do the same, ensuring that the scaffolding that is falling apart yet again is miraculously resurrected.

I end up appreciating that I am so blessed, not in the biblical sense, but in the sense of being recognised and acknowledged by my community. After this journey, I realise that I can no longer say that there is anything that I cannot be or cannot do. My 49th birthday present is the mental armoury to know that I can contend with just about anything. Fear will no longer blindside me. I know now that a panoply of possibilities lies within any misfortune. I fight against the pain down my right side with all my might.

The Path to Healing

Three weeks after the surgery and the infection, I still cannot shower, walk or exercise. I am exhausted by my patient status. 'The thing to hold onto,' Vicki says to me, 'is that the cancer is a gift which has shown you a path to growth and made it non-optional to deal with hurts that you have clung onto since childhood.' Her words are a reminder that healing is not just about getting back to normal life. It is also about retaining the new sense of me.

Vicki advises me to drop the cancer identity completely. 'It's time to tell people you are now cancer-free. The tumour has gone.' It is true that I am not simply in remission. I do not have cancer any more than the next person has cancer. 'The fire is out. Radiation is now about mopping up the ashes,' she says.

My meditation teacher is right. As I become more mobile again and reclaim the semblance of a normal routine, it is easier to feel less patient-like. I can now schedule regular meetings. The cogs of my brain are spinning freely again. One of my museum projects has seven months to opening, and it is exciting to have something to work towards.

Most importantly, I decide that the time has come to relinquish the variety of the adornments that have graced my head over the past eight months. My skull is now covered with a fine layer of soft baby hair that is straight and blonde. This is chemotherapy's final makeover.

It is easier than I imagined going around nearly bald. For a start, it is swelteringly hot and I enjoy the way the sporadic breeze tickles my head. It no longer punctures my heart when people I know walk straight past me. Those who do recognise me are positive and affirming: 'It's nice to see your face. You look young and fresh'. These are kind words for a nearly bald person with an unassailable air of vulnerability.

Then there is the thrill of being well enough to take my son to Cape Town to help him settle into his university residence. My chest and back are still heavily bandaged, but I am allowed to travel. On the flight down, I squeeze Josh's hand tightly as the plane takes off. He is leaving home.

As the metal bird heaves into the sky, the significance of the moment strikes me. Josh is leaving behind everything familiar and known and going into a space where there are no markers. He will be finding his path, creating his own trajectory. In a completely different way, he is embarking on a similar journey to mine. Luckily, his is about creating a life, rather than fighting to hold onto one. This contrast may explain the unbridled sense of joy I experience when we arrive at his residence. Bright young faces greet us at the door, and guide us through a labyrinth of administrative tasks. Young hands offer to carry the boxes of clothes and equipment to his new room.

The room is grotty and unkempt, a blank canvas waiting to have new hopes etched into its surfaces. Within a matter of hours, the coffee machine, record player and colourful espresso cups already create a personality. My son's ridiculously long legs hang off the bed but it is *his* bed in *his* new home. This is where he will live suspended between adolescence and adulthood.

Other youngsters continue to arrive with their families in tow along with myriad boxes large and small, carrying fans, fridges and microwaves. The air crackles with excitement. That afternoon, the parents watch as the newcomers are put through a series of bonding rituals. Anne, Lynn and I stand and watch as groups of ten boys, tied together by their ankles, race around a field. As the last group passes, we notice that one of the boys has a prosthetic leg making this group slower. It is clear that despite the machismo of the boys, no one in his group minds their disadvantage. These burly boys slow their pace to include their disabled mate. We all have tears in our eyes.

I leave Josh with an unanticipated sense of ease. Despite everything that has happened this past year, my identity as mother has not been unhinged. Josh is ready for his independence. His shooing me away when I arrive to help him the next day amply demonstrates this. I am stung, but also proud that Josh wants to create his own sphere where I am a visitor and not an inhabitant.

Too Scared to Look

Once back home, it is time to have my bandages removed. I avert my eyes from the multiple new scars that are revealed. The nurse assures me, however, that Dr J has done a really excellent job. While I am waiting for her to fetch the new dressing, I strike up a conversation with a woman in the adjoining booth. A curtain separates us and our respective cancer tales float across this cotton divide. The similarities are marked, but so are the differences. She is here voluntarily to 'touch up' on her reconstruction. I had no choice. When I say, 'I am too scared to look at my chest,' she bursts through the curtain, takes off her gown and exclaims, 'This is what you look like!'

She proceeds to give me a no-holes-barred demonstration of her various cuts and how they have healed. She shares exquisite detail of her hair regrowth post chemo. Her bold intervention forces me to reflect on my own squeamishness. Surely everything would be easier if I was this brave? In the end, her demonstration doesn't help me to look at my wounds. My willed state of blindness persists.

As the days tick by, there are more and more hours for me to forget about my surgery. I am not just suspended from my cancer reality, I am learning to divorce from it. A scheduled appointment with the radiation oncologist to plan for my radiation treatment rudely interrupts this respite.

The visit is badly timed. It comes directly after we attend an assembly at Josh's old school. He is the dux scholar of his year, and has returned from Cape Town to deliver a speech, as is the custom of his school. For Josh, this is not just an academic honour but also an opportunity to find closure on the 'Scarfgate affair'. In a calm and measured tone, Josh delivers a magnificent address. He carefully avoids controversy. He speaks from the heart about the lessons he has learnt during his school years, especially about facing difficulties. He implores his fellow pupils to 'bend the rules' and, most importantly, to 'be brave'. He gets a rousing reception. This is the start to his dealing with the immense trauma that he has experienced.

Jonny and I speed from the loud applause of the school hall to the quiet murmur of the hospital corridors. The radiation oncologist is paging through my rather thick file when we enter his room. He recounts to me the various chapters of my story as if I had not been the central character in it. I sit back and listen.

It turns out that there are bits that I don't know – or perhaps, that I had chosen not to know. I am surprised to learn, for example, that my tumour is classified a 'T4' – another of those seemingly anodyne medical terms that carries a sinister message. 'What does this mean?' I ask gingerly. 'In your case, it means that your tumour was localised but had not remained solely in the breast tissue. It penetrated your muscles and skin cells.' He emphasises 'A T4 tumour has to be radiated. In fact, a bigger area of your body has to be radiated because of the spread to the skin.' Once again, the worst possible news, the harshest treatment regime.

Prior to hearing these words, I had been planning to stage a mutiny against undergoing radiation altogether. I had declared myself out of the cancer woods and had planned to say to this doctor, 'If the cancer cells have been eradicated completely, why should I go through the nightmare of radiation?' As with everything else on this journey, my rebellious proclivities have no outlet. Dr C explains: 'Chemo kills the cancer cells that may have escaped from the breast tissue and entered into your bloodstream. Radiation kills any microscopic cancer cells in the breast that the surgeon may not have been able to see.'

As I walk out of the doctor's rooms into the harsh glare of the midday sun, I decide I am like one of those the 12 wooden pegs in a bowling alley that stand tall only to be knocked down by a powerful blow, swept away, and then pop up again ready for the next pounding. Despite my brave attempts to regain normalcy, radiation is here to knock me down again. Cancer patient. Respite. Cancer patient. Respite. Cancer patient. When will this endless cycle pass?

As is my reflex by now, I flee to the Meditation Centre for help. Vicki is clear with me: 'Think of the radiation as going to the gym every day. It's not necessarily enjoyable, but it helps you get fit.

This is the final stage of your marathon.'

A wise compass for my soul but, as always, easier to say than to put into practice.

PART FIVE
The Slow Burn

X Marks the Spot

27 FEBRUARY 2015

Preparation for radiation has its own peculiarities that I could not have imagined. The radiation oncologist has to figure out the exact position of the body on the 'table' so that the radiation beams are precisely directed to my chest area but avoid my lungs, heart and neck. As I lie on the narrow silver slab waiting to be scanned with my arms hoisted above my head and my neck turned at the oddest of angles, I struggle against the strong tide yanking me back into patient status. How is one meant to feel ordinary in such an untenable position?

I watch in dismay as four technicians with rulers and protractors in hand get my right arm positioned at the exact angle it needs to be, and my chest raised by small props so that it can rest at a precise distance off the bed. My chest area is then covered with a series of red ink dots. X marks the spot.

These crosses are made into permanent marks by needle pricks inserting a special dye which transform me from person to dartboard. My cancer tattoos are the furthest thing in the world from the sexy artwork that has come to adorn so many. X marks the spot.

My mind strays to the ghastly spectral mask that my father had fitted over his entire head each time he was radiated for his brain tumour. His only vision was through the punched-out holes in his visor-like helmet. Was I adequately sympathetic to the terror he must have felt at being pinned down in this way, I wonder. I realise in that moment how hard it is to truly empathise with another's pain.

In this contorted form, I experience a vast amount of self-empathy. 'How-much-more-does-my-body-have-to-endure,' I wonder.

෧

Sleep evades me on the night before radiation. It is no longer the terror of needles that prevents me from drifting away. My wakefulness is more inchoate, full of dread of yet another journey into the unknown.

I am extremely petulant when I arrive at the radiation centre. I am not at all in the mood for starting up a new cancer treatment – this time daily for six weeks. A part of me is trying valiantly to repeat the soothing wellness affirmations that I have worked out with Vicki, but a much larger part of me is screaming, 'Fuck you! Why am I here?'

I heap all of my rage onto the innocent technicians. I am irritated by their immense kindness. I don't want to be the recipient of their well-practiced empathy for the new patients. I hate the *sotto voce* tone of their voices. I don't want to hear that the upper quadrant of my body belongs to them for the duration of my treatment. I don't want to hear how aqueous cream will help my burns. I don't want to commit to a time of the day for the next six weeks that best suits me. I don't want to be assigned locker No. 3 for my dressing gown. I want to be anywhere but here.

Here is totally unlike the chemo centre. For a start, the reception area is thoughtfully designed and decorated. An expansive photo of the Nelson Mandela Bridge adorns the outer wall of the radiation chamber, undoubtedly chosen to remind us patients of the throb of downtown Jo'burg, the endless possibilities of this city of gold, the power of the greatest president ever to have lived. I reject the sense of hope implied in the image. I just want to run far away.

Unlike chemo, there is no long wait, no distractions of bald-headed patients and their significant others occupying every nook and cranny, no hustle and bustle of the staff or the calling out of the names of the next in line. This is a slick and well-oiled operation. X marks the spot.

So without a pause, I find myself in that badly designed blue gown, supine on that too-small slab under a vast and intimidating radiation machine. It is enormous, elephantine with three separate heads, a clear triumph of 21st-century engineering. Pristine and silent. The room is cavernous and no attempts have been made to pretty it up. There are no images of cities and bridges to keep the spirits afloat for those who lie beneath this contraption. Here, we are down to the nuts-and-bolts of cancer treatment.

The technicians use my newly acquired tattoos to align my body and prod me into position. The tattoos clearly do their job because it is not long before I am tangled up into the exact position as the week before. X marks the spot.

When the kindly nurse asks 'Are you comfortable?', I want to burst out laughing. 'Are you joking?' is what I want to reply. Instead I nod politely. 'It will go faster than you think,' she assures me. She is right. The 30 minutes of keeping dead still do go faster than I imagine, but not fast enough for my hand that is jabbed upwards not to experience intense pins and needles. And not fast enough for the tears not to trickle out of my eyes and down my cheeks without my being able to wipe them away. And not fast enough not to catch a glimpse of my husband's face which is contorted into the pain of the outsider, watching over the person he loves.

Once back home, I cancel a meeting I had blithely scheduled the night before. 'Such a trauma to the body must have an echo in the psyche,' says the wise friend and colleague I had planned to meet. How right Terry is.

Radiation is another kind of assault on my body, eerie and ghostly. There is nothing to feel. No sensation of needles in my veins, no ice packs on my hands and feet, no heat on my skin. Only utter silence and aloneness in the radiation chamber. Absence has become my challenge. The unfathomable, the un-seeable, the unknowable is now my mountain to climb.

The Four-Headed Monster

The second radiation session, late the next evening, is slightly easier. My interior landscape has adjusted somewhat, and I am less angry. Katya comes with Jonny and I wonder what it is like for her to be with her mother here. How may it affect her? I cannot possibly know. She appears sanguine, but does not want to engage over where she finds herself.

While calmer today, I am still startled by my experience. My rage during the first session had clearly dwarfed my senses. Today I hear how much noise emanates from the three-headed radiation beast. A wheezing and whining sound accompanies the overhead rotations. Then there is a whirr as the beams of radiation enter my upper quadrant. Lights come on and off. I could just as easily be watching a rock concert in a stadium.

In each subsequent session, I discover new aspects of the process. Over the course of the 1 080 hours that I lie under this machine, I learn the intricate rhythm of its movements across my body. Later, as I start to chat to the technicians, I get to know the function of the different parts; the flat rectangular board that rises on the left of my awkwardly positioned body takes the initial X-rays to check my position is correct; the twirling round glass face, that swoops over from left to right with its hypnotic moving teeth, shapes and curves the radiation beams that enter me; the final smooth white square that comes over like a rising moon sends rays into my lower chest quadrant.

One day, as I am waiting, I hear an animal-like groaning emanating from the treatment room. The strangled sound pierces my heart. I put on my headphones in an attempt to drown out the pain. After a few minutes, a stretcher with a writhing body is wheeled out of the radiation chamber. On it is a young girl of no more than 12. Her too-thin legs and arms are contorted in pain. Her mother looks on helplessly while a nurse is called to sedate her. 'What's wrong?' I ask the nurse. 'She has spinal cancer and struggles to stand so that she can be radiated,' he tells me. My heart breaks. I am to discover that many of the other patients who have radiation are at death's door. This is their last treatment possibility. It forces me to realise that I have a lot to be thankful for.

Despite knowing that I am one of the lucky ones, radiation is still torturous. Two weeks into my treatment, I take to bed with an extremely sore throat. This makes me weepy. Coping depends on my body staying strong. I call Dr C, who prescribes an ordinary pain killer.

Five days later, when I still cannot swallow, I call the radiation oncologist again and he says, 'It is possible that the field of radiation is catching the base of your throat. That could be the cause of your lack of improvement and intense discomfort.' Something about his casualness enrages me, particularly when he adds, 'You are probably being burned on the inside much like your skin is reddening on the outside.'

Why did he not mention this possibility when I first called him? Surely he knew that this was a possible side effect? What other parts of me are being scalded? I hate the idea of an invisible blowtorch slowly burning the walls of my gullet.

That night, Dr C comes to rearrange my position on the radiation slab. 'You need to turn your neck away more,' he tells me as he twists my head. In this newly knotted, highly uncomfortable position, I notice that the machine I am lying under is in fact a four-headed monster. If this last head has only become visible after 15 sessions of lying here, how much else is still to be revealed?

Two years later, my neck is still in severe pain from the stance I had to adopt that day. It is a daily reminder of my time spent under the four-headed monster.

I watch the film *Still Alice* about a woman of my age, battling the diagnosis of an early onset of Alzheimer's. 'I wish I had cancer', Alice, the character played by Julian Moore, says at some point in the movie. I do not know which of the diseases I would prefer. Alice's family suffers as they watch their mother deteriorate. It makes me wonder how my husband and children feel to watch me in the last throes of this treatment.

At the beginning of the radiation I am warned of the side effects of the process. The seven radiation plagues are:

1. *Nervousness*
2. *Burning*
3. *Itchiness*
4. *Skin tingling*
5. *Extreme fatigue*
6. *Sleeplessness*
7. *Lack of comfort*

As weeks go by, I suffer each of the seven plagues at different levels of intensity at different times. Fatigue is ever present, but the burning is the worst. First, the skin on my chest turns scarlet; then a darker shade of red; and then a complex purple. I don't know this from looking at myself. I know it from being told by the nurses who arrange me on the slab each day, and by Jonny who applies cream to my burnt skin each night.

Like the falconer that covers the eyes of the bird with leather patches to protect the bird from the world around it, I shield my own eyes by avoiding the mirror. My myopia protects me against the despair of my charred body. I do not berate myself for this avoidant behaviour. Jonny is my eyes.

Daily Dose of Gamma Rays

Regardless of what is happening, life stops at 3 pm for my dose of gamma rays. This daily interruption becomes more and more intrusive, but if I have learnt anything, it's that ongoing anger is as futile as chasing the wind. With gritted teeth, I push on.

Then, after a long uphill slog, the prospect of the final session arrives. 'How should I mark the end of the journey of these last 18 months?' I ask Jonny. I answer my own question: 'I must finish just like I started – surrounded by my family and friends.' I bash out an email to invite my girlfriends to come and drink champagne after Radiation Number 36.

Jonny accompanies me to my final session. He watches me don

the blue hospital gown for the last time. He helps me into position under the machine before he leaves the room. In these final 30 minutes, the twists and turns of the gargantuan machine appear strangely benign.

As the machine comes to its final rest, and the technicians come to help me off the slab, I fling my arms around them. I am walking on air as I pass through the big swinging steel doors for the last time. I watch the doors close silently as the next patient takes her place on the slab. My final act is to write my name on a flower which I attach to a tree alongside the flowers of others who have ended radiation. Tears spring to my eyes. At last, I am at the end of this monstrous journey.

On arrival home, I arrange my radiation card on a table next to my jar of 18 marbles. I have dotted loads of pink flowers in vases all over the house. Friends arrive and share in my jubilation. The air is threaded with joy. It is not just my celebration. We all desperately want to believe that this ordeal is truly over.

My outward elation continues, but my dreams tug me in a different direction. I have only dreamt of my father four times since his death eight years ago. Each of his nocturnal appearances has felt like a moment of great significance. On the night of my last radiation, my dream involves my father messaging me to say that he is waiting to take me for a walk. The dream scurries around in my head for most of the morning. I am terrified it is a portent of death that my father is there, beckoning me to be with him on the other side. The next night, I dream that I am diagnosed with incurable bowel cancer by a group of doctors who are peering into a toilet and then a cat dances on its hind legs in front of me, taunting me to kill it. I wake up seeing the malevolent gleam of the cat's eyes. Each dream suggests how difficult it is for me to put down my weapons of war, and let go of my terrors.

The threat of death is still so close by.

While death haunts me at night, the quotidian rhythms of life beckon me during the day. It is hard to know how to return to the ordinary after so many months in a foreign land. How do I return to light after becoming so acquainted with darkness? Jess sends me wise words: 'Do you know the saying 'You never step into the same river twice?' It's Heraclitus. The clever old Greek. I think it means that there is never a 'you' who can simply repeat things.' This saying makes me understand that I should not be trying to retrieve a previous way of being. I must embrace the new me and not imagine that 'recovery' is recovering the past or a permanent state of being.

PART SIX

The Aftermath

Burns and Liquid Sunshine

12 APRIL 2015

We land in Spain for a holiday with Jonny's brother and his family to celebrate the end of radiation. Once again, I am all too aware of how lucky I am to be able to do this. From the moment I step off the plane, the liquid sunshine of the Iberian coast seeps into my body. The warmth lubricates my muscles and my connective tissues; it is so different from the blaze of radiation.

Spain is a perfect place to recover. The spring light is incandescent and the cool breezes create a delicate cloak around me. The gastronomical delights sate my appetite. The colours of the buildings, churches and palaces are feasts for the eye. Each day, as 3 pm approaches, I pay homage to where my besieged body lay on the radiation table just a few days before. I grow wings.

Adam and Sarah are flawless travelling companions during this time of convalescence. Their perpetual laughter and whacky ways are medicinal, and my young niece and nephew bring an innocence and mirth to our days. My oldest niece, Gabrielle, also joins us. The love that surrounds me hauls me back into the kingdom of the well.

I discover that my proximity to death has brought with it a new proximity to life. There is a largeness and a godliness to each day, a new spiritual texture of clarity and order. I am tremulous with being alive, and in possession of a new compendium of dreams.

No one describes this transition to health after a serious illness better than Nietzsche in his most personal of books, *The Gay Science*: 'Gratitude pours forth continually, as if the unexpected had just happened – the gratitude of a convalescent ... the rejoicing of strength that is returning, of a reawakened faith in a tomorrow and the day after tomorrow, of a sudden sense of anticipation of a future, of impending adventures, of seas that are open again.'

When I look at my reflection, I feel like I have been forged and re-forged, and my dark forces have been redirected. This change is evident in my inner gaze. My face has been stitched and re-stitched into a series of new shapes, with refined borders.

While nothing about me is the same, there are two new features that most strike me. The first is a tenderness that emanates brightly from my soul, and is now a constituent part of my being. The second is my smile. It has kept the same outline despite all of the mangled toxic infusions and beams that have penetrated me these last months. Love and kindness have intensified its depth, shaping it anew.

I like this woman here more than the person from two years ago. I like that there is no dishonesty here at all.

Like the Moorish buildings that are so bland on the outside but bejewelled and dazzling on the inside, my exterior still shrouds excruciating rumblings of the months gone by. Underneath my T-shirts, the after effects of radiation are now at their peak. My skin on the right side aches, and is rough to the touch. I still cannot look at my charred outer casing. Jonny still applies the cream to soothe my burns.

By mistake, I catch a glimpse of my naked self in a change room with mirrors on three sides. I am too slow in getting on a magnificent white lacey Spanish blouse. My error leaves me horrified by the thousands of reflections of an aubergine-coloured torso. That brief flash discloses not only my discoloured flesh, but also the flaming red incisions from the operation. It is worse than I could ever have imagined. My carefully dissected and sewn-back-together body resembles one of those cows on the walls of the butcher shops and tapas bars all over Spain that illustrate different cuts of meat. It is my chuck and rib areas that are particularly raw and ugly. They would fetch a severely limited price.

I am sent into a panic by this image and much to the surprise of my daughter and niece who are trying on clothes in the next-door change room, I flee the store. 'What's wrong?' the girls want to know when they find me at the gelato store. I just smile and ask, 'Hazelnut or dark chocolate? One or two scoops?' As at other points during this journey, I bury my difficulties deep in the inner chambers of my heart in order to protect my children. There is no need for Katya to be exposed to this pain.

After this incident, I am far more careful about maintaining my sightlessness. Burnt skin is not compatible with morning coffee and croissants under the inky blue skies of Spain. My gaze lingers only on the bountiful pleasures that surround us for the remainder of the journey. Blindness is still what my soul demands.

Cocoons

4 MAY 2015

Arriving back home is not easy. I have been unceremoniously flung out from the cocooned world of cancer and all its predetermined rhythms. There are no more daily treatments. There are no more weekly doctor visits. No more pain. And yet ordinary life as I once knew it no longer exists. In this strange no-man's land, I try to refashion my reality.

'Are you in remission?', the masseuse at a day spa asks, when she sees that I have ticked the box 'cancer' on the information sheet. This question catches me off guard, and then plagues me for days. Remission implies the absence of the disease but also the chance of recurrence. Am I any more in remission than she is? Are my chances the same or worse than hers of having this deadly disease again? There are no answers to these questions, and so I go on as sure footedly as I can.

I am scared to feel joy. Will it be felled cruelly like it was after my last round of cancer? How much breathing space is there in between diagnoses this time round? Will another mutant cell require me to add an epilogue to this book?

In these unstable times, the Buddhist injunction 'to live neither in ecstasy nor agony but somewhere right in the middle' becomes my guiding principle. I continue to find solace in making lists. They quell my anxiety, and help me to discern my progress. I celebrate many 'firsts' as the days go by:

1. *Real hugs with friends without the worry of germs.*
2. *Dance classes with Yda where I feel so alive to be moving my body again.*
3. *Spinning classes where I feel muscles that have been dormant for so long.*
4. *Walking up and down the Westcliff stairs near my house.*
5. *Having my hair cut despite the lack of much hair.*
6. *Emotional outburst at Jonny.*
7. *Blood tests that shows the cancer is gone.*

I celebrate all the things that I do not miss at all:

1. *Paroxysms of fear*
2. *Disassociation from reality*
3. *Miasma in my brain*
4. *Self-absorption*
5. *Needles*
6. *Baldness*
7. *Tingling in my hands and feet*
8. *Hot streams of larvae in my blood*
9. *Weakened immunity*
10. *Endless intrusions in my body*
11. *Emotional swings between hope and despair*

With time, I make a list of the things that I *do* miss from Chemoland:

1. *Closeness of friends*
2. *A cocooned life*
3. *Enforced rests*
4. *Physical limits*
5. *Knowing when and where I have to be*
6. *A pampering routine*

7. *Intense emotions*
8. *Counselling and support*
9. *Not worrying how I look*

Most of all, I miss the island of tenderness and devotion that enveloped me. This is not unusual. In my cancer reading frenzy, I learn that 10 per cent of people who were depressed before being diagnosed with cancer stop being depressed during their treatment. 'This is because the support networks for a person with cancer are so strong,' I explain to Jonny. I think of all the support I have received from medical practitioners and wellness therapists.

Was I overzealous in my search for help to get me through the ordeal? Of course I was. But with hindsight, the only person I would eliminate from my array of healers is the acupuncturist who caused me such distress. Each of the others brought much-needed gifts: wellness (homeopath and pharmacist); fortitude, insights and inner calm (coach, meditation and mindfulness teachers); body and mind strength (Pilates and yoga teachers); soothing and relaxation (masseuse and reflexologist).

Together, these gifted souls forged my capacity to face cancer and mortality. They retrained my eyes to take in the fissures and the solids, my nose to smell the stench and the roses, my ears to hear the chants and the cries, my tongue to taste the bitter and the sweet. They bestowed upon me a new way to live life.

Besides, as an inveterate networker, I am now very well placed to provide the names and numbers of self-help gurus to anyone in need. I am able to weigh up multiple therapeutic modalities ranging from hypnotherapy to core strengthening exercises while on chemotherapy. I am able to speak to the benefits of tapping versus meditation to calm the nerves. I also have three brand new bullet points to add to my 'Who I am' list:

1. *I am slightly obsessive/quirky.*
2. *I am willing to travel in many different directions all at the same time.*
3. *I have the capacity to throw myself at difficult things.*

Pulse

After a few weeks, my cancer framework starts to corrode at an astonishing rate. An avalanche of work deadlines seems to have miraculously waited for my ordeal to end. Projects that have been quietly ticking along suddenly ramp up. I am hurtled back into the throng of meetings, presentations and deadlines. How soon can we install the *99% Alike* exhibition? When will the designs for the foyer of the Holocaust and Genocide Centre be ready? Can Clive and I present to our new clients on Friday? Are we interested in tendering for a museum on the story of diamonds? And on it goes.

Without any medical parameters, my diary is now full from morning to night. I dash from pillar to post in a way that belonged to my pre-cancer existence. Red traffic lights are an irritant once again. Nothing must stand in my way. I eat breakfast and lunch while driving. I talk on my cellphone endlessly. 'I am running ten minutes late,' returns as a constant refrain.

It is affirming to be an ordinary working woman out in the world again. But there are signs that it is too much. My neck is in spasm. My back aches. So much pain, so close to the surface. How did it take all of a few weeks to find myself in this state of wreckage? I believed that my transformation over the last year had been geological in nature, deep psychic shifts that meant that I would never repeat the same negative patterns of behaviour. Here I am once again in the midst of 'doing' rather than 'being'. Once again, I am drumming to the beat of others.

I am disturbed by my dismal failure to look after myself without the restrictions imposed by the kingdom of the sick. A kinder part of me sees that my deep desire for normalcy may be driving my behaviour. I remember in my very first session with Marissa when she said, 'Your mind is the instrument that creates wellbeing. Wellbeing is about harmony of the body and mind.' 'Fool!' I berate myself. 'How has this simple lesson escaped you so quickly?'

When I hear that an Ayurvedic doctor is running a seminar on self-healing through the pulse, I jump at the opportunity to attend.

Dr D, as he is affectionately known, walks into the room in his *khadi* cotton tunic and red silk pants. He sits in perfect silence for a minute or two, creating a god-like aura around himself while bringing us into his orbit. The first words he utters are: 'You have the infinite power to heal yourself.' His undulating voice with its strong Indian cadence soothes me instantly. I settle comfortably in my chair: 'The power of the universe has created you. You are supreme. You don't need anything external to feel the wellbeing within you.'

This is what I have come to be reminded of. I want to be reassured that the power of healing *is* within me. Dr D insists: 'Disease is disconnection in our soul when we lose compassion and belief in ourselves. It is the limitation of the mind.'

When he asks us to cup our hands around our left wrist and find our pulse, I am amazed. I have never felt my own pulse before. Through all the illness and treatment, I have not connected with my own heartbeat. This seems incredible.

Dr D deftly guides the 30 people in the room to create a heavenly state of mind. I follow his instruction to press my second finger, 'the knower', deep into my flesh. I am afraid of the beat at first. It feels too insistent and strange. But I love that I can touch my life force. The feeling intensifies as I move my third and fourth finger into position. The ultimate moment comes when I hold my pulse to my heart. It anchors me.

Dr D then instructs us to lift our fingers and then chants the words associated with the highest order of our being: life; bliss; healing; joy; purity; totality; and self-knowledge. 'Cling to these outcomes,' he says, 'Dispel those associated with the basic physical body – death; damage; suffering; pain; judgment; weakness; non-unity; distraction; reduction.' He ends the session by telling us, 'There are 56 outcomes in life. You are in charge of choosing yours.'

My head is whirling as I drive home, both hands on the wheel. As I round a traffic circle it comes to me to end this book by writing one last concise list of 'Who I have chosen to become'. This will provide a neat concise ending to the tumultuous journey that started 18 months ago, a manifesto of what I will try and hold on to. The list flows freely when I pull into my driveway:

1. *My body is not bounded by the cellular.*
2. *I accept pain as a challenge and not a threat.*
3. *I am able to transcend fear.*
4. *I listen to the skilful edges of my body.*
5. *I have learnt to add space to self.*
6. *I have experienced a deeper state of consciousness.*
7. *I believe that my life must be big, not long.*
8. *I seek a higher purpose.*
9. *I embrace the benefits of giving, gratitude and optimism.*
10. *I embrace moments of fragility and despair.*
11. *I am more authentic with others and myself.*

As the weeks and months go on, my list grows:

12. *I am in charge of my life.*
13. *My time is my own.*
14. *I have learnt to quiet the self.*
15. *I savour quietude.*
16. *I believe in my capacity to heal myself.*
17. *I know that self-mastery can be done on my own.*
18. *I have expanded my range of empathy.*
19. *My love for my family is more defined.*
20. *I am embossed with love.*
21. *I am at as much risk of a dreaded disease as everyone else.*
22. *I like the new me.*

I like this ending. It captures the multiple ways in which I have strengthened my resilience in the face of adversity. It displays a higher order thinking that Marissa, Vicki, Lucy, Hilde, Carla and Dr D have encouraged.

This is not to be. There is another shift in my tectonic plates. Another chapter to be written. And with it, the realisation that there are no endings. Life cannot be controlled by a set of lists.

PART SEVEN

Cancer Four – The Shopping Centre

NOOOOOOooooooo!!!!!

18 SEPTEMBER 2015

Just five months after I have glued my last typed list into my journal, I get another one of those calls. At the time, I am battling to find a parking ticket in a large oversized bag that holds my computer and work notes. It's Jonny. He utters the same sentence that started this story: 'La, it's malignant.' How I have come to despise those words.

This malignancy is a melanoma on my right upper arm. The only difference between this call and the one I received in Soweto over a year ago is that I already know the result of the biopsy. The dermatologist's face said it all when he looked at the mole on his screen two days before, even though I hadn't quite grasped the meaning of his words: 'It's time to have a conversation with the man upstairs.' I understand it now. He was trying to tell me that I really have the most god-awful luck.

Sweat starts to trickle down my forehead. A tiny cubicle in the ladies' bathroom is yet again the only private space I can find. An involuntary wounded cry rises from deep within my belly as soon as I close the toilet door.

I enter into a conversation with the persecutory 'man upstairs' who is governing my life: 'What kind of courage is being asked of me? Surely the Angel of Death is prepared to grant me a reprieve for a couple of years at least? Why this constant reminder of my mortality? How has all my hard work these last months ended like this?' Three cancer diagnoses is tragic. Four is a farce. It is not possible that I think of this disease as an unexpected 'gift'. Been there, done that.

In that small confined space, stability and solidity are expelled from my life once and for all. The only certainty I can conjure is that life will be punctuated by these instances of potential destruction. Bad luck is a certainty. These dark thoughts become a tempest. My newly acquired health is a fragile suit of armour. Barely five months old, and already there are chinks through which another poisoned arrow has penetrated. I can smell my own terror. I wish the toilet could flush away my enraged thoughts.

In the days that follow, the shape of my life yet again bears no resemblance to what it was a mere few days before. The liquid nature of my existence is frightening. There is no way to calibrate optimism. My mind shuts down. 'Resurrect the tools that you have gathered over this last year,' a fragile internal voice implores. While the news is still fresh, however, these tools slip from my grasp. My nerves are shattered. My pallor is deathly. My internal home feels as if it is at the foot of a volcano where the threat of eruption is omnipresent.

My breast surgeon says, 'This is not a big deal, but it's a warning that we need to keep an obsessive eye on you.' I feel no comfort in her words. Cancer may be an entire family of diseases with different characteristics, but I wish for a magic bullet cure to rid me of the whole gamut of these demons.

'You are so unlucky,' my son says when we pluck up the courage to tell him.

It is Jonny and my children who once again help me to know that safety *will* re-enter my field of vision. They somehow help the outline of my days to regain their edges. But before we can make our mutual adaptations, I punish myself for the painful contortions that I keep inflicting on their lives.

While my family should be kicking up our heels and recovering from the long ordeal that is now behind us, I am tugging them back into the kingdom of the sick. I am again exposing them to unsayable fears that are all too often projected onto the canvas of my life.

This time, I don't want anyone else to know. No group emails, no funky gifts, no flowers. My fractured reality has to be anchored without the voices of others ringing in my ears. I refuse to become a cancer patient again. Even if I wanted the comfort of friends, the words, 'I have a malignant melanoma,' won't come out of my mouth. My mind skitters. Life. Death. Life. Death. I am at a dangerous border crossing. X marks the spot.

Somehow, I manage to carry on working with Clive on a big tender. His brother has lung cancer and he is one of the few people who I tell of my plight. I appreciate his quiet empathy while we get our pitch together. Work is a good distraction, but the panic returns as soon as I step out of the meeting space.

When my friend Lloyd calls to ask for advice on how he can stay positive through a sudden diagnosis of colon cancer, I listen to myself talking about all the emotional lessons I have learnt through my ordeal. Why can't I resurrect the mental scaffolding that I describe with so much ease? In the months to come, Lloyd and I are to talk endlessly about the future selves we want to be despite our carved up bodies and the omnipresent threat of cancer. For now, we are both trapped in a negative internal dialogue that is very hard to escape.

I flee with my family to Cape Town to be with our son for *Yom Kippur*, the holiest day of the year in the Jewish faith. On this Sabbath of all Sabbaths, when a day-long fast marks the culmination of a ten-day period of introspection and repentance and when I am supposedly closest to God and to the quintessence of my soul, I try to think about my known and unknowable sins. Even with the might of religion inside me, I cannot fathom why I am back in this place.

I listen to the steady breathing of Jonny in the bed beside me. There is great assurance in the in and out of his breathe. My eyes drift from the sea to the mountains and back again. I seek out my future. 'I will not die from cancer,' is all I can find to say to my deep-in-the-belly-frightened self.

I repeat this mantra every day for the next week. Eventually, I feel the courage to break the gridlock of fear by drawing on the tools that are still so fresh to me. Slowly, the dark cast iron hold loosens its grip. My heart beats a little less fast, and I plod through the medical routines that I am by now so familiar with. Prod, prick, prod. PETSCAN. CT Scan. Untold anxiety. Untold fear waiting to hear if my melanoma has spread to the lymph nodes, or elsewhere in my body. A suspended life.

The scans suggest that the melanoma is contained but, because it is classified as Stage I B rather than Stage I or one and because of my history, I again have to undergo a large surgical procedure to remove a wide margin. With 'Cancer One', it was the plentiful flesh of my thigh that was removed. With 'Cancer Two', it was my breasts that were removed. With 'Cancer Three', a substantial part of my back disappeared. Now it is the scarcer flesh of my upper arm.

It is hard to contemplate this many incursions in my body. So I am thankful to come across Jon Kabat-Zinn's writing on stress reduction and mindfulness where he insists that so long as us patients are breathing, so long as we are interacting with the world, there is 'much more right than wrong with us'. I like his reminder that we are 'never not whole' and that the root meaning of the words health and healing is the word 'whole' and 'holy'. A map of my journey, perhaps? Hole. Whole. Holy.

Another Medical Safari

15 OCTOBER 2015

I wince at the thought of committing another hospital story to paper. It is too much for me, let alone a reader.

Suffice to say that I endure another scan; another three-hour surgery; another large wound. Dr J, my affable surgeon whom I have come to know all too well, makes a 'z'-shaped scar on my upper right arm that resembles the bolt of lightning on Harry Potter's forehead. It is angry and red for a long time, and continues to this day to draw the attention of strangers. 'What happened to your arm?' they ask.

What strangers don't see is that the surgeon also had to re-open the wound on the side of my chest to make sure that the melanoma had not spread beyond the skin to the lymph nodes in my armpit. This is the third time that I am cut at the same place. I bring home those dreaded drains yet again, although thankfully they are smaller and more bearable. This time, I don't hide them in my Ed Hardy bag.

By now the drill is all too familiar. There are visits. Chicken soup and chocolate cake. Conversations peppered with disbelief at what I have endured. A cacophony of sympathy. More fine chiselling of relationships. Although the surgery confirms that the tumour has not spread, the psychic rupture is profound. A fourth primary tumour and I am not yet 50. If I am to re-engineer my soul, much work lies ahead to expel the churning fear that engulfs me, the unspeakable inner sense of derangement.

We all carry within us the inevitability of our own death. But I am over-exposed to its existence, stripped of all delusion. It is hard to live with such a gossamer-thin wall between this life and the next. I long to reclaim the machinery of denial. Dissociate from the terror and rid myself of the sharp sword swinging over my head.

I discover that there is a word to describe the 'fear of everlasting life' – 'apeirophobia'. After a lengthy search, I find the word for the 'fear of a life foreshortened' – 'thanatophobia'. At least I have a word for my lack of internal quietude.

Tigers Above, Tigers Below

NOVEMBER 2015

Even though the world eventually comes to look similar again, the smells and textures return to their familiar guise, and the length of the hours of each day normalise, my inner conviction is fundamentally altered. My internal melody has a different pitch, lower than before, as if the private notes of my mind are now squeezed through thinner tubing. It is only those who have looked into the abyss, and have also lost their protective shields, that are able to hear this subtle change. It is only they who can observe the silent tears that glisten in my eyes as the world keeps turning with its geological certainty.

In an attempt not to be engulfed by anxiety, I add yet another person to my list of helpers. This time, it's an analyst. The theories of psychoanalysis have always intrigued me. I have read several books by analysts in which they describe their different patients' struggles to live a meaningful life. I have always imagined that one day, I might train as an analyst myself.

During the hurly burly of my various cancer treatments, I reached for forms of healing and wellbeing that were connected to my body. After 'Cancer Number Four', however, I am open to a 'talking cure'. I hope it will help me to refashion the story driving my own internal destruction, and to regain my optimism for life.

Resting my body on the analyst's couch necessitates a leap of faith. It is strange to talk into a void and I don't like the close-up photo of the male lion that stares down at me from the wall. Before long, I find comfort in this animal's eyes as I speak my story out loud.

My analyst reinforces what friends and counsellors have assured me – that 'Cancer Number Four' is another fertile piece of ground for self-discovery, that it will unmask still more versions of myself. I have heard this all too often. I worry about how much hardship I can take. During the first weeks, we move between my life before cancer, the last three years of treatment, and the universe more generally. I tell her, 'It is so hard to feel joy when my life has been felled this many times.'

I appreciate how she feels the unbearable pain of the hand that I have been dealt. She explains to me how hard it is to hold onto 'mature hope' when there is chaos and disorder in the soul. 'Omnipotence is what we reach for when we are frightened,' she says. 'As the trauma calms down, it will become more possible to grasp mature hope.' I respond: 'After my mastectomy, I chose a life of omnipotence. I see now how I have a chance to make friends with frailty.'

As the weeks go by, she gently prompts me to enter the dark patches in my mind. She holds my hand and shares my fears while she shines a torch to show me the way. Together, we start to build bridges over the breach in my sense of self. We slowly unfurl new interpretations that help me not to demonise my body's failings.

We circle again and again around my fear of death, a fear that now corsets my life. 'I can't stand there being no way to answer the agonising question of whether I will live or die from another diagnosis of this capricious disease,' I bemoan. She bears witnesses to my terror when it is time to have my three-monthly scans, and I have to wait for the results to see if the cancer has returned.

Little by little, my analyst shows me how to surrender to an awareness of death without becoming its captive. We spend hours talking about the human condition and the unknowability of our destiny. She helps me to face the fact that certainty is a futile quest. We start to rebuild my internal sanctuary without the speed bumps that cancer has created. Very slowly, I come to feel the benefits of having faced my mortality this many times.

I bring into the room the many inspiring stories that I am reading related to the nature of life and death. I have two favourites.

The first is by Oliver Sacks. This large-hearted genius falls in love at the ripe old age of 77, after three-and-a-half decades of celibacy and while battling an ocular melanoma that had metastasised throughout his body. His passionate love affair with Bill Hayes teaches me that everything is possible. The four essays he wrote in the last months of his life about coming to terms with his own death are an elegy to his unique capacity to celebrate life. In the last paragraph he ever wrote, when he was 'short of breath' and with his 'muscles melted away by cancer', he tells his readers that 'achieving inner peace within oneself' is what living a worthwhile life means.

While Oliver Sacks shows me how to think of death, Pema Chodron's story entitled 'Tigers Above, Tigers Below' is a parable of how to think about life. The story starts with a woman running away from tigers. She runs and runs, but the tigers get closer and closer. When she comes to the edge of a cliff, she sees some vines, so she climbs down and holds on to the vines. Looking down, she sees that there are tigers below her as well. She then notices that a mouse is gnawing away at the vine to which she is clinging. She also sees a beautiful little bunch of strawberries close to her, growing out of a clump of grass. She looks up and she looks down. She looks at the mouse. Then she simply takes a strawberry, puts it in her mouth, and enjoys it thoroughly.

Tigers above, tigers below. This is how I come to understand my predicament. Each moment is just what it is. It might be the only moment of our life, it might be the only strawberry we'll ever eat.

After speaking my thoughts out loud each week for months, I feel my deep fears starting to unlace, with the cavernous spaces created by cancer being re-stitched. My demons are once again my teachers. I gently watch my own 'black swan' – that bird that glides through my interior waters and brings with it weighty and unpredictable events – coming to a place of rest.

Cancer: A Love Story

14 JANUARY 2016

Cancer has averted a potential mid-life crisis when my 50th birthday arrives at the beginning of 2016. It feels like a magnificent achievement to be not dead. I choose to celebrate amidst a bunch of close family and friends. I don't touch alcohol, but I am drunk on the significance of the occasion, and spend hours on the dance floor in a state of ecstasy. In my speech that night, I talk about three words whose meanings have changed entirely for me. The words are kindness, gratitude and love.

About kindness I say: 'Each and every one of you here tonight – and those who are too far away to be here – has transformed the word kindness from something light into a weighty precious metal that has been my ballast and kept me steady in the eye of the storm. Just like I couldn't find a way to measure my fear all those months ago, I cannot begin to quantify your kindness or its import. Suffice to say that the sum of this kindness has allowed me to stand here today as a person who is both kinder to herself and, I hope, to those around me. You all have granted me the gift of self-compassion.'

About gratitude I say: 'Every day, I wake up feeling a sense of gratitude from deep inside. I feel grateful to be alive, living in this extraordinary community close in both geography and emotion. I am grateful that my challenges have allowed the colours of the world to become more saturated, my interchanges to be more satisfying. I am richer and fuller than I ever could have imagined. Again, it is all of you in the room tonight who are responsible for that feeling.'

About love I say: 'I have always treasured my husband, my children, and my community, but my love has been re-forged over these last years. In a world over which we no longer have an ounce of control – which is not an easy position for Jonny, Josh, Katya or I – we have built a temple of love to take shelter in. Jonny and I have formed a sublime duet. I have learnt to take agency in new ways while Jonny is always right there beside me. Given his medical background, he is uniquely placed to support me but his love goes well beyond that. It is constant, generous and all-encompassing.

Despite the difficulties and turmoil of having a mother with cancer, my children have remained steadfast besides me and have been the billowing sails that propel me through the stormy seas. Together, our family has learnt to find the treasures in the snow when it seems like there is only whiteness. Together, we have learnt to embrace the pathless path, one we might never have seen or found without suffering. Amidst the multitude of challenges, we grow our bonds. It's in this sense that cancer is my love story.

There is another sense in which cancer is my love story that I could not say out loud that night of my birthday party. My story has essentially been a journey towards self-love. Cancer's greatest paradox is that it is the loneliest of diseases, despite inviting so much support. No one could have had the chemo or the radiation or the operations on my behalf. No one could have taken away the physical and spiritual pain. No one could ultimately reassure me that I would live.

With hindsight, I see how easy it would have been to shut out the suffering. I am glad I found the strength to resist this deadly gravitational force, and to awaken myself to new discoveries in the face of the trauma. I am proud of what I have been able to gain along this lonely journey. I have learnt to observe the self-diminishing and destructive thoughts that cancer induces but not to cling to these as the only option before me. I have learnt to decide how to respond to trauma with a new awareness.

Choosing this as a path has made me confront the nature of my relationships, both intimate and more peripheral. It gave me my brother back. It helped me to discover new versions of myself. It brought me inner peace, something I had not experienced before in my life. It led me to find sources of internal nourishment. It allowed me to suspend judgements of others and myself. It acclimatised me to facing life's inevitable stresses. It is hard to say whether or not I am a better person. I know, at least, that I am better at identifying my own inhumanities and being wise about the realities facing me. I am better at releasing grudges.

Having cancer this many times is like starting life anew. I choose not to live with half a heart or a blighted soul. I have learnt that I am not my cancer. What started out as my own journey of potential destruction and self-hate has brought me more productive and intense ways to live with and love myself. I can only now grasp the counterveiling forces of love and cancer that have been enacted inside of me.

Despite – or because of – the story I have told, I am a happier and calmer person who looks forward to the next five decades of my life.

This is, for me, the ultimate love story.

PART EIGHT

Afterword

It has been a great relief to live 24 months free of the irredeemable grind of cancer. During this time, I have noticed how I don't whitewash my emotions, but neither do I live with the same exquisite intensity as I did during my years of treatment. Despite the three-monthly agony of waiting for the results every time I go for a scan or blood test, I feel safer internally. I think less of the room in the sky and see more swarms of brilliantly coloured butterflies in the lattices of my mind. I am glad that I captured my journey in words on these pages – as I read them, I see how it is both impossible to forget and yet difficult to remember all that I have been through.

I decide that this new chapter of almost normal life requires a new rendition of how I am going to spend my days in the future. I apply to train as a psychoanalyst. After a gruelling process, I am accepted into the training, although I am advised to wait for the next cohort that will start training in a few years' time. Wisely, one analyst tells me that after all I have been through, I need to take life slowly so that I can titrate my past and present experiences. I am invited to start attending psychoanalytic seminars and conferences in the meantime. I am thrilled. I don't know if I will ever practice as an analyst but from the first seminar I attend, I feel lucky to have the opportunity to better understand the workings of the mind. I am not sure I would be in this place without the journey I have undertaken.

New experiences in the cancer world have also afforded me new perspectives. A year after my last surgery, I felt a powerful urge to give back to others who find themselves with a similar diagnosis to mine. I have started to work closely with the Breast Health Foundation, an organisation established by Dr Carol Benn to promote awareness around the importance of early detection of breast cancer among South African women.

It is hard to believe that breast cancer kills one in eight women. Most of the deaths are caused because women do not have access to regular mammograms, and often arrive at the clinic with metastasised cancers. Shockingly, nine times more of these women die of this disease because of late-stage diagnosis, compared with breast cancer patients in the United States of America. I have the space to process the extent to which breast cance r is a scourge in South Africa even though I have been told this information before.

I have learnt how many women do not have even a sliver of the support that I have described in these pages. I have encountered horrific stories of husbands who will not look at their wives after a mastectomy; women who are too afraid to tell anyone that they have breast cancer because of the shame associated with the illness; women who are too poor to pay for transport to their chemo sessions; those who come to chemo in crowded taxis and throw up cytotoxic vomit into plastic bags all the way home; others with no access to treatment options at all. For many of these women it is impossible that the words cancer and love can appear in the same sentence. This is an invitation for me to give back to those who do not have the same resources or expectations.

I have understood my immense privilege. I remain unremittingly grateful.

Chemo Tips

For us patients, the treatments associated with curing cancer can be as frightening as the disease itself. Ironically, chemo turned into an opportunity for me to learn how to enhance my own health and wellbeing.

My first trick was to build a team of healthcare professionals around me. I quickly realised that it takes more than a medical oncologist to fight this devastating disease. I believe that the healers from the many different modalities that I engaged with made my conventional medical treatments more effective.

My second trick was to talk to as many people as possible who had been through chemo. No two people go through the treatment in the same way, although I discovered some basic tips that most patients seem to find helpful. I captured these in a 'Chemo Tips' list which I have now expanded for this book. (Thank you Coco Cachalia and Caroline Lambert for kick-starting this process. Your valuable advice has been incorporated into the information below.)

While working on this list, I was very encouraged to read about the growing field of Integrative Oncology. Practitioners in this field do not believe there are 'alternatives' to mainstream cancer care. Rather, they believe in additional 'non-pharmacologic' therapies that have been proven to be effective. They advocate complementary therapies (such as acupuncture, exercise, diet, meditation, massage and yoga) for managing cancer symptoms alongside mainstream cancer care as part of a patient's treatment plan.

I intuitively sought out these kinds of complementary therapies as I mentioned, but it is a great relief to know that many top cancer centres now recognise the need to treat patients holistically, rather than simply focusing on the disease of cancer or its symptoms.

1. Anticipating Chemo

The anticipation of the first chemo – what to expect and how you're going to cope with it – is really difficult. Like all things in life, however, once you have experienced it for the first time, it's not half as scary. In hindsight, the whole treatment process goes quicker than you can imagine when you are starting out.

Books

It helped me enormously to read accounts by people who had gone through treatment themselves, as well as to read the insights from healers, alternative practitioners and oncologists. The books often put into words fears and apprehensions that I was unable to describe. I have a long list of resources at the end of this chapter. In the first weeks after I was diagnosed, I found the following books invaluable:

Louise Hay, *Cancer: Discovering Your Healing Power*
Bernie Siegel, *Love, Medicine and Miracles*
Bernie Siegel, *Faith, Hope and Healing*
Bernie Siegel, *Preparing for Chemo* (Lecture available on Audible.com)

Buddies for Life

Buddies for Life is a bi-monthly, glossy lifestyle magazine, published in association with the Breast Health Foundation. It has essential medical, financial, nutrition and supportive information for breast cancer patients, survivors and their nearest and dearest. Survivors are featured in each issue, exposing readers to life after breast cancer. Subscribe to the magazine, or find back copies at www.buddiesforlife.co.za.

Emotional Support

Besides managing the physical side effects of the treatment, I can't emphasise enough the importance of getting into a positive mindset *before* treatment starts. Some women choose to stay silent about their diagnosis. This is a personal choice. For me, chemo was a marathon, and I needed all the seconders I could get. Speaking to people I knew who had breast cancer – and there are unfortunately so many in my wider circle of friends – offered me a chance to share my most intimate concerns and get advice. I found it very inspirational to witness people's tenacities and strengths, and their generosity in helping us new fellow travellers. There are specific moments when support and empathy of this kind feels especially important:

- At the time of the diagnosis;
- Deciding on and adjusting to the treatment plan;
- Dealing with difficult symptoms.

My friends (who have not had cancer) were also really appreciative when I invited them into my travails and asked for help. I found it liberating to learn how to receive gratefully. This ultimately deepened many of my friendships.

Formal Support

Formal counselling helped me to prepare mentally. Before my mastectomy, I went to a counsellor specifically trained to deal with breast cancer patients. She helped me to understand the intricacies and possible pitfalls of the operation. During chemo, my life coach, who had survived Stage IV pancreatic cancer, had invaluable advice, as did other healers that I went to.

Several South African organisations provide counselling to breast cancer patients. The one I know best is Bosom Buddies, which is initiated by breast cancer survivors and runs as a project of the Breast Health Foundation. It provides emotional and informative support to all those affected by breast cancer through telephonic care trees. Anyone affected by this disease can call 0860 283 343 to be put in contact with a support buddy. Bosom Buddies also hosts public meetings for breast cancer patients and their friends and families. Check out this network on https://www.facebook.com.

Your doctor or oncologist should also be able to recommend an organisation or counsellor who works in your area.

Integrative Oncology

Integrative medicine modalities such as acupuncture, massage, meditation, exercise, self-hypnosis, music therapy or yoga deal with symptoms ranging from anxiety to nausea. Check out the latest thinking and scientific evidence on this approach on websites such as that of the Memorial Sloane Kettering Cancer Centre – www.mskcc.org/.../integrative-medicine.

The Pink Parasol is a recently launched website-based directory for patients to find complementary health therapists that can aid them in their cancer journey. There is an "Ask us" section where patients can find answers and support. www.pinkparasol.co.za

Meditation

I can attest to the scientific studies which show the multiple benefits of meditation – learning to live more, worry less and sleep better. I learnt to meditate after my mastectomy, and I became a more regular meditator during my second round of breast cancer. The great thing is that you can meditate anywhere and at no cost.

There are many meditation training centres in South Africa. I was trained by the internationally recognised TM teacher, Vicki Broome, at the Transcendental Meditation Centre in Houghton – www.tminjoburg.co.za. Also investigate Varjrapani Kadampa Buddhist Centre's website www.meditation.org.za for other training centres.

Headspace, an app that can be downloaded onto a cellphone, is a very simple and accessible way to learn to meditate. Andy, the friendly meditation instructor, describes meditation as 'gym membership for the mind'. He expertly guides one through different course levels. If you are a person who likes tracking your progress, the app is great as it tracks your sessions and rewards you for consistency – www.headspace.com/headspace-meditation-app.

Mindfulness

Mindfulness is increasingly studied as a very useful practice in the arena of health and disease. Jon Kabat-Zinn, a professor of medicine and the founder of the Stress Reduction Clinic and the Center for Mindfulness, shows how mindfulness can enhance the quality of life for cancer patients and positively affect the way that the mind processes difficult emotions under stress. I highly recommend that you read Kabat-Zinn's book, *Full Catastrophe Living,* which describes his mindfulness-based programme. You can download his guided meditations on his website, www.mindfulnesscds.com.

I was lucky to be introduced to a most wonderful mindfulness teacher near my home, Lucy Draper-Clarke. She runs regular mindfulness courses and retreats. Her website www.heart-mind.co.za is a useful way to learn what is going on in South Africa's mindfulness community.

I also recommend that you read Elana Rosenbaum's *Here For Now: Living Well with Cancer Through Mindfulness.*

Needle Phobia

Given that my oncologist strongly dissuaded me from having a port through which the chemo could be given because of the risk of infection, I had to find other ways to overcome my fear of the constant jabs that any cancer patient has to endure.

Emla cream, a local analgesic that is available over the counter from pharmacies, became my new best friend. The cream effectively numbs the skin at the needle site, and is best applied 30 minutes before an injection. I was very happy to discover Emla patches, which are easier and less messy to use than the cream, but are more expensive.

Meditation, hypnotherapy, breathing exercises and listening to good playlists made by friends all helped to distract me while the needle was going in. Look for tips on how to deal with phobia on websites such as: http://journals.sagepub.com/doi/abs/10.

Writing

I recorded everything that was happening before, during and after chemo in a journal I kept with me constantly. The discipline of writing everything down helped me to track my challenges as well as my moments of triumph. It enabled me to create a sense of order over the chaos induced by cancer and gain a semblance of control. It also helped me to cope with the onslaught of new experiences that come thick and fast during this time. I had no idea at the time that the journal would become the basis for this book.

2. Preparing for Chemo

A Bag for Chemo

Chemo treatments are a lengthy and tedious business. You can spend up to five hours or more at the treatment centre. I had a special chemo bag that I kept packed with light reading material, aromatherapy massage oils, good luck talismans from my kids and friends, and a photo album of happier times. Each week, I added a flask of ginger tea (for nausea), green vegetable juice (for an extra immune boost) and some 'super foods' (listed below). The lazy boy chairs get uncomfortable after many hours of sitting, so I took extra cushions for my back, and a big fluffy blanket which was as much for 'protection' as it was for warmth.

Companionship

I asked a friend to accompany me to each chemo session. This is not only an excellent way of including people in your lonely journey, but it is also great to have someone who can assist you with accessing food, teas and drinks, putting on the ice packs, getting to the toilet, etc. while you are on the drip. I didn't realise how difficult it would be to accomplish these kinds of activities with one hand! Taking along a friend also relieved Jonny of needing to spend every hour with me at treatment, even though he was there for much of the time.

Counting Down the Sessions

One of the most innovative presents I got from a fellow breast cancer survivor was a jar containing 18 marbles (one for each chemo session). My kids took out a marble each time I returned home from chemo, and they also changed the number on the little black board on the front of the jar. Seeing the pile of marbles shrink made the weekly accomplishment feel very real.

Hair Loss

Hair loss was the most difficult side effect of the treatment for me. Some women are brave enough to go around completely bald, and still look and feel beautiful. From the start, I knew I would not be one of them. If you are like me, then I suggest that you go to a great local wig shop before your treatments start. You are much more likely to have a sense of humour about the new versions of yourself that appear in the mirror at this point.

Find out from fellow cancer patients where the nearest wig shop is in your area. Wig Beauty and Hair City are just two South African online wig stores: www.wigbeauty.co.za and www.haircity.co.za. Wyatt Hair also runs the Wig Library for cancer patients in and around Jo'burg. Here, patients can borrow from a variety of different wigs donated by former patients.

Many women choose to shave their head *before* their hair falls out. I understand this option, as it is very traumatic to loose clumps of hair. I chose, however, to keep my hair until it really wasn't viable any longer.

Patient Navigation

This is an emerging discipline in the world of cancer. A patient navigator stands by patients as their advocate, and helps them to navigate through the various medical disciplines and healthcare providers during the treatment process. The navigator supports the patient, assists them with their many choices and decisions, and helps to ensure that they don't fall through the cracks of the healthcare system. The patient can then use their precious inner resources for healing purposes. Ask your doctor or medical insurance if there is a patient navigator available to help you during your treatment process.

Visual Armour

Losing my hair, my eyebrows and my eyelashes made me consider my appearance in a whole new way. Before chemo, I had never made much fuss over doing my hair or applying makeup. Cancer changed that. Suddenly, I felt very exposed and makeup became much more important. My expert friend took me shopping to buy base, a highlighter, blush, eye shadow, and lipsticks. Annette gave me a quick tutorial, and I then spent much more time 'doing up' my face than ever before.

Tonnes of websites deal with 'makeovers'. I liked the Look Good, Feel Better website, lookgoodfeelbetter.org, which has step-by-step guides on how to apply foundation, blush, concealer, eyebrows, etc.

Yoga

Yoga is very helpful for its calming impact at all stages of the journey. There are many styles of yoga. I highly recommend Iyengar as the teachers are all rigorously trained in relieving a wide array of medical conditions. Check out the BKS Iyengar Institute of Southern African website at http://www.bksiyengar.co.za to find a teacher near you.

Yoga Warriors is a new chain of yoga studios that has sprung up around the country, although I would not advise going to the active yoga sessions as they are too strenuous for those undergoing chemo. Rather attend specialised passive/yin yoga sessions, and make sure that your teacher knows about your condition. http://www.yogawarrior.co.za

3. During Treatment

While the side effects of chemo are often cumulative, they can and should be managed from the beginning. I tried to find the right management protocol as soon as a symptom appeared. As time went on, I became more proactive and got much better at countering symptoms before they started to really bother me.

Anti-Cancer Foods

Chemo plays havoc with your metabolism, and all major cancer organisations recognise the advantages of a healthy diet as a way to give your immune system the best chance to fight back.

There are many approaches to what constitutes a healthy diet for cancer patients, but there is one thing that all nutritionists agree on – malignant tumours are addicted to sugar. I cut back on all forms of sugar, and refined and processed foods soon after I was diagnosed. I had been on a gluten-free diet for some time, so it wasn't hard to give up bread, biscuits, etc.

That was just the first step. The next challenge was to look at what I could eat. I was told by many people that an anti-cancer diet, particularly a ketogenic diet, can help eliminate cancer cells and enhance the effectiveness of chemotherapy and radiation.

This diet advocates minimal carbs, a moderate amount of high-quality protein and high amounts of healthy fats, as well as periodic fasting prior to and on the day of chemo or radiation. Supporters of the diet explain that, because cancer cells use glucose as fuel but do not have the same metabolic flexibility as regular cells, a state of nutritional ketosis can starve the cancer cells to death.

I suggest you do your own research if this approach interests you. I didn't stick religiously to this diet, although I did find the principles useful. Read more about nutritional ketosis at: http://articles.mercola.com/ketogenic-diet.aspx.

DO's

A key aspect of a cancer prevention diet is to find foods that reduce inflammation of the cells as this can damage your body's healthy cells and tissue, and weaken your immune system. The following foods appear on many of the 'good-foods-for-cancer' lists. I tried to include as many of these superfoods as I could in my diet.

- **Avocadoes** are rich in glutathione, a powerful antioxidant that attacks free radicals in the body.

- **Blackberries, raspberries** (especially the black ones) and **strawberries** contain many vitamins, minerals, plant compounds and antioxidants that protect against cancer.
- **Carrots** contain beta-carotene which which may protect DNA in the cell nucleus from cancer-causing chemicals.
- **Chilli peppers** and **jalapenos** are said to contain a chemical which may neutralise certain cancer-causing substances.
- **Citrus fruits** like oranges, lemons and grapefruit sweep carcinogens out of the body.
- **Curcumin** found in turmeric is considered the greatest cancer-fighting food. It is thought to inhibit the proliferation of tumour cells, decrease inflammation, and sensitise cancer cells to chemotherapy and radiation. Curcumin can be taken as a spice, as a fresh root in tea, or as a supplement.
- **Coniferous vegetables** such as cabbage, cauliflower, broccoli (especially broccoli sprouts), brussel sprouts, and kale all have a chemical component that converts a cancer-promoting oestrogen into a more protective variety.
- **Fermented foods** such as sauerkraut and kefir are very effective at restoring the gut bacterial ecosystem, and are believed to reduce inflammation.
- **Flax** contains lignans which may have an antioxidant effect.
- **Garlic** has immune-enhancing compounds that help to fight cancer, and indirectly help break down cancer-causing substances.
- **Green vegetables** including grasses (generally juiced) and sprouts are loaded with antioxidants, enzymes, chlorophyll and minerals.
- **Mushrooms** such as shiitake, maitake, reishi help to build the immune system.
- **Nuts** such as almonds, macadamia and walnuts contain antioxidants that are thought to suppress the growth of cancers. Cashew nuts and peanuts are strictly prohibited because they contain too much fungus.
- **Papayas** have high levels of vitamin C and folic acid which are believed to minimise certain cancers.
- **Red grapes** contain bioflavonoids which have powerful anti-

oxidant qualities.

- **Seaweed** and other sea vegetables contain important fatty acids.
- **Sweet potatoes** contain many anti-cancer properties, including beta-carotene.
- **Tomatoes** contain lycopene, an antioxidant that attacks roaming by-products of normal metabolism (known as free radicals), that are suspected of triggering cancer. They also have vitamin C, an antioxidant that can prevent cellular damage that leads to cancer.
- **Wheatgrass** and **barley grass juice** follow closely after curcumin as anti-cancer superfoods.

DON'TS

Avoid foods that cause inflammation, or that contain bacteria and fungi. These include:

- All **meat,** especially processed meats such as deli meats, bacon, sausage, hot dogs and pepperoni.
- **Fish** that is high in mercury, as well as eggs and milk that have hormones.
- Commercially stored **grains, rice** and **potatoes,** and all products containing yeast because of high levels of fungus.
- **Beans** that are high in carbohydrates and lectins, which trigger inflammation.

Other food tips:

- Buy organic foods whenever possible.
- Eat well-cooked food, soups and 'mushy' foods, so that your digestive system doesn't need to work so hard.
- Eat small regular meals rather than three large meals to help curb the nausea.

The following cookbooks provide good ideas and recipes to try during treatments:

Joan Fishman, *Something's Got to Taste Good: The Cancer Patient's Cookbook*

Rebecca Katz, *The Cancer Fighting Kitchen* and *One Bite at a Time*
Mohammed Keshtgar, *The Breast Cancer Cookbook*
The Taste for Living Cookbook: Mike Milken's Favorite Recipes for Fighting Cancer
Vern Verona, *Cancer Fighting Foods*

Constipation

Constipation is a common side effect of chemo, so be prepared. In the beginning, I took a laxative the night before and after chemo. This seldom helped. I only solved this problem when I was introduced to the Maharishi Ayuverdic Digestion tablet called Digestone by my meditation teacher. Unfortunately, these tablets are hard to access in South Africa, but may be purchased from: Ambrosia: ambrosiamap@gmail.com / www.mapinsa.co.za.

Exercise

Walking was often the last thing I felt like doing during my months of treatment, but it felt so good to overcome my inertia that I ended up walking every day throughout chemo, except for the day of chemo itself. I tried not to work up a sweat, but I walked for as long as my body would allow. The endorphins and fresh air changed my whole demeanour. I also made regular dates for friends to walk with me, so this also became a good time to connect with people.

In addition to walking, I did Pilates and Yoga throughout. Much research describes how exercise during chemo helps patients to sustain muscle mass, which is very important given that the average cancer patient may lose between 10 to 15 per cent of their muscle mass during treatment. Interestingly, one series of studies showed that breast tumours were slower growing in mice that had access to an exercise wheel as compared to sedentary mice, and there is a growing body of evidence that exercise is a significant factor in reducing cancer recurrence and prolonging survival of cancer patients.

Germs and infections

I tried as far as possible to stay away from people sniffing or coughing, because chemo severely weakens your immune system. Under Jonny's watchful eye, I did not hug friends and colleagues, so as to be completely safe. It was hard to stop people with outstretched arms from coming too close, but it was better than ending up sick. I never bought a face mask or latex gloves, although these are effective ways to deal with being immune compromised. If you do end up touching people's hands or kissing and hugging, try to wash your hands as soon as possible after contact.

Fluids

Drink as much as you can during chemo to try to wash out your system. These are all excellent fluids: ginger tea (helps with nausea); green tea (full of anti-oxidants); water and lemon (helps with nausea); turmeric tea (has amazing cancer-fighting properties); green vegetable juice of kale, cucumber, spinach, parsley and ginger (especially on the day of chemo when it's helpful in removing harmful bacteria and toxins from the intestinal trace and is an amazing energiser).

Massage

I have always loved a good massage, and this became a vital way for me to improve my sense of wellbeing during chemo. Integrative oncology centres have now studied the benefits of massage, and have discovered that patients who receive a massage before or after chemo suffer fewer symptoms.

Mouth Care

Chemo messes with your mouth cells, and your mouth PH. This can result in mouth sores, dryness, and/or candida. One easy solution is to rinse your mouth with warm water with a mix of a half teaspoon of salt and a half teaspoon of bicarbonate of soda several times a day (after each meal, and whenever you think of it in between). But don't swallow! This rebalances your PH. This also treats sores if they should develop. Brush and floss often. I went to the oral hygienist before chemo began to get my teeth cleaned, as you can't do this during chemo.

Nausea

My oncologist prescribed several meds to avoid nausea. The anti-nausea medications that were injected intravenously during the chemo prevented me from suffering from bad nausea, although many women around me were not as lucky. They told me that they also had to take additional medications orally for two to three days after chemo, which is the nausea risk period.

The oral prescription medicines are better taken preventatively. It is much harder to get rid of nausea once it has set in. A new wonder drug called Emend is supposedly the best anti-nausea drug on the market.

Ginger is the best natural anti-nausea remedy. I put fresh ginger into everything – my tea and my food – as often as I could. I found myself eating vast amounts of the pickled ginger that comes with sushi. I bought 'ginger shots', which are tangy and hot, and then I learnt to make my own from a chunk of ginger with some lemon or lime juice and a dash of cayenne pepper.

Neuropathy

Taxol, a very common chemo drug for breast cancer patients, has neurotoxic side effects that can cause neuropathy (sensory loss or pain) in your hands and feet. This tends to get progressively worse through the duration of treatment, and then stops after chemo is completed.

If you are on Taxol, there are ways to avoid neuropathy. Firstly, be diligent about wearing the ice gloves on your hands and feet during the Taxol infusion, as these stop the chemo drugs from reaching the peripheral nerves. Secondly, take Glutamine, a supplement usually sold to assist with weightlifting. This powder, which repairs muscle fibres, helped me enormously. Lastly, rub peppermint oil into your hands and feet to help wake up the circulation of the nerves.

Nutritional supplements

Chemo is a massive assault on the immune system, so staying well is a challenge. Much current data shows that, besides boosting the immune system, some nutritional supplements have molecularly targeted, anti-cancer effects. Specific commonly utilised drugs have also been found to increase anti-cancer activity. I would highly recommend seeking advice from an integrative medical doctor in your area. If there is not one nearby, a good homeopath or pharmacist should be able to help. I worked with both a homeopath and pharmacist to decide on which supplements I should take.

I checked everything I took with my oncologist beforehand, as some remedies are thought to interfere with the chemo by either increasing or lessening the effect of other medicines you're taking.

Antioxidants, for example, are excellent for your immunity, but they are not recommended the day before, during, or directly after chemo. Although my doctor was skeptical of the efficacy of many of the supplements, she did not object to my taking them. She agreed that Vitamin B is vital for cancer patients.

Reflexology and acupuncture

If you can cope with the needles in acupuncture, this 3 000-year-old Chinese practice is said to be remarkable in helping with common symptoms such as pain, hot flushes and dry mouth. If acupuncture is out for you, as it was for me, acupressure and reflexology work on similar principles.

Skin and nails

I was really worried that chemo would dry out my skin. Amazingly, I discovered that one of the best side effects of chemo was that my skin was as soft and smooth as a baby's bum. I am told that this is because the chemo kills the dead cells and takes all the toxins out of your skin. If this isn't the case for you, take vegetarian Borage capsules, or fish oil.

Chemotherapy can cause your nails and nail beds to change colour, become brittle, grooved, lifted or sensitive. Avoid keeping your hands in water for very long, as this can lead to fungal infections. Intensive moisturisers, cuticle cream, and olive oil all help to prevent dryness, splitting and hangnails. Avoid artificial nails during chemotherapy. Consult http://lookgoodfeelbetter.org/programs/beauty-guide/nail-care.

When to play the cancer card?

I suggest that you play this card when you are parked in the wrong spot, and any other time during this period when you feel really overwhelmed. You would have to be a real brute to argue that cancer patients are not entitled to some fringe benefits when undergoing treatment. My kids regularly said to me, “Now you are playing the cancer card!” when I said something they disagreed with, but they were often happy to go along with my needs.

Resources

You will discover an abundant number of books on cancer, healing, and the meaning of life along your journey, from memoirs to scientific studies. Books like those that listed below assisted me in coping with my diagnosis and subsequent treatments, and gave me a great deal of courage and reassurance. Many novels, such as *The Fault in Our Stars,* helped too, and I rediscovered the pleasures of Jane Austen and George Elliot over this time. The best non-fiction recommendations are:

Laura Bond, *Mum's NOT having chemo*
Mark Bunn, *Ancient Wisdom Modern Health*
Pema Chödrön, *The Wisdom of No Escape*
Pema Chödrön, *Coming Closer to Ourselves*
Viktor Frankel, *Man's Search for Meaning*
Atul Gawande, *Being Mortal*
Louise L. Hay, *Cancer Discovering Your Healing Power*
Louise L. Hay, *Cancer You Can Heal Your Life*
John Kabat-Zinn, *Mindfulness for Beginners*
John Kabat-Zinn, *Full Catastrophe Living*
Henry Marsh, *Do No Harm*
Siddartha Mukherjee, *The Emperor of All Maladies*
Bernie Siegel, *Love, Medicine and Miracles*
Bernie Siegel, *Faith, Hope and Healing*

Illness Memoirs

Diana Athill, *Somewhere Towards the End*
Amy Boesky, *What we Have*
Kelly Corrigan, *Glitter and Glue: A Memoir*
Kathlyn Conway, *Illness and the Limits of Expression*
Marion Coutts, *The Iceberg: A Memoir*
Jenny Diski, *In Gratitude*
Eve Ensler, *In the Body of the World*
Susan Gubar, *Memoir of a Debulked Woman*
Paul Kalanithi, *When Breath Becomes Air*
David Rieff, *Swimming in a Sea of Death: A Son's Memoir*
Fanice Mock, *Not All Bad Comes to Harm You: Observations of a Cancer Survivor*
Anita Moorjani, *Dying To Be Me; My Journey from Cancer, to Near Death, to True Healing*
Rebecca Solnit, *The Faraway Nearby*
Oliver Sacks, *On the Move: A Life*
Claire Bidwell Smith, *The Rules of Inheritance: A Memoir*
Brenda Walker, *Reading by Moonlight: How Books Saved a Life*
Mary Elizabeth Williams, *A Series of Catastrophes and Miracles: A True Story of Love, Science and Cancer*
Elie Wiesel, *Open Heart*

Audio Lectures

Pema Chodrom, *When Pain is the Doorway: Awakening in the Most Difficult Circumstances*
Bernie Siegel, *Getting Ready: Preparing for Surgery, Chemotherapy and Other Treatments*
Bernie Siegel, *Meditations for Enhancing Your Immune System*
Randy Pausch and Jeffrey Zaskow, *The Last Lecture*

A Very Last List of Lessons

Lesson 1: Face the thing that you fear most. There is nothing to lose and everything to gain.

Lesson 2: Ask for help. It is a gift to others to receive graciously.

Lesson 3: Keep taking charge of your health. Never avoid a procedure if you can help it. Avoidance is the enemy.

Lesson 4: Keep your mitochondria happy. This involves maintaining the healthy sleeping, eating and exercise regime that you create to fight off the disease.

Lesson 5: Write about your experiences. This is the best way of making sense of inner feelings.

Lesson 6: Gratitude helps heal. Find the positive even in the bleakest of situations. Laugh even when it is hard to do so.

Lesson 7: Practice the tools that you gain to centre yourself and to decrease stress and a sense of being overwhelmed, like deep mindful breathing and meditation.

Lesson 8: Give and be generous in the magnificent ways that you will witness.

Lesson 9: Live in the present, but plan for the future. Don't panic about things that are to come, but travel on new roads that may seem scary at first.

Lesson 10: Learn to be rather than to do.

Advocacy – The Breast Health Foundation

The Breast Health Foundation (BHF) is a not-for-profit established in April 2002 to educate the public on breast cancer and breast health, increase awareness and empower women. Over the past 14 years, the BHF has developed into a transparent and effective organisation that reaches our nation's women. The money that is raised is used to teach women – those who have had and those who have not had breast cancer – to spread the word of the importance of self-examination and medical examinations. The BHF aims to put to rest myths surrounding breast cancer, and to provide an open forum where women feel that they can come forward with their problems. Traditionally, women in Africa have been seen as the heart and soul of the family. By ensuring their health and educating them, the health education messages are passed on to children, husbands and partners. If you would like to contribute to the BHF, their details are:

Breast Health Foundation
Nedbank
Sandown – 193 305
Breast Health – 1933 176 741
Swift Code – NEDSZAJJ

The Cancer Alliance

The Cancer Alliance is a collective group of non-profit organisations and cancer advocates brought together under a common mandate – to provide a platform of collaboration for cancer civil society to speak with one voice, and to be a powerful tool to affect change for all South African adults and children affected by cancer.

Email: info@canceralliance.co.za
Web: www.canceralliance.co.za
Twitter: @Cancer_ZA

Acknowledgements

I am so grateful to the many people who stood by my side during my various cancer treatments. This book describes only a fraction of the acts of kindness that I was the lucky recipient of. I would like to thank the following from the bottom of my heart and apologise to anyone I may have overlooked:

My Anchors – Jonny, Josh and Katya – for giving me the courage and hope to live, and my mother, for standing beside me through thick and thin.

My Book Club – Jenny, Karien, Les, Lynn, Michi, Orenna, and Terry, for providing me with so much else besides good books to read.

My Cancer Spotter, and surgeon extraordinaire – Dr Carol Benn, without whom I would not be telling this tale.

My Chemo Comrades – Annette, Susie, Janine, Sharon, Michelle, Tali, Fiona, and Carol, for accompanying me to chemo.

My Chemo Doctor – Dr Georgia Demetriou, for her deep compassion and dedication to beating this disease.

My Chemo Nurse – Julian, for her indomitable spirit that got me through chemo.

The Coffee Girls – Janine, Karien, Sandy, Shireen, Theresa and Tina, for their magnificent generosity in their efforts to keep me laughing.

My Colleagues – Carina, Clive, Jackie, Jenna, Nabeel, Tali, Sharon and Terry, for being so supportive and understanding of my constraints during this time. Thanks also to Adrian, Ryan, Hilton, Emile, Brett and Susan for their unstinting support of

Jonny and our family.

My Children's Angels – Alice, Arthur, Divya, Gabriel, Grace, Jesse, Jonty, Julia, Kiah, Lula, Myles, Neville, Rachel, Rafi, Sam, Saul, Tali, for surrounding Josh and Kats with love.

My Dermatologist – Dr Gary Levy, for being the kindest person I know.

My Daily Walker – Susie, for being a magnificent pillar of support every single day of this journey.

My Editor – Sandy, for editing this and all my other books, for being my friend and a second mother to Josh.

My Family from Afar – Anita, Eddie, Mark, Ilana, Mandy, Stoy, Paul, Denise, Adam and Sarah, for batting for me in every way they could despite all the miles.

My Fellow Travellers: Caroline, Carrie, Coco, Denise, Helene, Lauren C, Lloyd, Malcolm, Merle, Penny, Sue, Susie, Tali – too many by far, but so important in giving me courage.

The Flower People – Lynn S and Michi, for weekly deliveries of poppies and roses.

My Friends from Afar – Caroline, Claire, Gary, Graeme, Hilary, Joan, David C, David F, Debbie, Pam, Keith, Lauren C, Lloyd, Max, Sue H and Tana, for consistently caring through an unquantifiable number of emails and calls.

My SA Family – Wendy, Tresa, Richard, Paul and Bianca, for always being there for my mom and me, and for growing me up.

My Other SA Family – Selma, Susie, Alan and their magnificent children, for so much love, support, mirth and shared Rosh Hashanahs. Tana and Sandy – my second mother and sister whom I adore.

My Food Soldiers – Cynth and Shirl, for showing me the true meaning of kindness and generosity. Your weekly deliveries never ceased to amaze me.

My Gym Buddy – Fiona, for all the sweating and laughing with questionable results.

My Golden Oldies – Carol, David J, Jess, Mark, Nicola, Phil, Steve, and their beloved partners, Neil, Indra, Chetty, Brynie and Monika, for being my other family for my whole adult life.

My Informal Nurses – Ilana and Adam, for coming to South

Africa when the going got tough.

My Inspirers – David and Pam, for magnificently standing by us and suggesting that I write this book.

My Hairdresser – Candice, who went well above and beyond the call of duty.

My Healers – Lucy, Marissa, Mary-Anne and Vicki, for gently and wisely tugging me through the hardest of times.

My Holiday Mothers – Janine, Mandi, Nic and Naomi, for giving Kats such happy holidays.

My Home Keepers – Cath and Jack, for supporting me in keeping the home fires burning.

My Informal Editors – David C and Simon, for sending reams of notes that radically improved this text.

My Masseur – Makwena, for massaging away my aches and pains every week.

The Mina Moms – Roz, Mandi, Sue and Naomi, for always being there for Kats.

My Mindfulness Mentors – Carina and Lucy, for creating a blissful hour of ease each week, and to Lauren G, for introducing me to Jon Kabat-Zinn and for her unbridled generosity, friendship and care at every point in this journey.

My Muse – Anne, for curating the poetry that guided my being.

The Music Makers – Phil, Yda, Mark, Jenny, Theresa, Irv, Paul and Simon, for creating playlists with music that reached my soul.

My Pilates teacher – Hilde, for bringing her healing touch to my house each week.

My Publisher – Melinda Ferguson, for bringing her immense enthusiasm, liveliness, empathy and writing acumen to the project from our first conversation.

The Publishing team – Bridget, for deftly steering the project from behind the scenes. Janine, Shay and their remarkable marketing, sales and editing teams for bringing this book to life.

My Pharmacist – Cheryl, for going well beyond the call of duty.

My Readers – Carol, Ilana, Jess, Judy, Kate, Lucy, Mark G, Mark S, Susie and Caroline, for reading early drafts and giving me such valuable feedback.

My Radiologist – for being an incredible human being.

My Role Models – Paul and Simon, for showing me how to celebrate life in the shadow of one's mortality.

My Surgeons – Dr Serrurier and Dr Slabbert, for so expertly stitching and re-stitching me.

The Sewing Circle – Lynn, Mandi, Janine, Karien and Shireen, for their love and dedication to my cause and for sewing the heart on the cover.

My Yeoville Mother – Pippa, for being a steadfast friend for so many decades.

The Yoga (and Chanel) Comrades – Annette and Carla, for creating a weekly circle of tenderness and friendship, and for tips on how to look good without eyebrows.

The Weekly Foot Soldiers – Adam, Dorothy, Janine, Jess, Lauren G, Michi, Pippa, Sandy, Sue and Tana, for calling to wish me luck before each and every chemo session.

My Weekly Walkers – Mandi and Lynn, for arriving at my door at 4 pm every Tuesday.

My Writing Workshop – Mia Botha from Writer's Write, for her invaluable book writing tips.

My Writing Group – Harriet, Michelle, Terry and Sandi, for kick-starting this extraordinary journey into writing a memoir, and for standing by my side every step of the way.